Nicholas Hobbs
Paul R. Dokecki
Kathleen V. Hoover-Dempsey
Robert M. Moroney
May W. Shayne
Karen H. Weeks

STRENGTHENING
FAMILIES

Jossey-Bass Publishers
San Francisco • Washington • London • 1984

STRENGTHENING FAMILIES
Strategies for Improved Child Care and Parent Education
by Nicholas Hobbs, Paul R. Dokecki, Kathleen V. Hoover-Dempsey,
Robert M. Moroney, May W. Shayne, Karen H. Weeks

Copyright © 1984 by: Jossey-Bass Inc., Publishers
433 California Street
San Francisco, California 94104
&
Jossey-Bass Limited
28 Banner Street
London EC1Y 8QE

Library of Congress Cataloging in Publication Data
Main entry under title:

Strengthening families.

(The Jossey-Bass social and behavioral science series)
Bibliography: p. 311
Includes index.
1. Child rearing—United States. 2. Parenting—Study
and teaching—United States. 3. Family policy—United
States. 4. Family—United States. I. Hobbs, Nicholas.
II. Series.
HQ769.S8864   1984   306.8'5'0973   83-49263
ISBN 0-87589-596-4 (alk. paper)

Manufactured in the United States of America

The paper in this book meets the guidelines for
permanence and durability of the Committee on
Production Guidelines for Book Longevity of the
Council on Library Resources.

Portions of Chapter Three are adapted from "The Place of
Values in the World of Psychology and Public Policy" by
Paul R. Dokecki, which appeared in the *Peabody Journal of
Education*, 1983, *60* (3), 108–125.

JACKET DESIGN BY WILLI BAUM

FIRST EDITION

Code 8408

The Jossey-Bass
Social and Behavioral Science Series

Preface

ଠା

This nation has experienced a revolution in work and family life over the past decades. Changes in birthrates, the economy, women's rights, and preschool education have raised significant questions of public and private rights and responsibilities in child-rearing. Issues at the center of the debate have varied with the waxing and waning of individual protagonists, but over time they have focused on questions central to this book: Who will care for children? How can parents be enabled to raise their children well? What are the community's interests and responsibilities in the development of children and their parents? In an attempt to answer such questions, we embarked on a five-year, interdisciplinary project. This book presents the procedures, findings, and recommendations of our study.

In exploring ways to fulfill human development needs, we focused on child care and parent education as two of the most promising paths. But because these areas are both complicated and value-laden, it is not easy to identify the best direction for the nation. Certainly they combine both private and public interests. In *Strengthening Families* we assess many of the ingredients involved in child care and parent education and weigh various options for public response to families' needs.

Chapter One elaborates on the necessity for improved child care and parent education programs, gives further details on our interdisciplinary project and our approach to analysis, and explains the organization and purposes of the volume. In brief, Chapters Two through Four examine the knowledge foundation on which various options for strengthening families can be formulated; Chapters Five through Eight look at major policies that could be adopted in relation to child care and parent education and recommend strategies that we believe should be undertaken; and Chapter Nine sums up the rationales and purposes underlying the specific recommendations. Our hope is that these chapters and the findings they contain will contribute to the ongoing development of child and family policy that is respectful of the strengths and needs of all families.

Acknowledgments

During the course of our project, we received significant support from many sources. The Carnegie Corporation of New York gave us generous funding, for which we have been most grateful. We were assisted by superb associates from several disciplines: Louise Barnes (child development), Barry Boggs (community and clinical psychology), Phoebe Cottingham (economics), Jane DeWeerd (special education), Paul Florin (community and clinical psychology), Erwin Hargrove (political science), Robert J-P Hauck (political science), Nancy Hendrix (sociology and demography), Sharon Innes (early childhood education), Bruce Mallory (special education), Randall McCathren (law), Jennifer McDowell (psychology), Florence Roberts (nursing; family and child relations), Nancy Stetten (political science), and Barbara Wheeley (psychology). Their contributions are woven throughout the volume and were particularly significant in establishing the state of knowledge in our areas of concern.

Two boards of advisors were most helpful in sharing their expertise with us. The National Advisory Committee of the Center for the Study of Families and Children, Vanderbilt Institute for Public Policy Studies, provided early guidance for development of the project. Garry Brewer, Wilbur Cohen, Whitty Cunninggim, Susan Gray, Alfred Kahn, David Kirp, Hillary Rodham, Lisbeth Schorr, Albert Solnit, Gilbert Steiner, and Edward Zigler were valued members of this group. The Parent

Enablement Seminar provided on-going advice and response at various points throughout the project. We were privileged to have as participants in this group Mary Jo Bane, Carolyn Brown, Steve Cobb, Mozelle Core, John Dill, Barbara Finberg, James Harrell, Douglas Henry, Jr., Laura Knox, Stanley Kruger, Peggy Pizzo, Robert Rice, and Marilyn Smith. David Harman, Algund Hermann, A. Sidney Johnson III, and Sara Smith provided advice at specific points during the project that proved most helpful. Barbara Finberg, our project officer from the Carnegie Corporation of New York, was consistently gracious and supportive; her involvement and that of her colleague, Gloria Brown, are deeply appreciated.

The full manuscript emerging from this project was reviewed at various stages by Mary Jo Bane, Scarlett Graham, Erwin Hargrove, John Masters, and Frank Sloan. Their general and specific responses were very helpful in clarifying and revising the final product. Scarlett Graham provided, in addition, valuable editorial guidance prior to final revisions of the manuscript. Sally Robinson was expert in tracking down bibliographic references. Support provided by the Institute for Public Policy Studies at Vanderbilt University took many forms. We particularly appreciated the many opportunities for interdisciplinary interaction, and the gracious and competent help given by several staff members: Lottie Strupp, Regina Perry, Frieda Knight, Louise Patton, Nannette Fancher, Mary LeBlon, Patricia Harrison, and Dane Wadkins.

As coauthors, we have valued deeply our collegial relationship throughout the project. Individual contributions to this volume were woven together long ago, and we are—in a sense perhaps rare in contemporary scholarship—coequal in authorship. The order of authorship we have chosen reflects our equality of contribution and the profound respect in which we hold Nicholas Hobbs, director of the project before his death in January 1983. His loss was felt deeply by all of us, for we were privileged to count him as friend, mentor, and colleague. Although the final revision of the book took place after his death, he was involved in all of the decisions it presents; indeed, he argued vigorously for some of them when others of us were in doubt.

We believe the book would please him, for it reflects the vision that was his and continues to be ours: a caring and competent society, strong in its commitments to the individuals, families, and communities that comprise the social whole.

January 1984   Paul R. Dokecki
                                                   Nashville, Tennessee

                                          Kathleen V. Hoover-Dempsey
                                                   Nashville, Tennessee

                                               Robert M. Moroney
                                                   Tempe, Arizona

                                                   May W. Shayne
                                                   Nashville, Tennessee

                                                   Karen H. Weeks
                                                   Nashville, Tennessee

Contents

    Families, and Communities   303

    References   311

    Index   336

The Authors

Nicholas Hobbs was professor emeritus of psychology at Vanderbilt University and senior research associate at the Vanderbilt Institute for Public Policy Studies prior to his death in January 1983. He was awarded the B.A. degree from The Citadel, the M.A. and Ph.D. degrees from Ohio State University, and honorary degrees from the University of Louisville, The Citadel, and Université Paul Valéry in Montpellier, France.

Hobbs taught at the Teachers College of Columbia University, Louisiana State University, and George Peabody College for Teachers. At George Peabody College for Teachers, he was the first director of the John F. Kennedy Center for Research on Education and Human Development. He was provost of Vanderbilt University from 1967 to 1975, then joined the Vanderbilt Institute for Public Policy Studies, where he was director of the Center for the Study of Families and Children for five years. He served on a number of regional and national bodies concerned with children, health, and education; was the first director of selection and research for the Peace Corps; was a member of the advisory committee on child development of the National Research Council; and was a member of the Select Panel for the Promotion of Child Health established by Congress in 1979. For the American Psychological Association, Hobbs chaired the committee that first developed the *Ethical Standards of Psychologists* and, in 1966, served as the association's president. In 1980, he received the American Psychological Association's Award for Distinguished Professional Contributions and the award for Distinguished Contributions to Psychology in the Public Interest.

Hobbs's previously published books include *The Futures of Children, Issues in the Classification of Children,* and *The Troubled and Troubling Child* (Jossey-Bass, 1975a, 1975b, 1982).

Paul R. Dokecki is professor of psychology and special education in the George Peabody College for Teachers at Vanderbilt University, where he is also associate director of the John F. Kennedy Center for Research on Education and Human Development, senior research associate in the Vanderbilt Institute for Public Policy Studies, and editor of the *Peabody Journal of Education.* He received his B.A. degree (1962) from Manhattan College in psychology, and his M.A. (1963) and Ph.D. (1968) degrees from George Peabody College for Teachers in clinical psychology.

Dokecki's main research activities have been in the philosophy and history of science, early child development, psychopathology, intervention programs for at-risk and handicapped children, and public policy affecting the ecology of family life and human development. His experience with parent education and child care includes founding and directing one of the Parent Child Development Centers and serving as an advisory board member for the federal project throughout its ten-year history, directing the Demonstration and Research Center for Early Education (DARCEE), and directing the Peabody Child Study Center. Dokecki's books include *Conscience, Contract, and Social Reality* (1972, with R. Johnson and O. H. Mowrer) and *Exceptional Teaching for Exceptional Learning* (1979, with Nicholas Hobbs and others). He has chapters on parent education and public policy in *Changing Families* (Sigel and Laosa, 1983) and *Parent Education and Public Policy* (Haskins, in press).

Kathleen V. Hoover-Dempsey is associate professor of psychology and education in the George Peabody College for Teachers at Vanderbilt University and senior research associate at the Vanderbilt Institute for Public Policy Studies. She received her B.A. degree (1964) from the University of California at Berkeley in political science and her M.A. (1969) and Ph.D. (1974) degrees from Michigan State University in educational psychology.

Hoover-Dempsey's main research activities have been in young children's development and education, public policies affecting children and families, stress and support in relation to teacher, parent, and school effectiveness, and women's mental health and career development. Her experience with child care and parent education include public school teaching, Head Start program coordination, early childhood program development and evaluation in East Africa and Mexico, and consultation with varied early childhood and parent support programs. Her publications (some under her former name, Dunlop) have appeared in *Education and Urban Society, Exceptional Children, Interamerican Journal of Psychology, Journal of Applied Developmental Psychology, Professional Psychology,* and *Young Children.* Currently, she is co-directing a study of school effectiveness for the National Institute of Education.

Robert M. Moroney is a professor of social policy and planning in the School of Social Work at Arizona State University. Previously he spent twelve years as a professor of city and regional planning at the University of North Carolina at Chapel Hill, where he was also a faculty member of the Bush Institute. He received the B.A. degree (1960) in philosophy, the M.A. degree (1962) in social work, both from Boston College, and the M.A. degree (1965) in public health from Harvard University. Moroney received the Ph.D. degree (1970) from the Florence Heller School for Advanced Studies in Social Welfare at Brandeis University. He has also held a number of policy-related jobs and consultantships, including work in the Office of Planning and Coordination of the Commonwealth of Massachusetts, the U.S. Public Health Service, and the Massachusetts Department of Public Health. More recently, Moroney has worked as an affiliated faculty member of the Center for the Study of Families and Children, Institute for Public Policy Studies at Vanderbilt

University, and is currently the editor of the *Urban and Social Change Review*. Moroney is the author of some thirty-five books, chapters, and papers in professional journals. His recent books on analysis of family policy include *The Family and the State* (Longman, 1976) and *Families, Social Services, and Social Policy: The Issue of Shared Responsibility* (U.S. Government Printing Office, 1980).

May W. Shayne is research associate and liaison officer at the Center for the Study of Families and Children, Institute for Public Policy Studies, Vanderbilt University. She received the B.A. degree in English (1956) from Radcliffe College and the M.S.S.W. degree (1958) from the New York School of Social Work.

   Shayne's clinical experience has been mainly in psychiatric casework with emotionally disturbed children and adults. She has engaged as a volunteer in community and governmental activities concerning social services, public welfare, juvenile justice, and mental health. She serves in a dual capacity at the Center for the Study of Families and Children. As liaison officer, she maintains contact with policy makers in government, voluntary and professional associations, and the media. As research associate, she has studied child care, social services, and health care. Recently, she co-authored "Chronically Ill Children in America: Background and Recommendations" (1983, with Nicholas Hobbs and others), the preliminary report of a major national study of children with severe chronic illness and their families that is underway at Vanderbilt.

Karen H. Weeks is research associate at the Institute for Public Policy Studies, Vanderbilt University. She received her B.A. degree (1962) from Duke University in political science and her M.A. degree (1965) from Duke University in history.

   Weeks's main research activities are in intergovernmental relations as they affect the financing and implementation of programs in child care, health care, social services, and education. She has served on several community-wide task forces on public education and financing of local government services.

Currently Weeks is coordinating the Educational Excellence Network, a national organization of education scholars and practitioners. She contributed a chapter on private health insurance and the chronically ill child to a forthcoming work on chronically ill children in America, edited by Nicholas Hobbs and James M. Perrin.

STRENGTHENING FAMILIES

Strategies for
Improved Child Care
and Parent Education

ONE

CIOIOIOIOIOIOIOIOIOIOIOIOIOIOIOIOIOIOIOIOIOIO

Introduction: Strengthening Families

The central thesis of this book is that the rearing of each new generation of children is a public trust of vital consequence to our future as a people. Alan Pifer (1978, p. 7–11), former president of the Carnegie Corporation of New York, stated the issue this way:

> Every child alive today or born in the years just ahead, whether male, female, black, white, Hispanic, or otherwise, will be a scarce resource and a precious asset as an adult in the early part of the next century. At that time, the nation's standard of living, its capacity to defend itself—perhaps its very viability as a nation—will be almost wholly dependent on the small contingent of men and women who are today's children. . . . No nation, and especially not this one at this stage in its history, can afford to neglect its children. Whatever importance we attach as a people to expenditure on armaments, to programs for older Americans, to maintaining high levels of consumption and to a hundred other purposes, the welfare of children has to be our highest priority. Not only are they our future security, but their dreams and ideals can provide a much-needed renaissance of spirit in

1

what is becoming an aging, tired, and disillusioned society. In the end the *only* thing we have is our young people. If we fail them, all else is in vain.

Human development is the central concern of this volume. And we believe that child care and parent education are the instruments most readily available to increase the nation's capacity to achieve its human development aspirations and fulfill its human development needs. Human development, properly understood, focuses not only on individuals and their personal developmental potentials but also on the *contexts* in which individual development occurs. The most influential of these is the family, and the family, of course, is set within its own developmental context, the community. If we fail to take account of these pervasive influences on the course of human development, we fail to understand human development itself. We believe that the strengthening of families within supportive and caring communities is a desirable goal in and of itself. More importantly, however, we believe that competent families and supportive communities are indispensable elements of any effort to realize the full potential for human development in our society.

Every society makes choices about its own perpetuation. How the society is to be maintained and nurtured and how each new generation is to be reared are questions always on the public policy agenda. In simple and stable societies, tradition often determines the choices that are made, with little awareness of the process of decision making. But in a complex and rapidly changing society such as ours, the swift course of events, often unpredictable, requires constant reexamination and frequent revision of public policies.

Far-reaching changes in the structure of our society have increased the burden of childrearing for many families, demanding a reexamination of how children are to be cared for and how parents are to be helped to rear their children well, in ways satisfying to themselves and responsive to the needs of their children and the broader community. Much is at stake: not only the rights and responsibilities of parents and children but also the strength and character of the nation. With stakes so high, the way in which policy decisions are made becomes important, a matter itself of public concern.

In assessing the prospects for children's programs in this country, Gilbert Steiner (1976) emphasized the need for an adequate theory of child care backed by an effective coalition of politically competent interest groups. The demographic and social changes discussed in Chapter Two provide one theoretical rationale for systematic, public address to the problems of child care and parent education. For example, the declining birthrate means that there will be fewer children to nurture. Children will therefore become more precious (more highly valued) than they have been during the recent decades, when the very abundance of children and youth created social problems, from crowded classrooms to crowded juvenile courtrooms. The changing age structure of the population, as well as the growing significance of technical knowledge to the nation's productivity, will also mean that new generations of children must be helped to become increasingly competent just to maintain the nation's current levels of economic vitality and quality of life. Any enhancement of national life will require yet an added investment in the competence of new generations. Thus, a child development theory for the immediate future may well have a demographic basis for the major goal of building competence in children.

But competence alone is not sufficient for a society worth living in. Suppose that the nation is successful in nurturing new generations of highly competent people but that the people turn out also to be selfish—that is, long on ability but short on commitment to community. The result could be disastrous; a society now threatened by incompetence could, with competence achieved, be torn asunder by a deficiency of caring. All the divisions that now run through our society like great geologic faults—age stratification, racial and ethnic divisions, economic inequities, and discrepancies in opportunities to achieve competence—could grow into irreparable fissures signaling the moral and spiritual decline of the nation. Thus, another theoretical rationale for the systematic public address to child care and parent education is based on social values—a vision of the relationships for which we strive in this nation between individuals, the families in which they are nurtured, and the communities in which they live and work. Much of the theoretical and empirical evidence in the field of human development, as we will see later (Chapters Three and Four), supports the wisdom of taking such a position, for it adds up to the critical importance of viewing children, parents, families, and communities as significantly interrelated components of the social fabric. When these relationships are mutually supportive, the nation as a whole and the individuals who constitute this society benefit. Thus, we suggest that a theory adequate for promoting a sensible approach to child development in this society should have as one of its major rationales the nurturance of caring. The rationale we propose in this volume for national attention to human development, focusing on programs of all kinds but including especially child care and parent education, thus calls for the creation and support of a *competent and caring society*.

While it is heartening to have demographic and economic pressures come into play in support of services to children and families, our concerns clearly extend beyond the productive capacity, military strength, and economic vitality of the nation. We are equally concerned with the quality of life available to citizens; with the encouragement of invention and discovery; with the nurturance of poets and playwrights, musicians and mathematicians, scientists and philosophers and social critics; and with the refurbishing of individual responsibility and community purpose. We are concerned, in sum, with laying the groundwork for specific policy attention to the development of competence and caring in our nation.

We have elected to focus on child care and parent education as means of enhancing society's capacity to develop competence and caring for two major reasons. First, we are at a critical point nationally in addressing with sensitivity the needs of our nation's families for support in wise and effective child-rearing. As discussed in Chapters Two and Four, families are now experiencing a need for assistance in effectively meeting the multiple and sometimes conflicting responsibilities inherent in contemporary life. We have elected to deal with child care and parent education as two properly linked facets of the same need: the need of families for community support in gaining the time, energy, resources, and knowledge critical to the societally indispensable function of effective childrearing. Thus, we examine not only alternative approaches to helping families care for their children, but also the utility of parent education and the notion that all services for families and children, including but not limited to child care, should include the component of parent education. We do not define parent education as instruction in caring for children in the narrow sense, but extend it to include the enhancement of parental competence in all areas that affect the family. To be sure, parent education may provide increased understanding of children and a heightened competence in caring for them. But it may also provide instruction and experience in enhancing the community, in strengthening the family as a mediating structure, and in perfecting the rights and well-being of each family member.

A second reason for examining child care and parent education as linked functions is that we believe in enabling society's regular socializing agencies to do their jobs well. The institutions normally responsible for nurturing children, in addition to the family, include the neighborhood, school, church, and community. Communities have come to provide (over and above identity, friendship, and mutual assistance) a myriad of agencies, both public and private, that make available specialized, supplementary services to families and children, without which the rearing of children today would be an impossible task. Of all the regular social institutions responsible for nurturing children, however, the family is most important.

The American ideal is for children to be brought up by two caring parents in a stable home, a potential circumstance for over 80 percent of America's children, the percent of children who now live in a household with a father and mother. That such a large proportion of children live in traditional families is sometimes overlooked in our well-warranted concern for children with potentially special needs (for example, children in one-parent families, children in poverty, or children with no

families at all). Insofar as policies have tended to overlook traditional families, they have neglected the greatest opportunity for
contributing to the effectiveness of parents as care givers as well
as to the stability of families.

When young children are cared for out of the home, either
in shared arrangements as in child care or in long-term or permanent arrangements as in foster home or institutional placement,
the corollary to the "rule of the regular" is that the child should
be removed the least possible distance from his or her family—
in space, in time, and in the psychological significance of the experience involved. The younger the child, the more rigorously
should the corollary apply; but even with older children, it
never ceases to be important altogether.

What happens to young children, whether parents care
for them at home or receive help in caring for them out of the
home, is not altogether a matter of private convenience. The
public interest is directly involved, just as it is involved in the
education of all children, in their protection against abuse and
exploitation, in their health and nutrition, and in their physical
safety. Yet, it is clear that casual intrusion into family life or
infringement of parental responsibility is destructive. The nation needs an approach allowing for community involvement in
the provision of child care and parent education that will
strengthen families by enabling parents to rear their children
better than they would be able to do without a community response. The community response should serve both family and
community interests. What is needed, in sum, is a rationale for a
public response in the service of private *and* public interests,
with parents centrally involved in defining where one leaves off
and the other begins. It is the goal of this volume to examine
and assess, in as systematic and thorough a manner as the subject will allow, some of the components of an appropriate public response to families' need for child care and parent education.

An Approach to Policy Analysis

When a group of academicians (deliberately chosen from
such diverse disciplines as psychology, child development, social
work, political science, law, and economics) commits itself to

an enterprise involving the complex task of analyzing public policies related to the strengthening of families and communities through child care and parent education, the group obviously has to work out some policies for itself, some common understandings to guide its own work. This we have done, and it seems to us wise to share these understandings with the reader, if for no other reason than to lay bare our presuppositions, our biases, our idiosyncratic inclinations. We may thereby reduce surprise, and perhaps annoyance, on the part of the reader expecting a different type of policy study. Further, the reader can assess the value of the effort in reference to its stated intentions and not to standards alien to its purposes.

Making Existing Knowledge Available to Policy Makers. There appear to be about as many approaches to policy analysis as there are practitioners of the craft. Much inventing is yet to be done before the craft can be called either art or science; indeed, even the word *craft* may promise too much. Be that as it may, we obviously think it important to try to bring to bear in the shaping of public policies affecting families and children knowledge from the university, from research in the behavioral and social sciences, the medical and health sciences, and the humanities.

In the shaping of public policies and programs, academic knowledge is only part of the broad range of knowledge and understanding needed to arrive at a wise and effective course of action with respect to some problem of public concern. In our society, the policy-making process is and should be largely a political matter, informed by experience, common sense, and political wisdom. Interest group politics have a legitimate role, and due attention to upcoming elections appropriately modulates the process. Policies and programs are a consequence of a myriad of political interactions. The process is not always highly rational, although we are impressed by how rational the product often turns out to be. Our aspiration is to make a modest contribution to a complicated process for which other people are largely responsible. We believe deeply in the utility of knowledge from library and laboratory, insufficient as it may be, and we seek to make that kind of knowledge available, in usable form, to people who influence, shape, make, and carry out policies and programs affecting families and children.

A Policy Liaison Function. We found it useful to conceptualize our task as involving, in part, the transfer of knowledge. Based on our group's prior experience and the growing literature in the area, we developed a policy liaison strategy for positioning our project in the network of individuals and groups playing roles in the areas of child care and parent education research and policy (Dokecki, 1977).

Schematically, the liaison function identifies the knowledge *needs* in an area of public policy, develops usable knowledge as a *resource,* and makes this resource available to potential *users* through translation into forms amenable to fashioning policy *solutions* (Havelock and Lingwood, 1973). This need-resource-user-solution function entails integration, the synthesis or interpretation of existing research knowledge; translation, the transformation and transmission of existing or potential solutions derived from the knowledge base; and linkage, bridging the gaps between researchers and policy makers (Short, 1973). Done effectively, knowledge transfer through a liaison function entails early and continuing involvement of key potential users through a number of communication channels, but most importantly through personal contact (Glaser, 1973).

As we have employed it, the liaison function has involved continuous communication with policy makers and policy researchers at every stage of our study. Means employed for purposes of communication included breakfast and luncheon meetings and a series of informal seminars with parents, media representatives, resource providers, legislators and their aides, and federal and state officials. Although planning the liaison function was the responsibility of one staff member, it is reflected in the work performed by every member of our project group.

Short- or Long-Term Goals? In accepting the opportunity to study child care and parent education, we were faced with the issue of whether to address the problem from a short-term or a long-term perspective. Economic conditions at the time the study was conducted strongly suggested that we settle for short-term solutions, solutions that would make maximum use of existing resources, rely heavily on private-sector initiative, emphasize voluntarism and self-help efforts, and, above all, cost little money. To recommend any bold new programs in such stringent times would be an exercise in futility, argued some advocates and the political climate of the early 1980s.

What this book offers are suggested directions and dimensions that are appropriate for a comprehensive approach to family needs but that will also be usable for more modest purposes. What we attempt to do is not to lay out specific plans, small or large, but to *define the issues and bring knowledge to bear upon them* in such a way that policy makers can use the results of our work in addressing either short-term or long-term solutions to the problem of child care and parent education.

After working out this position, we found an admirable statement in its support by Kenneth Prewitt, president of the Social Science Research Council, given in testimony before the House of Representatives Subcommittee on Science, Research, and Technology: "The social and behavioral sciences are not going to solve the nagging, persisting problems of this or any other nation. These disciplines are not a substitute government. Rather economics, anthropology, demography, and statistics are sciences. They are sciences whose progress is marked, and whose usefulness is measured, less by the achievement of consensus or the solving of problems than by a refinement of debate and a sharpening of the intelligence upon which the collective management of human affairs depends" (U.S. Congress, House Committee on Science and Technology, 1980). So we have sought "a refinement of debate and a sharpening of the intelligence" with regard to the strengthening of families through child care and parent education, with the public interest primary in our minds.

Values in the Policy Process. Values permeate the policy process. The initial choice of a policy issue, the way the problem is defined, the kinds of data that are marshaled to throw light on the problem, the selection of one solution over alternative possibilities, the strategies preferred for the implementation of programs, and the criteria for assessing outcomes all are profoundly influenced by the values held by the participants who make the choices involved.

In national policies and programs affecting families and children, values and aspirations are paramount in determining choices among options. Data on the effects of programs on families are important, but the frequency with which data are selectively seized upon to buttress already-held value-laden positions gives testimony to the preponderant weight of values in this area. The values involved in policies related to family life and child development seem largely intuitive, heavily influenced by economic and sociocultural experiences, highly sensitive to political considerations, seldom examined, and almost never made public.

It has thus seemed important for us to make clear our own value position, to reduce the intuitive component, to detach ourselves as much as possible from personal economic and sociocultural interests, and to set aside immediate political considerations. The reader can then know where we stand and make appropriate adjustments, if necessary. We have gone to great lengths to clarify our own assumptions about values and to reconcile differences among us.

At the outset of this study, the staff reviewed many of the major works of the past decade that bear upon public policies affecting families and children, including reports of commissions and advisory groups. All of these are highly useful documents for the refinement of debate and sharpening of intelligence about public policies, families, and children. Each work presents a strong and cogently argued position; taken together, they follow and extend a tradition of commissions, study groups, and individual scholars to discover and champion particular solutions to policy problems. There is no doubt merit in this strategy. The argument is certainly sharpened by hard-edged positions, confidently held.

However, we found compelling the possibility that policy makers in the decades immediately ahead may gain the most help from an analysis that lays out reasonable options and assesses the relative advantages and disadvantages of each, at the same time making clear the nature of the criteria used in the assessment. The options to be addressed should be those likely to be encountered in debate by the policy makers, and the assessment should enable the policy makers to sort out their own values and aspirations as well as to anticipate the sorting that will be done by others. The strategy does not preclude advancing preferred policy specifications; in fact, we do. The only requirement, and it is an exacting one, is that we make clear the values that inform our judgments. A measured analysis of recognized options may in itself generate new insights, and we have attempted to remain free to propose solutions as cogently as we can while keeping a broad vision of the possible.

An Overview of the Volume

As alluded to earlier, two lines of argument are interwoven throughout our work. Although not inherently congenial, both of these rationales are intended by their proponents to justify public policy attention to child care and parent education programs (Dunlop, 1978, 1980). The broader rationale, and the one we find the more compelling, we have called the *human development rationale*; the narrower one, the *human capital rationale*. The human development rationale is universalistic in its orientation, arguing that *all* families and *all* children, as well as the communities in which they live, have much to gain from public attention to questions of child and family policy. It is also heavily oriented toward service delivery programs designed to enrich the lives of all participants as well as enhance the quality of life within communities and the nation as a whole. The human capital rationale is far more specific in its orientation, more often geared toward particular measures— based on demographically based indicators and economic analyses of benefits—intended to remedy particular problems among specific populations within society. These problems are seen as threats to the future social and economic viability of the nation, and specific policy measures are often aimed at minimizing those threats.

The coexistence of these two rationales in one study reflects the state of opinion that exists among experts and advocates of child and family policy. Both rationales are based on sound reasoning; although they sometimes conflict, both may be sincerely motivated by a desire to improve the lives of those who would be touched by the policies and programs they recommend.

To bring the broadest range of considerations to bear on the problems that are the focus of our analysis, we felt that it was preferable to bear with the inconsistencies between the two rationales, rather than ignore a sizable portion of the thinking being done about child and family policies and programs. We aspire to contribute to a dialogue among those concerned with the problems we treat. It is our hope that this dialogue will help the nation transcend unproductive divisions of opinion over questions of child and family policy, resulting in a commitment to the best possible public policies concerning children and their families. In the end, the primary beneficiary will be the nation itself, for society cannot long survive as it would choose to unless the adults of future generations have the competence to guide its affairs and the sense of caring to do so with wisdom and commitment.

In Chapter Two, we present and analyze data on a sample of now well-established social and demographic trends that have important implications for families and our society. We are persuaded that these data strongly suggest the need for public consideration of programs designed to enhance the capacity of families to realize the full developmental potential of their children, for the sake of the children and for the sake of the nation. The data presented in this chapter are among those most frequently included in a human capital rationale for public attention to child care and parent education.

We are further convinced, however, that if the goal of human development is to be realized, communities will play an important role in its realization. Chapter Three examines the importance of community and its contribution to human development. The model of human development that unfolds in this chapter implies standards for judging the adequacy of different policy approaches put forth as part of our national response to the needs of families and children. The human development standards we suggest in Chapter Three are applied to a range of proposed policies in subsequent chapters.

Chapter Four examines the literature on child care and parent education programs developed in this country over several decades and analyzes research measuring their effects on children and parents. However, if programs in child care and parent education are to be successful in realizing human development goals, a productive relationship must exist between parents and professionals who provide services to families. Chapter Four concludes with an examination of important dimensions of that relationship and explores the complementary roles of parents and service providers in promoting the full development of the nation's children.

The first four chapters of the book thus provide the foundation we believe necessary for an adequate examination of a broad range of policy options that might be selected to promote the strengthening of families, the care of children, and the national goal of sound human development. In the following chapters, we examine five major policy options for child care and parent education. Selected for their salience in the national debate on child and family services or their relevance to our national practice in those areas, each option is examined in terms of the standards we believe important if the broad notion of human development, including the development of a competent and caring citizenry, is to be realized through public policy.

In Chapter Five, we examine four major policy options: to do nothing and accept the status quo; to build a comprehensive national family policy; to develop options that provide flexibility to families; and to provide resources to families. Our analyses indicate the potential usefulness of the latter two courses of action in particular. All, however, fall short in some areas of our values analysis, and in Chapters Six and Seven we turn to the analysis of a fifth major policy option: the provision of services to families.

In Chapter Six, we describe and analyze major recent federally funded programs designed to provide child care and parent education services: Title I of the Elementary and Secondary Education Act (ESEA), Head Start, and Title XX of the Social Security Act. We follow this analysis in Chapter Seven with the presentation of two case studies, describing exemplary state-initiated efforts in child care and parent education services. Throughout these two chapters, we examine national and state experience in service provision with an eye to deriving guidelines for the development of national policy that more closely meet the human development and community criteria central to the development of a competent and caring society.

In Chapter Eight, we present recommendations and supporting analyses for the future development of policy in these areas. While our recommendations are clearly not without their limitations, we believe that they represent the best of the possible approaches and we offer instrumental analyses with reference to optimizing their chances for successful implementation.

We conclude in Chapter Nine with a review of the rationales and purposes underlying our recommendations. And we urge again an understanding of child care and parent education within the broader social context of enhancing both the competence and the caring capacity of children, their families, and their communities. Only in this context, we suggest, will our individual and societal well-being be successfully and humanely served.

TWO

Changes
in American Families

American families have witnessed a revolution in the last generation. They have become smaller. They have come to incorporate
an increasingly large proportion of older, dependent people as
the age composition of the population has shifted upward.
Women have entered the work force in significant numbers and
their earnings now account for an important portion of many
families' total income. The number of single-parent families has
increased. And parents are turning with increasing frequency to
out-of-home sources of supplementary child care and information about childrearing. If, as is often said, the family is the
basic building block of society, then we in the United States
clearly have cause for examining the foundations of our social
order. Scholars dispute whether the American family is "besieged" (Lasch, 1977) or "here to stay" (Bane, 1976), but they
agree unanimously that the family is undergoing profound and
rapid changes that are major by-products of this nation's development during the last century (see, for example, Hendrix,
1979).

    These changes are at the heart of a demographically ori-
ented, or human capital, rationale for systematic public policy
address to the issues of child care and parent education. In es-

15

sence, claims this rationale, the demographic changes in family structure and related changes in family functions make imperative systematic attention to the national need for the development of competence in the younger generation. If, for example, the combined effect of lower birthrates and increasing numbers of older people is that more older people will be dependent on fewer productive, working-age citizens, then we need to ensure that the younger generation will become increasingly productive and able to care for the growing number of postretirement dependents. Similarly, if increasing numbers of women are working outside the home for reasons that may involve choice but may also involve economic necessity tied to family well-being, we may need to develop policies that ensure that the out-of-home care replacing in-home care for children is of the quality necessary to promote competence in children and that the information parents need to rear their children well under conditions of multiple role responsibilities (for example, combined work and family demands) is readily available.

Describing a situation that requires public attention is perhaps the most important, and at the same time the most difficult, aspect of public policy analysis. A general sense that something is wrong or that opportunities for individuals and society are being overlooked may be widely shared, but such generalized notions provide a poor foundation for policy analysis. In this chapter we highlight some of the social and demographic trends that give focus to a concern for the condition of children and families. As will become evident, data presented here are amenable to both a human capital and a human development argument. They are perhaps most directly relevant, however, to the development of a rationale based on the issue of human capital, a rationale addressed to the question, How do we ensure that society's need for an adequate base of productive adult citizens is met?

Selected Population Trends

Two population trends in particular—changes in the birthrate and changes in the age composition of the population—have immediate and potential implications for the development of public policies related to children and their families.

During much of the twentieth century, birthrates and death rates in industrialized countries declined steadily, with two temporary war-related reversals. In the United States in 1910, for example, there were 30.1 births per thousand population; in 1940, just prior to World War II, there were 19.4 births per thousand; and in 1980, there were only 15.9 births per thousand. These figures amount to a reduction in the birthrate of almost 50 percent in seventy years. At present, the U.S. birthrate is below the rate required to replace the population in the long run (the replacement rate is 2.1; the present U.S. rate is 1.9), a circumstance obscured by the fact that the absolute number of children born each year will increase because of the large number of women born during the baby boom who are still in their reproductive years. Also of importance in these figures is the fact that the declining birthrate is not evenly distributed among various economic and geographical groups in the population. Birthrates are higher among families with the fewest economic and educational resources; similarly, they are higher among families concentrated in urban centers, where opportunities for children are most constricted.

The policy implications emerging from these figures are many. Smaller family size, for example, may produce a new demand for early socialization opportunities, important for the development of some socially valued characteristics in children (for example, sharing and learning to interact productively with peers). In an earlier age of larger families and more stable communities, siblings and neighbors frequently filled this function very effectively, albeit informally. Clearly implied in these figures is also the need for investing substantial public resources in the growing proportion of children born to families in less advantaged circumstances if the children are to grow up as healthy, competent adults able to enter the mainstream of economic opportunity in this country. Their ability to do so has personal importance, but it also has societal importance, for the country is likely to need the productive capacities of all its citizens. If birthrates remain low, as seems likely, we might also observe that each child's value as a future resource will increase significantly, making the fullest realization of each individual's potential not only desirable but imperative. Such an accomplishment would benefit any nation in any time, but the broader implications of the trends in birthrates, in combination with the trends in the age composition of the population, suggest that such an accomplishment may be a necessity for the well-being of this nation. Barring substantial shifts in the birthrate, U.S. Census Bureau projections indicate that although the *number* of children born in 2050 will be approximately the same as the number of children born in 1980, the *proportion* of children and adolescents in the population will decline sharply (see Figures 1 and 2).

There are a number of ways to describe the significance of these shifts. One way is simply to note that the United States has been, through the years, a relatively young society. But we are entering a period when the average age of the population will rise steadily, from a median of 30.3 years in 1980 to a median age of 38.6 in 2050. Demographers and economists use a *dependency ratio* to refer to the ratio of the number of potential (age-eligible) members of the work force to the number of dependent members of the population, defined as those under eighteen and those over sixty-five (Hendrix, 1979). It is also possible to derive more precise projections of the size of the work force in relation to the number of dependent young people and old people. It is expected that the dependency ratio will remain relatively stable over the next thirty years; in other words, there will not be a significant decrease in the ratio of workers to dependent people. This is because although the birthrate has declined, the baby boom infants, now adults, are still in their work years and because women are moving into the work force in increasing numbers. Not until 2010 will the picture change substantially. Then the wave of people who were born in the two decades after World War II will begin to move into the retirement years. Then dependency ratios will change dramatically, and the cost of maintaining our Social Security system will grow even beyond present levels.

In the meantime, there will be an important shift in the

Figure 1. Age Structure of the Population of the United States,
1980–2050 (by Number of People).

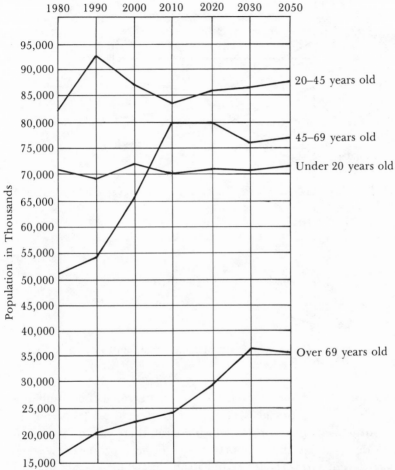

Source: U.S. Department of Commerce, Bureau of the Census,
1982.

age composition of the potential work force, defined here as
the number of people between the ages of twenty and sixty-
nine. (We use the upper age sixty-nine instead of sixty-five to
make these estimates conservative. Better health makes it possible for older people to work longer, and it seems probable that
there will be incentives for older people to work longer to main-

Figure 2. Age Structure of the Population of the United States,
1980–2050 (by Percent of the Population).

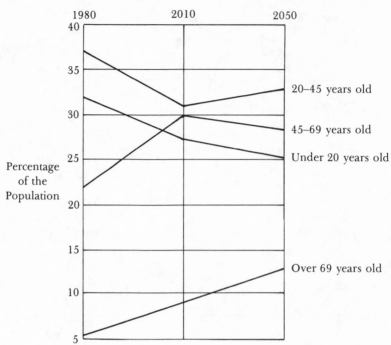

Source: U.S. Department of Commerce, Bureau of the Census,
1982.

tain the size of the work force and to decrease the number of
people drawing Social Security.) Although the absolute number of age-eligible workers will increase, there will be a substantial decrease in the proportion of younger potential workers
(ages twenty to forty-four) and a substantial increase in the proportion of older potential workers (ages forty-five to sixty-
nine). Between 1980 and 2010 (a thirty-year period, or one generation), the absolute number of younger adults will increase
slightly despite the fact that they will constitute a smaller percentage of the work force (there were 82 million younger adults
in 1980 and there will be 83.75 million in 2010). During the
same period, however, the absolute number of older adults will
increase substantially from 51.5 million to 79.5 million. In

1980, younger adults constituted 61 percent of the potential work force; by 2010, this figure will shift to 51 percent. While the number of younger adults will increase by 2 percent, the number of older adults in the work force will increase by 55 percent.

These trends indicate that we may be approaching an inversion point marking the reemergence and recognition of children as an economic asset rather than a liability. Until recently in Western societies (and today in less well-developed countries), children were expected to take care of their parents in old age, thereby providing a form of Social Security; thus, children were highly valued for economic reasons. The forces of industrialization and urbanization in the twentieth century, however, worked to reduce the perceived economic value of children. Indeed, children are more often perceived today as economic liabilities by potential parents. It seems entirely possible, however, that children will come to be appreciated in the years immediately ahead as a scarce resource vital to the well-being of the nation and its citizens, young and old alike.

Birthrates and the size of the work force are clearly related, with a time lag of about twenty years. The recent experience of European nations indicates that when birthrates decline to or fall below replacement levels, various incentives for child-bearing will be instituted, such as family allowances, housing subsidies, low-interest loans for setting up housekeeping, extended leaves for both parents on the birth of a child, and extensive public programs for child care. When the labor force shrinks, additional policies may be anticipated that will encourage women to enter the work force, keep skilled older people employed, relax child labor laws and mandatory retirement ages, import "guest workers," conscript youth for public service and the military, and facilitate the combination of careers with homemaking and childrearing by various means, including flexible working hours and public assistance for the care, education, and general development of children and youth.

These population data increase the probability that today's wave of empty classrooms will become a wave of empty workbenches in the near future. Between 1980 and 2010, the proportion of younger workers will decline sharply and the proportion of older workers will grow. Although older workers contribute experience to the work force, younger workers bring new skills, the most recent training, and new potential for innovation into the work force. Beyond 2010, older workers will move into retirement, and the total work force will decline sharply in proportion to the number of people. The economic well-being of the nation, its military strength, the security of older people, and the quality of life in general will depend on offsetting the reduction in the proportion first of younger workers and then of all workers by an equivalent increase in the competence of the work force. If increasing the competence of the work force does become a national goal, then the competence of *all* children must be of concern. These population trends may be seen as compelling attention to some basic questions related to family life: how children are to be reared; how parents are to be educated for new and evolving roles; how social institutions—most notably in education, health, and social services—are to be made responsive to changing realities in the structure of the population and family life.

Women in the Work Force

Another set of demographic trends important to the development of a rationale for examining public policy in the areas of child care and parent education is related to the entry of significant numbers of women into the paid labor force. Technological changes that have led to increased longevity and the efficient control of reproduction have paved the way for social changes of great consequence for public policy. These changes—and significant advocacy—are leading gradually to the recognition and acceptance of the right of women to the full realization of themselves as individuals unencumbered by nonfunctional role restrictions imposed by law or custom. Inexorably, changes in the roles of women demand complementary changes in the roles of men, thus signaling a profound social revolution. This revolution, fueled by worldwide economic pressures not likely soon to abate, is yet incomplete. Its full consequences are impossible to predict, but its impact is already deeply felt.

The increased entry of women into the labor force, and especially of mothers with young children, is probably the most dramatic and significant of all changes faced by families. In 1900, only 18 percent of the labor force was composed of women, but by 1979 that figure had increased to 42 percent. The incentives and pressures toward women's employment outside the home pervade the economic structure.

Not only do women now constitute a significant proportion of the labor force, but patterns of female work force participation have changed over the years. Up until 1950, women were likely to work when they were young (sixteen to twenty-four), drop out of the labor force to marry, and then reenter the labor force after age thirty-five, if at all. Those who reentered (at a lower rate than those who left) usually did so only after their children were in school. This pattern changed during the 1970s, when the employment rate for women aged twenty-five to thirty-four rose from 43 percent in 1970 to 65 percent in 1980 (Waite, 1981). Increasingly, women in the twenty-five- to thirty-four-year age group—the group most likely to have preschool children at home—are not dropping out of the paid work force. And indeed, the most rapid increase in labor force participation in recent years has been among those very women. The labor force participation of women with children under six rose from about 29 percent in 1970 to 43 percent in 1980, which represented a more rapid rate of increase than for mothers of older children (six to seventeen) or for women with no children under eighteen. Labor force participation for single mothers in 1980 was even higher at 55 percent (U.S. Department of Labor, Bureau of Labor Statistics, 1980). Although the number of children under six declined during the 1970s, the number of children under six whose mothers work increased. Demographers and economists—who differ in numerical projections but not in overall trends—predict that the percentage will continue to rise substantially (see, for example, Waldman and others, 1979). The Census Bureau estimates that by 1990, fully 10.5 million children under six, or 45 percent of the total, will have mothers in the labor force (U.S. Department of Commerce, Bureau of the Census, 1977).

Just as labor force participation is rising, so is labor force attachment, reflected in full-time, year-round employment. While labor force attachment of mothers of children of all ages increased during the 1970s, standing at 35 percent of mothers of school-age and preschool children in 1977 (Waldman and others, 1979), the most pronounced increase was among mothers with children between the ages of three and five. In 1978, about one third of these women (and about one fifth of those with children under three) who had work experience were year-round, full-time workers (Masnick and Bane, 1980).

The trends toward greater labor force participation and attachment among mothers of preschool children do not enable us to predict the number of preschoolers whose mothers will work full-time year-round over the next decades; however, there is no sign of decline. Masnick and Bane (1980, p. 63) were cautious, stopping short of making a forecast, but believe that in addition to increased participation, "a second revolution is just under way in attachment, particularly among women of the young generation born after 1940 who also are revolutionizing family structure."

While there are many reasons for the increased labor force participation and attachment among women with children, the contribution to family income from their employment clearly constitutes one major factor promoting these trends. The inflationary economy has become a powerful incentive to women's employment as family purchasing power has failed to keep pace with prices. The advantage to being a two-income family became pronounced in the 1970s, a period that experienced recession accompanied by the steepest inflationary spiral since World War II. During this period, children living in families where both parents worked were, on the average, better off economically than those living in two-parent families where only the father was employed; they were substantially better off than children living in families in which only the mother was employed. Although the portion of family income contributed by wives in two-worker families remained fairly constant between 1955 and 1977, for more than two decades families in which the wife was employed have had consistently and significantly higher incomes than families in which the wife was not in the labor force (see Table 1). The median contribution of

Table 1. Median Income of Families, 1955–1977.

	A Married, Wife in Work Force	B Married, Wife Not in Work Force	Income of B as Percentage of A
1955	$ 5,622	$ 4,326	77
1960	6,900	5,520	80
1965	8,633	6,706	78
1970	12,276	9,304	76
1975	17,237	12,759	74
1977	20,268	15,063	74

Source: Adapted from U.S. Department of Labor, Bureau of Statistics, 1977.

full-time working mothers to family income was about 38 percent during the period 1969–1977; the contribution was somewhat less among women who worked part-time or part-year (Masnick and Bane, 1980). The impact of these data is augmented by the following survey information. In 1975, 60 percent of the employed women with children under the age of fourteen indicated that they worked "for economic survival" (*National Childcare Consumer Study: 1975,* Vol. 3, p. 54). In 1980, another survey found that almost half (48 percent) of the women interviewed worked because they needed the money, while another quarter (24 percent) indicated that they worked for both money and personal satisfaction (The Gallup Organization, Inc., 1980). Some women were asked why they did not work: 22 percent indicated that their husbands preferred that they not be employed, 18 percent cited the unavailability or high cost of child care, and 13 percent stated that they did not need the money; the remainder were retired, disabled, or unable to find a job.

Thus, a variety of factors have merged to produce a significant and profound change in the relationship between wom-

en, families, and the labor market (Dunlop, 1981). Technological innovations allowing for reproductive control have resulted
in smaller families; these changes in combination with increased
longevity mean that women today live much longer after the
completion of childrearing responsibilities than was true for
their predecessors, and the personal value of a career (meaningful work for the decades following the maturation of children)
has increased concomitantly. At the same time, economic pressures have pulled women out of the home and into the labor
force; the importance of women's contributions to family income, particularly in inflationary times, demands acknowledgment and attention. The fact that increased levels of labor force
participation among women are most pronounced among mothers of young children only supports these demographic variables
in calling for a policy response that will help this growing group
of "normal" families to perform their sometimes conflicting societal, familial, and parental responsibilities.

Changes in Family Composition

While changing trends in birthrate, longevity, and employment have all had an impact on family functions, changes
over the last few decades in family composition have also become a factor of importance to the demographically oriented
rationale for systematic attention to the issues of child care and
parent education. While most children, as we noted in Chapter
One, live in a home with a mother and a father, the last decade
has seen a large increase in the number of children living in
single-parent families, most of which are headed by women. The
trend toward an increasing number of single-parent families is
likely to continue through the next decade (Ross and Sawhill,
1975). According to census data, the proportion of children under six living with both parents declined from 87 percent in
1968 to 81 percent in 1977. During the same period, the number of preschoolers who lived only with their mothers rose from
2.1 million to 2.8 million, while the number of preschoolers living with both parents declined from 19.9 million to 15.0 million. A related factor of potential importance is that the likeli-

hood of living in a single-parent family varies across different groups in this country. For example, the proportion of black children who lived only with their mothers in 1977 was 41 percent; this figure was substantially higher than that for white children who lived only with their mothers (10 percent). Also noteworthy, however, is the fact that differences in total group size meant that in absolute numbers, there were more white than black children living in single-parent, mother-headed homes (Moore and Hofferth, 1979).

In contrast to earlier decades when widowhood accounted for a large proportion of families headed by women, divorce and separation have now become the major determinants. Further, a small but growing number of mothers have never married. In recent years, the divorce rate has slowed its rapid rise, but at present about 40 percent of the children born in the 1970s are expected to experience the divorce of their parents. Single-parent status is becoming less of a final, or permanent, state, however. It is now predicted that as many as four out of every five divorced persons will eventually remarry, implying that a small but increasing number of children will live in stepfamilies (Glick, 1979).

Also important in these data on family composition is the fact that families headed by females are much more likely to have young children than previously. In 1950, only 10.4 percent of families headed by females included their own children under six. By 1975, however, the percentage had risen to 24.5 percent (U.S. Department of Commerce, Bureau of the Census, 1950, 1975a). The influence of single-parenthood on the need for extrafamilial child care is apparent. The factors affecting all families—for example, loss of traditional sources of child care (extended families, older siblings)—affect single-parent families even more sharply. Such factors are likely to cause single parents to rely on nonrelatives for child care, especially since most single parents experience strong financial pressures to work full-time. Similarly, the need of single parents for additional parent education may well be a factor. The strongest traditional sources of information about childrearing—one's own parents and extended family—are less likely to know about the multiple demands of single-parenthood, particularly if combined with employment, than about more traditional family forms and parent needs. Thus, yet another set of demographic variables may be construed as contributing to the need for public policy attention to the care of children and the education of parents.

The Trends in Perspective

The trends described here are familiar facts of modern life. They are but a few of a large number of social and demographic realities reported regularly by the media. The tendency has been to treat these trends as individual statistical phenomena with little attention to their broader or combined implications. If one looks at them as a group, however, with an eye to discerning their effects on family life and the rearing of children, it is but an easy step to assert their relevance to those concerned with the society's store of human capital *and* to those concerned more broadly with the quality of human development and the quality of life available to individuals, families, and their communities.

In considering these demographic trends from either perspective, we believe it is important to eschew the romantic view that families were once better off than they are today (Laslett, 1977). It is not appropriate now—if indeed it ever was—to look back nostalgically and devise policies whose primary purpose is to recreate things as we imagine, usually erroneously, they once were (Cohen, 1976). Families are not worse off today than they were in the past. They have undergone changes, to be sure, and those changes have taxed the coping abilities of many families, just as they have sometimes taxed the coping abilities of the society itself. But families have always been under pressures of one sort or another in this country and they have survived well as a viable social form.

Specific pressures on families over the last decades, however, have taken new forms having particular relevance for families' abilities to rear children well. Many "normal" families have experienced difficulties in performing "natural" child care and parent education functions. Because we have generally believed in this nation that families are the most desirable and effective agents of children's development (and indeed, we would strongly support this belief), it is significant—from both the human capital and the human development perspectives—that the capacity of families to realize the developmental potential of their children is, in a very direct sense, the capacity of the nation to realize its potential. In other words, factors influencing the abilities of parents to rear their children well are significant to the national well-being. This is true if one takes either the economically oriented human capital perspective or the more broadly construed perspective of concern for human development set within a socially responsive community.

It is our value position that human development should encompass more than the transmission of marketable skills to children, more than the development of competence alone. We suggest that human development necessarily entails the notion of the *quality* of existence, as well as the functional competence for existence. We believe that human communities are the sphere in which these two aspects of development can most readily be achieved for families, their individual members, and the society as a whole. While we find the demographic trends highlighted in this chapter important and the human capital rationale useful, we find them insufficient to a full consideration of the needs of children, parents, and families in contemporary society.

THREE

ଠା

Importance
of Community Support

We believe that the quality of the human community plays a
major role in determining the strength of families and, in turn,
the ability of families to raise their children well. We believe further that the adequacy of community support for families is
especially important for the effective performance of childrearing functions. While we find the demographic trends presented
in Chapter Two compelling and significant in justifying policy
attention to the needs of children and families, we find a
rationale based only on those trends—the economically based
concern for the development of an adequate supply of human
capital—to be insufficient. We believe that those trends underlie
a worthy case for public attention to child care and parent education needs. We also believe, however, that the case grows in
power and significance when set within the broader context of
values related to human development and community. We have
chosen in this project to emphasize a rationale based on concern
for human development, nurtured in community. Our choice of
emphasis implies many value issues.

Systematic value-based policy inquiry requires the expli-
cation, based on past experience, of the values that are worth
fostering in the future. It requires also the application of appro-

priate methods in the development of public policy as an articulation of those values (Dewey, 1939). Public policy may therefore be seen as the development of fact-value appreciations (Vickers, 1968), necessary to make valid decisions. Within this perspective, policy analysis becomes the attempt to improve the quality of decision making by identifying the fact and value implications of alternative courses of action.

Our overarching concern in this project is to identify ways in which policies affecting families with young children—specifically in the domain of child care and parent education—can be designed so that parents are enabled to maintain and enhance their capabilities for making intelligent choices and managing resources in the interest of their children. Underlying this concern is the belief that if families are to be strengthened, not only should they be viewed as means to societal ends (for example, means to the production of human capital and social stability), but also their well-being should be recognized as a valid end in its own right. Interdependence should characterize optimal family-society relations; neither the family nor the society should be wholly dependent on the other. We believe that if families set within appropriately supportive communities are effective in childrearing and caring for their members, the quality of their own living and the quality of life in the society as a whole will benefit.

Overview of American Social Policy Values

The debate on the most appropriate approach to social policy ultimately reduces to the relationship between individuals and the society as a whole. In regard to family policy, the basic issue is the relationship of individuals and their families to the society.

The prevailing approach to social policy in the United States has emphasized two primary values—individuals and families that are independent and competitive, and a government that intervenes very little, consistent only with the well-being of the economy and limited social means. In apparent contradiction of these individualistic and minimalist values, however, we

have witnessed, particularly in recent decades, an increase in the
scope and quantity of social interventions. The use of individualistic and economic values as a basis for justifying and developing any intervention, however, has remained virtually unchanged.

Two important principles generally shape the way in
which government in the United States intervenes in areas normally considered the domain of families. The first principle requires a case-by-case determination of need for intervention; the
second emphasizes treatment, rather than prevention or insurance against risk, as the preferred intervention strategy. Thus,
services and supports are usually provided only when reasonably
convincing evidence can be generated to make a case for need.
Without such evidence, intervention is usually deemed inappropriate because it is seen as undermining and weakening the independent family.

The current framework of social policy values does not
discount the appropriateness of some attention to families.
There is concern, in fact, that families may need support in limited circumstances. It is often feared, however, that "unnecessary" intervention will result in families giving up responsibilities that they and the society as a whole would prefer they
keep. A pervasive concern centers around the belief that support for families, rather than helping them remain strong care-
giving units, might actually weaken families, since intervention
can easily become interference and lead to dependence.

For these reasons, it appears to many that the appropriate role of the government is to intervene only when there is
clear evidence of family breakdown or pathology. It is argued
that there is such a fine line between support and substitution,
between intervention and interference, that caution is the preferred course. In using this residual notion of social welfare,
each case is judged on its own merits, and intervention decisions
are assumed best made by competent professionals. In this way,
the troublesome issue of unnecessary interference in family life
is said to be minimized. This value framework assumes that limited policies to strengthen families are sufficient to meet existing needs. The concern of such policies is usually the amelioration of poverty and other social pathologies, with families whose

resources are below some level deemed minimally adequate. All in all, it is believed that government's involvement should be restrained and indirect, its aim being to increase economic stability and to guard privacy.

If we examine American social policy historically, we can see clearly its derivation from the belief in competitive individualism and the related notion of laissez-faire economics. As a society, we have assumed that the free enterprise, capitalist system is good and that the state's primary function is to support the market's continuing operation. Social policies have been viewed as acceptable in relation to special needs not adequately addressed by the economic system. Thus, they have been viewed as corrective measures in the interest of individual and social welfare. This attempt to balance individual and collective welfare—with its roots in utilitarianism and the principle of maximizing overall satisfaction in the society—is consistent with a decision to distinguish between the few dependent people who need assistance and the vast majority who do not. Our social policies thus have tended to ignore the enhancement and well-being of the majority on the assumption that the majority of citizens are self-sufficient and benefit most from societal economic well-being (the "trickle down" effect).

Even with the advent of the Great Depression and our national acceptance at that time of some of the principles of the modern welfare state (for example, the assumption of societal responsibility for a threshold of minimally adequate financial resources for retired workers), social policy was seen as part of general economic policy, not as an independent area of public concern governed by separate, noneconomic principles. The Social Security Act went far beyond the provisions of the poor laws, but remained rooted in the economically derived concept of a social minimum. Although many current social policies seem to contain the recognition that modernization and industrialization have created risks and consequences that potentially affect all people and not just a small percentage of the population, social policies continue to function primarily as correctives to an economic system that has not achieved a just allocation of goods and services. Social policy thus continues to emphasize provision of a minimum standard of living and the provision of services only when crises threaten socially acceptable norms. Social services, such as child care and parent education, thus function much as an ambulance at the bottom of the cliff, intended to help those who have fallen, rather than as a fence at the top that prevents people from falling over.

Another value underpinning of current social policies is very closely linked to the human capital rationale. For example, it is felt that resources should be allocated to children because children are *economic* resources for the future. Our programs for the handicapped, another example, are justified on the grounds that rehabilitated handicapped persons will become independent and contribute to the general well-being of the economy (at the very least, they will cost taxpayers less to maintain than if they had no employable skills). This argument is cast in cost-benefit terms: For every dollar invested, a given return should be expected. One difficulty with this, of course, is that some individuals are better risks than others, requiring less investment for comparable or better "payoff" and economic return. Thus, many people with serious needs are often overlooked.

We believe that if the values shaping current social policies—particularly those related to individualism and economic return—remain unquestioned, families will continue to be seen primarily as means to ends, usually economic ends. "Strengthening" families will relate mostly to the contributions of families to economic growth. Policies will continue to focus almost exclusively on the needs of clearly defined and limited special populations, will focus in response to crisis, and will assume that most families are able to function adequately without resources and supports beyond those they are able to muster for themselves. To ensure that intervention remains appropriate, policies and programs will continue to be justified only when there is clear evidence of pathology; the services and supports that may emanate from family policies will be restricted to clearly inadequate families. In this framework, any expansion of child care and parent education policies will be claimed to weaken some families and waste scarce resources.

We propose, however, that traditional policy values in this country be reevaluated and that consideration be given to shifting social policy emphases from a valuing of the atomistic individual and family to a valuing of the individual and family within community. We propose to consider moving from valuing a society based solely on economics to valuing a society in which economic priorities, while important, are secondary to human development priorities. Shifting our value emphases would signal a move from a residual approach, one that is primarily reactive to crises, to one that is preventive, proactive, and universalistic. Elimination or amelioration of poverty and social pathology would continue as an appropriate goal of policy, but it would not be the ultimate goal. The purpose of public policy would be expanded to include the enhancement of the general welfare of families and children by going beyond guaranteeing the social minimum and toward promoting a *caring and competent society*. It would be recognized that industrialization and modernization have given rise to situations that affect *all* people in our society, not just an exceptional portion of the population. We would build the society on the premise that social welfare is a collective responsibility, resting its moral claim on the ethics of mutual aid and cooperation.

Liberty, Equality, Fraternity

The aspirations that inform choice among policy options and rationales in a democracy such as ours should reflect the historical and contemporary goals of the society. They should acknowledge, as well, the inescapable conflicts among these goals.

Although the armies of the French Revolution marched explicitly behind the banner of liberty, equality, and fraternity, they had been deeply influenced by American revolutionaries. The French, in turn, influenced further American thinking, for these three aspirations have permeated American political values throughout our history. Taken together, these goals offer an inspiring challenge. However, they also constitute a set of aspirations in which exist profound conflicts, for it is not possible to achieve, simultaneously, fullness of liberty, equality, and fraternity. They are rights and ideas in conflict. All three cannot be maximized at once; more of one usually means less of another. Indeed, much of American politics, especially in the twentieth century, has involved significant conflict between the goal of liberty—with its emphasis on individual freedom—and equality, focused on the just distribution of social and economic rights and goods. Often lacking in this debate has been serious consideration of the idea and ideal of fraternity (McWilliams, 1974), which we call community. We suggest that the idea of community should be reintroduced into the nation's ongoing political debate.

The formulation of liberty, equality, and fraternity may at first appear too abstract to be of much value in the practical world of child care and parent education policy. It seems far removed from the conflicts of interest groups, child care standards, the desirability of parent participation in early childhood programs, the role of industry and churches in providing services to families, the appropriateness of certification and licensing, the relative merits of block grants, and so on, through the thousands of specific issues in which policy ultimately finds its meaningful expression. However, we contend that the differences that divide people so deeply on these issues, the differences that make it so difficult to gain consensus on child care and parent education policies, spring from passionately held commitments to one or another of these three democratic aspirations.

Thus, we suggest that national policies for child care and parent education take shape in response to deeply held, often unexamined assumptions regarding the relative importance of these three aspirations. And we make two corollary assertions. First, we believe that public discourse about child care and parent education policies will be far more intelligent if the assumptions concerning basic goals are made clear and explicit than if they are allowed to remain obscure and unstated. Second, we believe that the political debate concerning child care and parent education will benefit from increased and explicit attention to the idea of community, making the strengthening of families a more feasible and meaningful enterprise than if we attend only to the aspirations of liberty and equality. We turn now to a brief analysis of the meaning and import of each aspiration for policy making in relation to families.

Aspirations for Liberty. An emphasis on liberty will lead in general to a society focused on individualism, competition, and productivity. And indeed, the American tradition honors work, individual initiative, competition (within limits), and corporate enterprise, all sometimes tempered by a charitable concern for the unfortunate.

The system has been extraordinarily productive. It has resulted in one of the most open societies in history, for those who can "make it," as many have. The system, however, must reckon with the allegation that its survival is contingent upon a substantial number of people of marginal competence who can absorb (through employment and unemployment) fluctuations in the economy; a class of workers who live in the "worlds of pain" (Rubin, 1976) that is frequently the lot of those who are involved in physically demanding and low-paying jobs; and recourse to war, if necessary, for economic vitality. In the eyes of critics, this free enterprise system justifies its support for very limited welfare programs as an "overhead" cost related to the containment of discord that might undermine the system. Social service programs are just sufficient to keep marginal populations reasonably content, but insufficient to prepare marginal individuals for full and rewarding membership in the society. Whatever position one takes on the accuracy of the criticisms, the mood of the nation today seems more in harmony with the aspiration for liberty than for any other.

An emphasis on liberty leads to a focus on the family as a strong, autonomous, and detached unit. This goal emphasizes the centrality of individual family units to the social structure and assumes that policies geared toward maximizing the autonomy and strength of families will lead to the appropriate rearing of children and reasonable security for family members. Government intervention in this perspective should be quite limited and policies should be oriented to increasing economic stability, guarding privacy, and enhancing the "executive function" of the family (that is, the ability of parents to manage family resources, time, and decisions). Such policies assume that the common social good is best served by existing diversity and family self-reliance and that choices made by independent family units will in the end produce outcomes more desirable than those ensuing from any alternative policies. The implications for both child care and parent education are clear. The government has little, if any, role, save perhaps for the granting of small tax breaks to families where parents are employed and use child care or the provision of some care services to the children of the very poor. The government's role in parent education is even smaller, arguably nonexistent from this perspective.

Aspirations for Equality. An emphasis on equality calls for an egalitarian society, a society committed to reducing age-old and worldwide social inequities. In the United States, there are great disparities in the distribution of resources and access to opportunity, and these disparities are apparently increasing. Many citizens regard these inequities as intolerable and profoundly inconsistent with traditional American ideals. Very recently in our history, during the Kennedy and Johnson years, social policy was in fact characterized by a widespread effort to reduce inequities and injustices while preserving—to the extent possible—the more traditional emphases on liberty. Multiple programs were mounted to increase equality of access to social resources and benefits to poor people, women, minority groups, old people, handicapped people, and others whose opportunities had been limited historically by de jure or de facto policies.

Although gains have been made in opening opportunities for members of several groups, many feel that the national commitment to equality of recent decades is waning. And a major criticism of the policies growing out of the aspiration for equality has been that the gains in equity have been made at an unreasonably high cost to traditional liberties.

An emphasis on equality leads to a view of families as having primary responsibilities for the care, nurturance, and maintenance of their members, but also as sometimes limited in their abilities to fulfill those responsibilities as well as they might (Dunlop, 1980). Government intervention in the interest

of increasing the abilities of families to promote the competence of their children—and thus the abilities of children to gain
equal access to the responsibilities and benefits of full membership in the society—is seen as justifiable and useful. The benefits
of such intervention are assumed to accrue to the families and
individuals who participate in the intervention and to the society as a whole as more families gain in strength, access to social
opportunity, and ability to rear their children well. Policies
growing out of this perspective assume that the social good is
best served by helping families and their individual members
overcome disadvantages and deficits by increasing their abilities,
skills, and access to opportunity through direct or indirect
means. The policy implications for child care and parent education center on the provision of developmentally and educationally sound services to augment the existing resources of families.
Services in both child care and parent education would be focused on increasing the competence of children and their parents in the primary interest of enhancing and realizing the full
developmental potential of children.

   Aspirations for Community. An emphasis on fraternity
underscores the importance of community in our national life.
It is significant that debates about social programs, including
the proper role of government in child care and parent education, have centered mainly on concerns for liberty and equality.
The libertarians want the government to stay out of child care
and parent education or, at most, to make resources available
for purchases on the open market, made on the basis of private
preference. The egalitarians want the government to provide
child care and parent education to close the gap between the
fortunate and the unfortunate. And policy makers for the most
part have cast the problem in terms of the interests of individuals or the economic good of the nation (for example, child
care should be provided to enable women to work outside the
home). Seldom has the debate been shaped by concerns for
community. In the section that follows, we explore this issue—
and the implications that flow from a societal commitment to
community—more fully.

The Value of Community

The concept of a caring and competent society in relation to community and human development is neither new nor radical. Indeed, concepts closely related to it were espoused by Thomas Jefferson (Wills, 1978). It is different from prevailing American social thought, however, in rejecting the concept of an atomistic society with its emphasis on self-interest and competition. It is an image of society built on the idea of community, a society in which individuals and families avoid alienation and have a sense of social identity and belonging. Self-interest is expanded in meaning to include concern and action on behalf of the well-being of others (Dokecki, 1981).

However, there has been long-standing conflict between traditional moral values, which have focused on community and mutuality of responsibility for individual well-being, and liberal Enlightenment values, which emphasize political impersonality, competition, and material power (McWilliams, 1974). As McWilliams has so clearly shown, much has been written on American fraternity and community as an abstraction, an end to be achieved *after* liberty and equality issues are settled. True community as an ongoing means of conducting public life, while an occasional theme in American letters (for example, in the writings of Thoreau, Hawthorne, Melville, Twain, Baldwin, and Emerson), has been effectively dismissed from concrete political considerations.

Both McWilliams (1974) and Nisbet (1969) have argued that our politics have been shaped through the use of liberal Enlightenment ideas and that any deviation from them, as, for example, when we seriously discuss community, "has had a suspect, alien quality" (McWilliams, 1974, p. 96). Although the ideas of the Enlightenment have shaped much of what is good in America, "American culture is deeply dualistic [and] the domination of its formal thought by the Enlightenment does not exclude an informal tradition in symbols, rituals, and arts and letters based on very different notions of man and politics" (p. 98). Thus, lurking somewhere in the background over the course of American history have been several traditions of fraternal and communal ideas, which, in their best form, "have expressed a wisdom and truth which the Enlightenment did not possess, and they have always provided the emotional and symbolic basis for the appeal to fraternity in American politics as an immediate need rather than a distant goal" (pp. 99-100). Nisbet (1969) in fact argued that the frequent public dismissal of community is related to historically influenced misconceptions in the Founding Fathers' views of individualistic liberalism. The systematic application of the philosophy of individualism growing out of the aspiration for liberty in American politics has led, in Nisbet's view, to our current situation in which we earnestly seek elements of community, in spite of their conflicts with a wholly libertarian perspective.

We suggest that a community is an immediate social group that promotes human development. Its full meaning is elusive, however, and we do not explore it exhaustively here. We do subscribe to some empirically verified aspects of a psychological sense of community: In communities, individuals experience a sense of membership, influence members of the group and are themselves in turn influenced by others, have personal needs fulfilled, and share a psychologically and personally satisfying connection with other people (McMillan, 1976).

Community basically involves the coming together of people around shared values and the pursuit of common cause. We suggest that it also involves reciprocal obligations. It is clear that communities offer support for their members, be they individuals or families. It is somewhat less clear, however, that communities may appropriately make demands on their members. We believe that individual acceptance of personal responsibility for contribution to community is a necessity of national life and that reciprocity of responsibility among individuals, families, and communities has been and is vital to our national well-being.

Membership in community influences individuals in many ways, among them the shaping of behavior to correspond with group norms and expectations (for example, becoming "good citizens"). Membership in community also brings with it rewards, such as peer support, a right to education, entitlement to

protection from crime, and so on. Membership in community—
which we suggest also entails an obligation to contribute actively to community—enhances individual well-being and contributes to the well-being of others.

Community can be construed on two levels: the immediate, local, face-to-face community of family, friends, and neighbors and the broader, more distant communities inhabited by
people with whom we share a common heritage (fellow citizens) but who are nonetheless strangers to us. Concern for national community grows out of an awareness of the intercon-
nectedness of all people in a society and a valuing of those
broad social groupings—be they related to personal interests,
avocations, professions, special political interests, or the nation
itself—that transcend geographical and local boundaries. Concern for local community grows out of an awareness and valuing of both the many benefits derived from families, friends,
neighborhoods, places of employment, and so on, and the often
critical importance of informal support systems in helping all
individuals and families function well.

If local communities are to support families and the resources they need to meet their responsibilities, they must have
the autonomy necessary to determine community members'
needs and the most appropriate means for meeting those needs.
The national community, most often expressed through the federal government, has a responsibility to help ensure the effective
functioning of local communities. At the very least, it has an
obligation to refrain from interfering unduly with their operation. It is clear, however, that local communities must sometimes defer to the national interest, as in matters of macroeco-
nomic policy, national defense, and equity on those occasions
when local communities fail to guarantee the basic rights of citi-
zenship to their members. It is apparent that in a modern state,
the national community, through the agency of the national
government, must be quite active. But this activism should not
be unlimited. Where there is tension between local and national
community, its resolution should be based on assessment of the
most appropriate means of meeting the human development
needs of citizens. Although the national community should be

fostered and a sense of national purpose enhanced (in part for its value in strengthening local community), the needs and goals of local communities—to the extent that they adequately meet the needs of individual members—should generally have higher priority.

Our consideration of community at all levels leads us to suggest that the essence of community is caring and that the maintenance of community requires competent members. Individuals—children, parents, families—need the support of relatives, friends, neighbors, churches, clubs, self-help groups, and service agencies of many kinds if they are to develop well. And they need opportunities to contribute to the well-being of others. It is in the interest of both local and national community that all children grow up with basic needs for security, affection, and discipline satisfied; that they learn to read, write, do arithmetic, and use technology well; that they are well prepared for their future roles as parents, workers, and citizens; in sum, that they grow up strong in body, quick in mind, and generous in spirit. We believe that strong communities, focused on the enhancement of human development, are the best means to those ends.

Human Development, Community, and Families

The companion principle to an emphasis on community in moving toward a caring and competent society is that human development—social, intellectual, moral, and physical—should be the aim of society. We use here John Dewey's sense of human development as a continual broadening of human experience and the perfection of human social relations over the life cycle. We should strive in the present to develop ourselves, and especially our children, into socially competent people, into better future citizens, into citizens who will create and support a just, democratic, humane, and caring social order.

Families, we believe, are critically important in the development of a caring and competent society. By virtue of our value orientation and evidence from much of the early childhood intervention research of the 1960s and 1970s, we believe that parents and families are of primary significance in the optimal development of children. Strengthening families, in the context of a concern for community and for human development, is therefore an important subject of public policy attention.

Bronfenbrenner (1978), based on several extensive critical reviews of the behavioral research literature, suggested four propositions central to the development of competence in children:

> *Proposition I.* In order to develop, a child needs the enduring, irrational involvement of one or more adults in care and joint activity with the child [pp. 773-774].
> *Proposition II.* The psychological development of the child is brought about through his continuing involvement in progressively more complex patterns of reciprocal activity with persons with whom the child develops a strong and enduring mutual emotional attachment [p. 774].
> *Proposition III.* The involvement of caretaker and child in patterns of progressively more complex reciprocal activity generates an emotional bond, enhanced motivation, and cognitive and manipulative skills that are mutually reinforcing to both participants, are then reflected in the child's competence and cooperation in other situations, and thereby facilitate the child's future development [p. 775].
> *Proposition IV.* To develop the enduring involvement for one or more adults in care, activity, and so forth, requires social policies and practices that provide opportunity, status, encouragement, example, and approval for parenthood [p. 776].

Although children's needs relative to the specifics of their development may vary across cultural, economic, and ethnic groups, Bronfenbrenner's propositions suggest that developmental needs for all children are best met in meaningful relationships with primary care givers in the context of families or familylike settings. The environment provided in such settings is probably the single most important influence on the development of children's cognitive, affective, and social competence, particularly during the first six years of life (Bloom, 1964; Bronfenbrenner, 1974; Clarke and Clarke, 1976; Hunt, 1961). In addition to their significant role in promoting children's healthy development, parents also serve a critical function in mediating between their developing children and the larger society (Berger and Neuhaus, 1977; Keniston and the Carnegie Council on Children, 1977).

Thus, families are the critical element in the rearing of healthy, competent, and caring children. We suggest, however, that families—all families—cannot perform this function as well as they might unless they are supported by a caring and strong community, for it is the community that provides the informal and formal supplements to families' own resources. Just as a child needs nurturance, stimulation, and the resources that caring adults bring to his or her life, so, too, do parents—as individuals and as adults filling socially valued roles (for example, parent, worker)—need the resources made possible by a caring community if they are to fulfill their roles well.

We now move from our understanding of the social and developmental significance of both communities and families to the derivation of specific statements of value that will guide our evaluation of policies related to children and their families.

A Value-Analytic Framework

In this section, we develop a framework that suggests criteria for assessing public policies consistent with the principles just presented.* The framework reflects our preference for a developmental and social ecological perspective and its attendant value positions (Bronfenbrenner, 1977; Emery and Trist, 1972;

*We have reviewed a number of works with an eye toward identifying both implicit and explicit value propositions. They include Berger and Neuhaus (1977), Brim (1959), Craig and Craig (1973), Dolbeare, Dolbeare, and Hadley (1973), Education Commission of the States (1971, 1975), Emery and Trist (1972), Goldstein, Freud, and Solnit (1973),Greenblatt (1977), Keniston and the Carnegie Council on Children (1977), Ladd (1978), Lasch (1977), Marmor (1971), National Academy of Sciences (1976), Rice (1977), Ross and Sawhill (1975), Steiner (1976), and White (1973).

Hobbs, 1975a). We have attempted to make the framework broad enough to be of general use for developing policies to strengthen families. We believe that the framework is useful for the formulation of policy-related questions to be asked of existing research and scholarly literature; the organization of existing data, information, and opinions; the analysis of the existing policy context; the presentation of arguments for and against proposed policy options and implementation approaches; and the formulation of policy evaluation strategies.

We offer as a basic value position that a central goal of public policy and program development in relation to children and families is to *enhance human development through community*. This value position can be stated in two forms:

1. The aim of public policy should be to *enhance community* (both the local, face-to-face community and the broader national community) so that individuals and their families have a legitimate claim on community resources and support in the performance of their developmental tasks.
2. The aim of public policy should be to *enhance human development* so that individuals and their families can participate effectively in the community. The community can legitimately expect individuals and families to master their developmental tasks and engage in relationships of reciprocal responsibility with the community.

We suggest here several specific value-based questions and associated criteria, which we will later apply to the assessment of major policy options in the areas of child care and parent education.

Value Element 1: Does the Policy Enhance Community? Policies that promote the coming together of people around shared values and the pursuit of common cause enhance community at both the local, face-to-face level and the national level, where people also concern themselves with the well-being of citizens who are strangers to them.

This first criterion is, *Does the policy increase shared heritage, mutual aid, and community building?* Policies are valued that actively bring people together both locally (diversity of communities) and nationally (overarching communities, encompassing diverse local communities). These policies highlight human commonalities and aspects of shared heritage, thereby encouraging people to form socially around shared values and common goals. They encourage placing human differences in appropriate perspective, recognizing that the uniqueness of individuals is not a cause for suspicion and separation but is, rather, socially valuable. Nationally, these policies help raise consciousness about matters of far-reaching societal concern. They are implemented fairly and evenhandedly so that all citizens feel equitably treated; all citizens therefore agree to the policies and seek to achieve their goals. Developing "commons" —community areas and functions shared by all, such as public schools—and setting up representative policy bodies to govern these community functions are among the means to achieve these purposes. These policies also encourage the formation of self-help groups, caring opportunities, and community organizations that work to better their members as well as promote community well-being.

The second criterion is, *Is the policy demeaning to any group?* Policies are opposed when they demean people by their nature or by specific forms of implementation. Demeaning policies subject people to humiliating circumstances and communicate that those who participate have an inferior status. Demeaning policies are most often implemented through means-tested eligibility determination, a process by which eligibility for a program or service is assessed on the basis of a combination of factors, including income, assets, and family size. Any conspicuous setting apart of groups of people (as in some school lunch and health-screening programs) also communicates the status of inferiority. Participants are thereby devalued and stigmatized, often suffering a loss of self-esteem. Many people are loathe to seek the supposed benefits offered by such policies and may thereby suffer harm. Demeaning policies deny the existence of common needs among people and clearly reinforce the idea that not all citizens are equal.

The third criterion is, *Does the policy bestow unwar-*

ranted advantage? Policies that give unwarranted advantage are opposed. Comparative justice requires that like cases be treated alike and different cases be treated differently. Certain differences—those based on the notion that special needs, justified as societally important, call for special help—may result in policy-produced advantages that are *warranted.* In this case, all members of a justifiable special-need group should have entitlement to the policy's warranted advantage. Where advantages are bestowed that do not respond to justifiable societal need, however, they are *unwarranted* (Watson, 1980). Income tax credits for child care may be an example of unwarranted advantage; persons not earning enough to pay taxes, but with equal or greater needs than those of higher incomes, are denied the benefit.

The fourth criterion is, *Is the policy divisive?* Policies that are socially divisive are opposed because, by definition, they work against social coherence and solidarity, which are required for meaningful community. Divisive policies separate people for unwarranted reasons on the basis of age, sex, racial and ethnic group membership, socioeconomic status, religious preference, educational level, handicapping condition, and the like. These policies create situations that allow, even encourage, invidious social comparisons, which tend to divide people who might otherwise engage in fruitful social relationships. Certain policies that divide people may be warranted if they allow receipt of warranted advantages (as defined in the previous criterion). Although a core of shared values is necessary for fostering a sense of community and a sense of group identity, impermeable boundaries that arbitrarily define people in and out of social groupings are destructive of community.

The concern in this criterion is with numerous policies and practices that divide major groups. These include de jure and de facto segregation; the separation of old people in nursing homes; and the continuing inequities between men and women at work and in regard to eligibility for Social Security and insurance benefits. Further examples include those human services that are delivered in decidedly different ways for rich and poor people or that use separate modes of payment (for example,

Blue Cross versus Medicaid), often leading to differential quality of service. In child care specifically, current policies may lead to two systems, one through profit-making centers for families who can afford it and one through public agencies such as Head Start and the public schools for those who cannot.

Value Element 2: Does the Policy Strengthen Families? Strong families are the foundation of meaningful community, and they provide the context for the human development of their members. In addition, the family as a system has developmental tasks to master and has responsibilities for relating to other systems within society.

The first criterion is, *Does the policy improve the capacity of families to master a broad range of developmental tasks?* Policies are valued that create conditions or provide services enhancing parental competence, especially in relation to intrafamily and extrafamily factors that influence childrearing. Such policies improve the knowledge, skill, and decision-making capacity of parents in dealing with family developmental issues, such as pregnancy and childbirth, children's growth and developmental tasks, children's health and nutrition, family needs for child care provision because of parental work responsibilities, and children's entry into school. Such policies provide for assessing the diverse needs of individual families, recognizing that different families face different developmental tasks and that the same family has different developmental needs at different times in its life cycle. Of importance here are policies and programs that enhance family functioning both in and outside of the home. Many other public programs are also relevant, for example, mental health services and other public programs that train human service specialists to provide family-related services to individuals. Education-for-parenthood programs are relevant here, as are various government publications on child development.

The second criterion is, *Does the policy improve the liaison or linkage functions of families as they relate to the social resources and supports they need?* Policies are valued when they recognize that families exist within a network of informal social support and formal human service agencies and when they help parents identify and make use of these networks as necessary. Valued policies here do not necessarily require the involvement of formal service bureaucracies, but rather help parents look toward more primary kinds of social support, such as family members, kinship groups, neighbors, and voluntary associations. When the use of formal services is required, information, referral, and liaison services are provided. The goal of such policies is to identify family needs, locate the informal and formal resources necessary for meeting those needs, and help link families with the identified resources. Of concern here are programs that inform families of available resources and facilitate access to those resources. For example, schools have an obligation to inform parents of special opportunities for handicapped children under Public Law 94-142, and numerous programs (like Head Start) foster parental participation and link parents with other specific social services as needed.

The third criterion is, *Does the policy protect the family from unwarranted intrusion and allow parents choice within the constraints generated by other criteria?* Policies of voluntary participation in human service programs and policies that intrude as little as possible into private family matters are valued. Short of the danger of physical harm to a family member, participation should not be coercive. Both de jure coercion and the use of blatant or subtle social pressure should be avoided. Beyond these initial criteria of intrusion and choice, policies that provide a variety of options, as well as adequate information about options, are valued insofar as they allow parents to have real choices on decisions they will make regarding their families.

Value Element 3: Does the Policy Enable Parents To Do Their Job Well? Enabling parents is the primary program and policy means to strengthen families. Policies that enable parents to make competent decisions for their family strengthen the family and enhance the well-being, developmental status, and rights of all family members.

The first criterion is, *Does the policy minimize stress by making essential resources available to parents?* Policies are valued when they help ensure that parents have the time, energy, knowledge, and resources (and consequent satisfaction in the form of positive affect and feelings of worth) necessary to carry out their parental functions well. Necessary time and energy might be provided through sensible schedules of work, flexitime, shared jobs, maternity/paternity leaves, good-quality child care, adequate periods for recreation and vacation, and general good health and nutrition. Knowledge regarding parental roles comes from many formal and informal sources, including parent education programs. The term *resources* refers to the wide range of supports that communities, sometimes through governments, make available to people, including various tax benefits that are associated with family membership and family functioning (for example, income tax exemptions for dependents, earned credit for low-income families, and credit for child care provided by grandparents). A large number of other policies are relevant here, including unemployment compensation; assistance in the care of handicapped, chronically ill, and infirm family members; and leave time to facilitate caring for a baby or a sick child.

The second criterion is, *Does the policy promote shared responsibility among parents and service providers, including professionals?* Policies that operate according to enabling and empowerment principles are valued. Parents become able to develop and to become effective decision makers when they are treated as capable adults and are helped by service organizations and professionals to become even more capable. Enabling involves the enhancement of knowledge and skill through appropriate education for adults. Empowerment involves providing parents with resources and legal rights so that they may negotiate effectively with social institutions. Many professionals, primarily because of their training, often behave as imperious experts, an approach decidedly counter to this criterion.

Value Element 4: Does the Policy Enhance Individual Development and Protect the Rights of Individual Members of the Family? All family members—parents and children—have ongoing developmental tasks to master. Similarly, all family members, including even very young children, have fundamental human rights. Clearly, this value element is closely related to, in fact is part of, the second and third value elements given earlier. There, the argument was that the strengthening of families and the enabling of parents will have salutary effects for all family members. But it is worthwhile to repeat the issue here with a focus on individual family members.

The first criterion is, *Does the policy enhance individual opportunities for the development of competence and self-realization?* Policies that create conditions or provide services to enhance individuals' physical, cognitive, affective, and interpersonal development are valued. Such policies emphasize that the developmental and educational opportunities of specific family members should not be ignored in the general quest to strengthen the family. This is central to the idea of building a competent and caring society, for it is important to each citizen that there be developed in the nation a diversity of competencies essential to its economic and humane development and that there be a minimum level of competence in basic and special skills above which *all* citizens will be sustained.

The second criterion is, *Does the policy protect individual members of the family from abuse and severe neglect?* Policies are valued that recognize the importance of parental rights to the maintenance of the family unit but that stop short of allowing these rights to work to the significant detriment of individual family members. Issues of child abuse and spouse abuse are involved here. One of the intended effects of many human service programs—including parent education and child care programs—is to help prevent abuse and severe neglect. Fundamental to this criterion is the concept of the dignity of each human being, but also stressed is the idea that individuals exist in social context and that individual rights, inside or outside the family, imply corresponding social responsibilities. Policies that come into play here are concerned with foster care, prevention of child abuse and severe neglect, the termination of parental rights when abuse so warrants, the equitable sharing of property, the prohibition of child labor, and so on.

These, then, constitute the values and criteria that guide our analysis of policies affecting children and their parents. We believe that they go a significant step beyond a reliance on demographic trends and the human capital rationale in considering the course this nation should take as it formulates policies related to children and families. We also believe that this step into community-based values criteria, grounded in concern for human development, is necessary if this nation is to have the competent and caring citizenry it needs for its movement into a sensible and humane future.

FOUR

ଠୀଠୀଠୀଠୀଠୀଠୀଠୀଠୀଠୀଠୀଠୀଠୀଠୀଠୀଠୀଠୀଠୀ

The National Experience with Child Care and Parent Education

With our goal of strengthening families so that they are enabled to raise their children wisely and well in the context of communities, we turn now to examining a large body of evidence on the nature, use, and effects of child care and parent education programs. Our intent here is to analyze and integrate what we know about child care and parent education so that we may make the best use of past experience in moving forward with the development of future policy options.

Programs of Child Care and Parent Education

Child care and parent education have been offered for many decades by a variety of public and private sponsors. Across the years and sponsors, definitions of both child care and parent education have been marked by changes and shifts in emphasis. In this section, we examine the purpose and content of those programs.

Out-of-home child care was first formally provided by

day nurseries, as early as 1822. These programs focused on the provision of *daycare* for unfortunate children of all ages—the poor, the orphaned, the neglected, and the abandoned. Historically, they took a custodial approach to service delivery, but in recent years, that approach has been expanded in many child care programs to include an educational component based on developmental principles. *Kindergartens,* serving five-year-olds only, were established in the mid 1850s as private programs and introduced into the public schools in the 1870s. Although characterized by a variety of purposes, kindergartens traditionally have taken an educational approach to program development and service delivery. *Nursery schools,* usually serving children between the ages of two and four, have existed as private programs since 1922. Historically, these programs focused on training adults in parenting skills, home economics, social work, or child development research. Moving from an early "laboratory" function, their purpose expanded subsequently to include the well-being and total development of the children enrolled in the program.

Although their initial and continuing orientations have grown from different purposes and goals, all three types of early childhood programs—daycare, kindergarten, and nursery school —now share significant characteristics. For the most part, all focus on the development and health of young children, include some educational component in program activities, and frequently attempt to involve parents. Their differences have diminished over time, and all are now important in providing some portion of care for large numbers of young children, albeit with some variation in emphasis. We will review the evidence on all of these programs as they have affected participating children between infancy and five years of age.

Like child care, parent education has been marked by major shifts in purpose, content, and approach. Parent education is typically defined as dealing exclusively with childrearing (Harman and Brim, 1980), but some extend its scope to the family as a system and a variety of parent needs (Wandersman, 1978). Some construe parent education to mean experts imposing values upon families (Keniston and the Carnegie Council on

Children, 1977; Lasch, 1977), while others see parents as defining their own needs and using experts as resources (Dokecki, Roberts, and Moroney, 1979). We view parent education as the process of enabling parents to obtain information and skills useful to them in performing the array of functions broadly related to their parental role. Parent education includes learning opportunities relevant to childrearing functions, to parents' executive function (providing for the family, interacting with other institutions), and to meeting the personal needs of parents. We will discuss what is known about child care and parent education as offered by different sponsoring agencies (see also Florin and Dokecki, 1983; Innes and Dunlop, 1979, 1980; Roberts and Dokecki, 1980).

Individual, Private Provision. Individual, private provision has been and continues to be the most prevalent form of child care and parent education in the United States, probably because it seems the most natural means for supporting parents in their childrearing functions. When parents want help (child care) or advice (parent education) regarding their children, they traditionally turn to the resources perceived as most convenient, most trustworthy, and least expensive: kin, friends, and neighbors. If *advice* is not available or is unsatisfactory, parents usually turn to one or more sources of parent education described in the sections that follow (for example, courses on childrearing or church-sponsored programs). If informal *help* resources are not available from the immediate network of kith and kin, many parents turn to in-home baby-sitters or individual daycare providers (Bane and others, 1979). Indeed, family daycare, provided by unrelated individuals in their homes for pay, constitutes the most frequently used form of child care help in the United States today. Fully 45 percent of the 7.5 million families who use child care use family day homes, 35 percent choose in-home baby-sitters, and 17 percent use other forms of child care (*National Day Care Home Study Final Report,* 1981).

Early on, individually provided child care came to be defined as part of the public interest and therefore subject to regulation and licensing (Goldsmith, 1978). Despite this, however, most individually provided child care is not regulated or licensed;

the *National Day Care Home Study Final Report* (1981) estimated that over 90 percent of family daycare—serving approximately five million children for ten or more hours per week—is
unlicensed. Family day homes that are licensed constitute approximately 6 percent of the total day home care providers; an
additional 2 percent of day home providers are both licensed
and sponsored. Licensing requires that providers and their
homes meet local and state standards. If the home serves children whose fees are subsidized by a federal program, the provider must meet federal standards as well. Sponsored day homes
are those that meet licensing requirements and are affiliated
with some organization (for example, an association of day
home providers, a child care center, a university) that provides
access to training, client referral, and services such as participation in the U.S. Department of Agriculture (USDA) Child Care
Food Program.

Keyserling's (1972) frequently cited survey of 166 daycare homes presented a bleak picture of family day home quality. The homes she studied, which usually served neighborhood
children between the ages of two and four years, made only in-
frequent attempts to involve parents and offered activities that
were very restricted in nature, reflecting little familiarity with
children's educational or developmental needs. Adams and
Macht's (1976) later survey of forty-five providers revealed that
most received their training from being parents, although half of
the group had taken at least one course related to child care.
The providers usually supervised free play activities but did not
plan for specific activities or goals. In spite of these limitations,
Adams and Macht found enough encouraging information to
conclude that as a group, the care givers provided "safe and
often enriching care for children" (p. 304).

The results of the National Day Care Home Study presented a still more positive view of the quality of care offered in
family day homes. The homes studied (unregulated, licensed,
and sponsored) reflected high levels of care giver–child interaction (46 percent of the total day's time). Care givers usually
spent an additional 17 percent of their time each day preparing
for or supervising the children. The interaction time was found

to be "appropriate, [given] the needs of children in care as indicated by their ages" (*National Day Care Home Study Final Report*, 1981, p. 27). In general, care givers in the sponsored homes tended to show higher levels of involvement with children and higher frequency of teaching behaviors than did providers in the other homes. Homes in the study served an average of 3.5 children, about half of whom were toddlers (the remaining half was made up of preschoolers, infants, and school-age children). Funding usually came from parent fees, which averaged $21 per week. Parents were generally satisfied with the way their children's social needs were being met. Most were pleased with the children's social growth, although some wanted more emphasis on conceptual and language development. In general, the study results supported the positive possibilities inherent in individually provided care, as well illustrated by Galinsky and Hooks's (1977) description of an exemplary family daycare program. The positive findings and potential suggested by the latter two studies, however, must be understood within the still limited state of knowledge concerning much of this primary source of child care.

Parent education, of course, is most frequently derived from individual informal sources (other parents, neighbors, grandparents) in countless major and minor exchanges over time. Evidence concerning the specific content and impact of such advice, however, is sparse indeed, leaving us to conclude for the time being that it is very prevalent and probably quite influential, but elusive insofar as any possibility of systematically examining its effects is concerned. Thus, our attention in parent education has focused on that offered by more formal sources.

Cooperatives and Self-Help Groups. Parents who choose individually provided care for their children sometimes do so for reasons related to both geographical and psychological proximity; there is often a motive to ensure that the care children receive is much like the care that would be received at home. Parents who cannot or choose not to use family day homes may elect—to keep their sources of parent education and child care "close to home"—to work with other parents in the development and provision of care and education services for themselves and other families. Such motivations form the sources of a small but significant movement in cooperative child care and parent education.

Parent cooperative nursery schools were begun in the 1920s and have grown in number and influence since that time (Frost and Kissinger, 1976; Lazerson, 1972). Focused on providing care and education of high quality at a reasonable price, parent cooperatives have usually employed professionals to provide leadership in program design and implementation and then supplemented this leadership with active parent involvement and work (Leeper and others, 1974). The programs frequently offer curricula focused on children's social as well as cognitive development. Many offer an "intensive program of parent education" because all parents are regularly involved in program teaching (Leeper and others, 1974, p. 95). An international organization of parents involved in cooperative preschools, Parent Cooperative Preschools International, has an active membership of about 10,000. While somewhat limited in usefulness to parents who need child care to maintain full-time employment, parent cooperatives nonetheless represent a creative effort to maintain the benefits of strong parent involvement and parental influence in child care while developing access to the benefits of a group program led by well-trained personnel.

Cooperative groups similarly have been the source of a good deal of parent education, particularly in the last two decades. Unlike professionalized helping services, these groups involve helping exchanges between people sharing a common experience. First-hand experience with the same difficulty, not specialized training, is the rationale for the help offered by group members to one another (Silverman, 1976).

Help delivered through mutual aid groups may address several issues in parent education, one of which is coping with the adjustments demanded by transitions in the parental role (Hirschowitz, 1976). Group discussions and interactions between people who have experienced similar transitions are seen as providing several elements of help to parents: an environment conducive for the sharing of feelings and experiences; a source of information and new perspectives on the transitional situation; and an arena in which to plan, rehearse, and receive feedback concerning the behaviors demanded by new roles. In this way, these groups form a social support system that facilitates adaptive coping behavior (Caplan, 1974).

Another mutual aid program, the Post-Partum Education Project, was organized by certain members of the American Association of University Women who felt unprepared for the arrival of their children and accompanying life changes. It was designed to help ease others' adjustment to parenthood. Volunteers, all recent parents themselves, take part in a two-day training program conducted by physicians, psychologists, and other professionals. They then aid other "newborn" parents through emotional support, the sharing of ideas and potential solutions to problems, and encouragement to seek professional advice when appropriate. Parents Without Partners is another group focused on providing mutual help for specific parental needs. It has grown from its founding in 1957 to over 170,000 members. It offers a wide variety of activities seeking to meet the educational, instrumental, social, and emotional needs of single parents.

Mutual help groups in parent education also engage in advocacy designed to influence public attitudes, policies, and even legislation. The Parent Educational Advocacy Training Center in Alexandria, Virginia, for example, offers a fifteen-hour training course for parents of handicapped children. The course teaches parents to become full participants in educational planning for their child. The center hopes to build a network of parents who will be ready to assist one another in educational planning.

Neighborhoods, too, may serve as the locus of mutual help parent education groups. For example, on the basis of data gathered in neighborhoods in Milwaukee and Baltimore, the Neighborhood and Family Services Project recommended that a "network of helping systems" be designed to provide needed supports to all families—single-parent, two-parent, and extended (Naparstek and others, 1978).

The experience of cooperative, mutual help groups strongly suggests the utility of emphasizing "natural" community-based settings for child care and especially parent education (see also Harman and Brim, 1980). Among other advantages, mutual help groups offer strong opportunities for parent determination of program goals and content.

Private, Nonprofit Organizations. Another source of child care and parent education includes a wide variety of private, nonprofit organizations such as churches, community organizations, and private, nonprofit corporations.

Private, nonprofit sponsorship of child care began in the charitable day nurseries founded in the early 1800s. Although philanthropic sponsors viewed them as a temporary expedient to be eventually phased out of existence, private, nonprofit programs continue today as a major source of out-of-home child care. In general, they continue to reflect the initial interest and concerns of the day nursery movement, but almost all now include an educational component in program design. This educational influence was felt in the early 1900s, when the nursery school movement began to affect child care programs. The major impetus for the change, however, came from research on the early childhood development and intervention programs of the 1960s and 1970s (for example, Bloom, 1964; Gray and Klaus, 1970; Hunt, 1961; Weikart, Deloria, and Lawson, 1974).

Like their predecessors, many contemporary programs sponsored by private, nonprofit organizations deliver services primarily to low-income families, although some are aimed at middle-income families or mixed income groups. These programs traditionally have received their funding from one or more federal sources (for example, Titles IV and XX of the Social Security Act, as amended; Head Start; and the Handicapped Children's Early Education Program). Some funding also comes from state and local governments as well as private sources (for example, charitable organizations, labor unions, parent fees, and private fund raising).

Most care that is center-based is offered today through private, nonprofit groups. To a great extent, the "basic" needs of children and specific needs of families are the foci of their services. These groups are often oriented toward the provision of child care in keeping with a larger social goal (for example, improving educational levels), rather than the provision of child care as an end in itself. Many include supplementary services, such as counseling, job training, social work, and family planning, as an integral part of a comprehensive approach to helping families improve their life situations.

Private, nonprofit child care centers tend to have a variety of goals, among them the development of children's self-confidence and independence; the preparation of children for formal schooling; the development of identity with "American" and ethnic group culture; the development of family relationships; the freeing of older siblings from responsibility for the care of young children; the training of professionals and paraprofessionals; the development of strong parental involvement; and the strengthening of communities. These goals are addressed through several specific activities complementing the care and education of children: medical, dental, and health services; nutrition programs; services for handicapped children; parent education; toy-lending libraries; information and referral services; social work and other support services for families; assessment of community needs; community organization; and consultation to families and family day home providers.

The curricula used in these programs vary from an emphasis on individual expression and creative activity to unit-based planning. Commercially developed programs and materials, such as Sesame Street or the Peabody Language Development Kit, are used and formal mathematics and reading readiness activities are included in some programs. Some use specific early childhood curriculum models; others design programs to meet the specific needs of the children served.

In almost all private, nonprofit programs, parent involvement is considered very important, although often difficult to implement. Many programs have formal means of involving parents, such as parent meetings and home visits, and many operate under funding-related mandates to include such opportunities for involvement in their programs. Education services, through family counseling, for example, may also be offered.

Some agencies have recently shifted to programs of parent education that focus on more intensive preventive (rather than remedial) services in support of family functioning (Beck, Tileston, and Kesten, 1977). Consider, for example, such programs as family life education; neighborhood discussion and action groups; and the use of drama, such as the Family Service Association's Plays for Living program. Other voluntary organizations offer additional kinds of programs focused specifically on parent education. The American National Red Cross, for example, developed a Mother and Baby Care Course (later renamed Preparation for Parenthood), designed to help expectant parents, particularly in the areas of infant care, human development, and parenthood responsibilities. The course reaches nearly 200,000 new parents each year. The Young Men's Christian Association (YMCA) offers the Family Communications Program, based on concepts developed by family therapist Virginia Satir, all of which focus on helping family members develop insight into their communication patterns and develop new ways of managing family conflict. Churches also have been involved in parent education, particularly in the areas of family guidance and counseling. A history of informal involvement in these areas currently reflects an effort to develop more structured activities, all of which acknowledge the concept of churches as naturally occurring contact points for families. There is enormous potential for family support inherent in the churches of this nation, which may be channeled into an organized, cooperative resource system.

Private, nonprofit groups thus have been integrally involved in the provision of both child care and parent education from the inception of formal offerings in both areas. While the amount of child care provided by private, nonprofit organizations—when compared with that provided by private individuals —is small, nonprofit programs have been among the most visible and significant of the formal providers of group care. Their traditional focus on serving the needs of disadvantaged populations has put them at the forefront of efforts to improve social conditions in this country. Interestingly, some of them, especially churches, are now also involved in meeting what is perceived as a new social need, supplemental care for the children of *all* families, and are offering increasing numbers of mothers' and parents' "day out" programs on a regular basis. The amount of parent education offered by private, nonprofit groups also seems to be increasing, particularly as existing social institutions move to support parents and families in a variety of ways.

   Public Schools. Perhaps no other sponsoring agency, outside of individual private providers, has been so involved in child care and parent education as the public schools. It is also likely that no other sponsoring agency has been so lauded as an excellent vehicle for delivering those services, so castigated for the shortcomings of its efforts, and so complex in the mix of promise and problems that have seemed inherent in the structure of its efforts to provide child care and parent education.

   As a provider of early child care and parent education, public schools have long served as a locus of initially experimental programs designed to improve the well-being of a portion, or all, of society. Kindergartens were introduced into the public schools in the 1870s as an experimental effort borrowed from philanthropists to "overcome the handicaps of growing up in an urban slum [and] transform family life in the slum through the education of parents" (Lazerson, 1972, p. 40). The goals inherent in philanthropic support of kindergartens, as well as the programs' developmental emphasis on socialization and nurturance, came early into conflict with institutional demands for disciplined classrooms and financially viable organization. The conflict between the developmental and reform orientations of the proponents of kindergarten and the organization and control orientations of the school institution is in fact cited by Lazerson (1972) as one of three abiding themes of conflict in the history of early childhood education in the public schools. The other two themes are related to assertions by early childhood educators that the early years are uniquely important in the education of the child and that their more flexible approach to classroom organization should serve as the impetus for reform of elementary school practices.

   In spite of conflicts between public elementary schools and programs for young children, such programs have grown and flourished—albeit at times with difficulty—as a part of the school system. Kindergartens served less than 15 percent of the eligible-aged children in the mid 1920s (Lazerson, 1972), but by the 1980s they were available to virtually all of the nation's five-year-olds as a regular part of the public school offerings in most states.

Not only have public schools seen the introduction and integration of kindergartens into their midst; they have also served as a significant locus of more recent attempts to improve the conditions and education of poor children. In the 1960s and 1970s, armed with new scientific information concerning "the staggering rate at which the preschool child acquires skills, expectancies, and notions about the world and about people [as well as] the degree to which culturally specialized attitudes shape the care of young children during these years," social reformers turned to early childhood education as a means of fighting the War on Poverty (Bruner, 1972, p. 8). With these efforts, there came into the public schools a new variety of curricular innovations under the banner of Head Start and early intervention, all intended to increase the school readiness of poor children, improve the lives of their families, and introduce reform into the practice of elementary education. Although many of these programs were at least partially dependent on federal funding, they created professional and public acknowledgment that the schools, on their own initiative, may appropriately be involved in preschool education. Conclusions as to the effectiveness of early intervention programs have varied across studies and time (Beilin, 1972; Weikart, in press), but the programs appear to have had increasingly positive effects on children's lives and they have become a regular part of many schools' offerings to preschool-age children, especially those from poor families.

While the primary focus of kindergarten and early intervention has been the education of children (and, in varying degrees, their parents), they have also served as providers of care for children, sometimes offering programs whose primary orientation, in fact, is care. In the early 1900s, the boards of education in a few cities began to sponsor day nurseries; these beginnings saw significant expansion in the 1930s, when approximately 1,200 nurseries were established in schools under the authorization of the Work Projects Administration (WPA). In the 1940s, the Lanham Act authorized funds for school-based child care programs and the number expanded still further. However, because both the WPA centers and the Lanham Act centers focused primarily on providing jobs or freeing mothers for the labor force, standards for the programs were often sketchy, with resulting variability in quality of service (Steinfels, 1973). The end of both the economic and the war-related crises that spurred federal support for daycare in the public schools saw a marked decline in school support for child care programs per se, although some states (California, for example) continued the program of children's centers in the schools. Only in the 1970s —influenced by early intervention efforts and political pressure from many quarters to increase public school involvement in child care—did more schools again involve themselves in the sponsorship of programs explicitly and primarily intended to provide care for young children (see, for example, Levine, 1978).

The goals and curricula of all types of preschool efforts undertaken by public schools—kindergarten, early intervention preschools, and child care—share similarities and reflect variety. All are oriented toward preparing children for elementary school. Kindergarten programs, serving almost all families who use public schools, generally focus on academic readiness activities as well as a varied mixture of creative activities, language development, group interaction, and play (Evans, 1978). Among kindergarten programs, however, orientations may vary in patterns that have been defined loosely as focusing on the socialization of children, the maturational development of children, and the instruction of children (Davis, 1963). Early intervention programs also display substantial variety in program content and approach (see, for example, Parker and Day, 1972), although most are characterized by orientation to a specific model of early development that is assumed to be effective in supporting the learning of young, disadvantaged children. School-based child care programs display similar variability; almost all emulate the intent of the early intervention preschool programs to enhance the learning potential and cognitive skills of disadvantaged children, but they also usually include an expressed intention to provide supplemental care to the children of low-income working parents (Levine, 1978).

Orientations to parent involvement in these public school programs are quite varied. Kindergartens usually reflect a pattern of parent involvement similar to that of the elementary grades, a pattern that may vary from school to school but is often characterized by formality and infrequency of contact. Early intervention preschool programs and school-based child care, on the other hand, often function under funding mandates to involve parents and provide some form of parent education. In one evaluation of parent participation, Kaplan and Forgione (1978) concluded that in the states they studied, parent participation in ESEA Title I programs was hampered either by the reluctance of educators who were uncommitted to parent involvement or by failure to generate participation among those willing to try. Parent involvement often drops off rapidly as children approach first grade, and parent education programs under ESEA Title I have been almost universally reported to be characterized by poor attendance and high attrition rates.

There are some notable examples of successful parent involvement in school-based programs, however. The Brookline Early Education Project (BEEP) is a locally funded, school-based comprehensive program for all families with preschool children. It began in 1973 and was designed to use research findings and program components that had worked elsewhere in developing an optimal program. In addition to a diagnostic program, which provides early health screening and follow-up for each child from early infancy until school entry, the program concentrates on providing parents with information and support to facilitate their childrearing tasks, primarily through home visits and small discussion groups. Center-based educational activities are initiated when the child is two years of age, and parents continue an active role through observation of their children in play groups and regular consultation with teachers. Home visits continue on a regular basis until the child is three years old; after that they occur as needed. Families are also offered some child care services, the loan of books and toys, and referrals to other community agencies. Programs similar to BEEP have been established in a few public schools through a variety of funding sources.

Another exemplary program, the Minnesota Early Childhood and Family Education (ECFE) project, was established in 1976. Six programs in elementary school districts throughout the state were funded with an appropriation of $250,000. By 1979, the program had expanded to twenty-two program sites with a budget of $777,000, and in 1980 there were thirty-six programs with state expenditures of $1.45 million. Each program is operated from an elementary school and serves all the families having preschool-age children within the attendance area. Each is overseen by an advisory committee, appointed by the local school board, that must have a majority of participating parents. The programs offer a variety of services but do not provide child care and do not duplicate services available through other agencies. Evaluations of the program have concluded that local groups have successfully implemented the concept of early childhood and family education, generated overwhelmingly favorable responses from participating parents, and steadily increased the quality of program services and administration.

Public schools and state education agencies are thus involved in a variety of parent education efforts offered through or in conjunction with early care and education programs. Schools are involved in other parent education efforts as well.

One such area focuses on people who are not yet parents. Parenthood preparation programs are offered to many junior and senior high school students, providing information and experience related to child development and the responsibilities of caring for young children. These programs may serve as a means of preventing "premature parenthood"; they also provide a foundation of knowledge and skill for competent childrearing. Education-for-parenthood programs have been developed both locally and under the auspices of various levels of government. One of the most widely disseminated was developed by the Education Development Center, Inc., of Newton, Massachusetts, called Exploring Childhood. Adopted for use in over

2,600 schools, it is one part of a nationwide program launched in 1972 by the U.S. Children's Bureau in cooperation with the Office of Education and the National Institute of Mental Health. High school home economics departments also play a significant role in parent education, offering thousands of courses on child development, family living skills, and family relations. For example, the Education for Parenthood Pilot Project in Austin, Texas, combines parenthood education, vocational training for the child care field, education for school-age parents, and child care for the infants and toddlers of school-age parents.

Schools have been active recently in developing programs specifically for the increasing number of school-age parents, most of whom are women with low income, limited education, and low employment status (Aaronson, 1978). The Park School in Grand Rapids, Michigan, is illustrative of such programs. A public alternative program for pregnant students and school-age parents, it provides a complete junior and senior high school curriculum, special instruction in all areas related to pregnancy and childbearing, group and individual counseling, and referrals to appropriate community agencies. An Infant Care Center provides child care for mothers who continue in the program after the birth of their babies. Students attend an Infant Stimulation Project in the Infant Care Center one evening a week, where they receive information and training in infant health care, diet, and social and intellectual stimulation.

Public schools also offer adult education, and many of these courses are relevant to parents. These courses may be especially attractive because they are usually quite accessible and offer help to parents in an educational mode, which is frequently preferred over definitions of parent education as "help" or "treatment" (Hirschowitz, 1976).

Overall, therefore, there is substantial public school activity in the areas of child care and parent education, continuing a long history of involvement in these areas. While some people have questioned aspects of this activity (for example, the appropriateness of school involvement, the sometimes tenuous nature of school relations with other community agencies, the introduction of bureaucracy and rigidity into early care programs), the public schools nonetheless represent considerable experience and potential for child care and parent education. This potential has been demonstrated through a large number of successful programs representing a wide variety of approaches to service delivery.

Colleges and Universities. In the early 1900s, several universities established laboratory schools to complement the demonstration and training functions of their undergraduate programs. The programs for children emphasized growth and development and provided activities in an enriched, stimulating environment. From these university-based laboratory, demonstration, and nursery schools came a developmental approach to early childhood education that is considered contemporarily to be "traditional," based as it is on a variety of theoretical and developmental approaches to educating the whole child. While many of the demonstration and laboratory schools stayed within the university setting, nursery schools were gradually absorbed into the fabric of many communities, offered by various organizations and individuals.

During the 1960s, colleges and universities renewed their involvement as sponsors of preschool programs, but with major differences in the populations served and program content. The children in most early programs were from middle- and upper-income homes; in contrast, university programs established during the 1960s generally served low-income families, reflecting a change in political climate and academic research interests. They began in the 1960s to serve as a research base for learning more about the effects of enriched care and educational opportunities on the development of children, particularly poor children.

Colleges and universities also began to sponsor a third type of program for young children, one intended to provide child care for student and employee families. Ravenscraft (1973) estimated that nearly 40 percent of the 1,000 accredited senior colleges and universities in the United States offered some form of preschool program, including child care centers, nursery schools, and laboratory schools.

Parent education has generally been a priority of college- and university-based programs. Almost all focus on parent education and involvement, although the approach and extent of involvement may vary. In some cases, parent education courses, discussion groups, and support groups are provided as an additional service to parents (see also Galinsky and Hooks, 1977). Regardless of their specific offerings, college-sponsored programs generally seem responsive to expressed parent needs; for example, arrival and departure times are frequently flexible and parents seem welcome in most of the centers at their convenience.

Programs sponsored by colleges and universities are often of high quality, a result of several factors: the availability of skilled teachers, teacher trainees, and volunteers seeking experience; the relatively high levels of funding available to selected research-oriented programs, the public nature of most university programs; and the relatively high level of knowledge or education among many parent-users, who tend to demand and monitor quality in the programs offered. This clustering of characteristics seems unique to college- and university-sponsored programs.

Although the programs seldom report family income levels, many serve low-income populations: designated low-socio-economic status (SES) children in research and intervention efforts; student-users who live at or below the poverty level; and low-income families living in the nearby neighborhoods. Other users include children from the broader university community, including children of faculty and staff. Private funds support most of these programs, although some programs charge fees and others use financial support from student organizations, fund-raising events, donations, and in-kind contributions. Still others, especially those serving low-income populations, receive federal funds. In some programs, sliding scale fees based on parents' income are used.

The purpose of most campus-based child care services is to provide child care through activities designed to enhance children's self-concept and language, as well as their general cognitive, social-emotional, and physical skills. The content of many campus-sponsored programs appears oriented toward developmentally based curricula; many use an open classroom approach to educational activities and focus on unit-based planning or teaching through play. Research-oriented programs often compare, deliberately and experimentally, the effects of different types of curricula on children's development. This research effort in university-based programs has contributed significantly to the state of the art and what is known concerning the effects of group care participation on young children.

Workplace-Sponsored Child Care and Parent Education. Notable involvement in child care by private industry in the United States emerged during World War II when the Kaiser Child Service Centers, located in two shipyards, were established. The industry employed 25,000 women, and 1,005 children were enrolled in the centers at one point. The centers were unique in part because of their size and intense service delivery (twenty-four hours a day; 364 days a year) (Stolz, 1978). However, with the need for women in defense employment waning after the war, workplace involvement in the sponsorship of child care declined. By the 1970s, 200 employer-sponsored centers served 6,000 children, although by 1979, estimates had declined to approximately 5,000 children in 150 to 200 centers (Boocook, 1979).

For the most part, employer-sponsored child care is found in industries whose employees are predominantly women (Steinfels, 1973). Employer motivation for involvement in child care has been related primarily to the attraction of new employees, the retention of current employees, and hopes for increasing the productivity of employees through the reduction of absenteeism, tardiness, and turnover (Sassen and Avrin, 1974; Boocock, 1979). The success of employer-sponsored child care programs in achieving these goals has been mixed, and many have shifted the rationale for offering child care from business-related reasons to an expressed intention to do something beneficial for a group of employees or the community. Because child care programs seldom generate income for the organization, however, they may be eliminated quickly if they are underutilized or become administratively problematic.

When employers do offer child care programs, they tend to be of good appearance and quality, for it is important to most businesses that the program be seen as a positive contribution to the community. In general, they serve the preschool children of employees, although some allow the enrollment of neighborhood children as well. Curricula are infrequently based on formal designs or early childhood education models, but focus on "positive experiences" and child-oriented activities. Services are generally limited to child care and supervision, although informal visiting by parents may be encouraged and health consultations may be included.

Funding for employer-sponsored programs has come from a variety of sources, most frequently from a combination of parent fees, state funds, and organizational subsidies. Federal funding has been used at times, although usually during demonstration projects or other special programs. Parent fees vary across the centers and include flat fees, sliding scale fees, and fees calculated as a percentage of wages.

Although examples of workplace-sponsored parent education are few, some have been developed over the last several years, among them a program conducted by the Texas Institute for Families. With funding from the Levi Strauss Foundation, the institute presented parent education programs in corporations around the state. The program consisted of several one-hour seminars for working parents, usually offered during the lunch hour. The first series focused on "how to get along with your kids while getting along with your boss," stressing ways of having quality time with children and such "executive functions" as time management and selection of care programs. Other programs in the series dealt with the stress of management jobs and its effects on families and also the problems faced by single parents. The institute's goal is to have corporations, impressed with the benefits to their employees, eventually finance the programs themselves.

Considering the access to parents that the workplace offers and the important influence of work on family life, it seems likely that these beginning approaches to linking family and workplace will continue. The area is clearly not without problems, however. Some corporations have offered child care programs only to find them underutilized and ineffective in combating employee absenteeism or turnover. Others have found such programs costly and difficult to maintain, causing some to suggest that employer involvement in child care—if it is to continue at all—should be limited to subcontracting with private providers or granting child care subsidies as an employee benefit. Parent education in the workplace is, similarly, a complex issue. Parents may or may not show enthusiasm for participation in such programs when they are offered (Yankelovich, Skelly, and White, Inc., 1977), and issues of family privacy and undue workplace intrusion may be raised.

Private, For-Profit Sponsorship. Private, for-profit child care emerged as a significant sponsorship form in the late 1960s, when investors were attracted to child care as an industry promising the quick profits associated with a growth enterprise. The promise of ready profits was not often realized in the early stages of this sponsorship form, and professional opinion, predominantly hostile to the idea of profit making with young children, calmed somewhat as several centers closed. Estimates made between 1973 and 1979, however, indicated that profit-making centers were indeed growing again, as 40 to 50 percent of all preschool-age children enrolled in *center* care were located in profit-making programs. Profit-making centers, in spite of their checkered history, had become a significant force in the field (Bane and others, 1979; *National Day Care Study,* 1979; Steinfels, 1973).

For-profit centers include traditional single-owner centers, operating as very small enterprises, and corporate chains or franchises operating regionally and nationally (Ginsberg, 1978; Steinfels, 1973). Some profit-making centers receive federal funding when they enroll eligible children (as per Title XX, for example), although most operate without government funds (*National Day Care Study,* 1979; Steinfels, 1973). Income is derived primarily from parent fees, usually assessed on a flat-rate basis. For the most part, the programs serve predominantly middle- and upper-income families.

To attract sufficient numbers of customers, profit-making child care centers must be conveniently located and offer services that parents want. They tend to be flexible with respect to full-time and part-time care, before- and after-school care, and transportation (Steinfels, 1973). They are usually open more hours per day, more days per week, and more weeks per year than nonprofit child care centers (*National Day Care Study*, 1979). Only infrequently do they provide supplementary services (health examinations, developmental assessment, social services), although centers receiving federal funds are more likely to offer such services than are centers receiving no such funds (*National Day Care Study*, 1979).

In general, profit-making centers seem to be based on the assumption that parents know what they want, and what they want is good-quality child care offered at a reasonable price. Perhaps because they emphasize the provision of service at a price within the range of parents' ability to pay, most for-profit programs do not emphasize parent education or involvement. While many maintain regular channels of communication with parents, they usually do not view the education of parents as a significant program goal.

The major program goal of most for-profit centers is the provision of educationally appropriate activities for participating children. Emphasis on academic activities per se appears to vary across different programs, as does the emphasis on social, cognitive, and physical aspects of development. Some centers use curricular models developed by the corporation, while others use locally or more eclectically derived guides for curriculum.

For-profit sponsors have also entered the field of parent education. Perhaps the prime example is Thomas Gordon's Parent Effectiveness Training (PET). Gordon conceived PET in 1962 as an educational approach to helping improve parent-child relationships. The twenty-four-hour program (eight three-hour sessions) emphasizes communication, conflict resolution, and problem-solving skills applied specifically to the parent-child relationship. Instructors take a special course and then operate as independent agents. Over 13,000 PET instructors have been trained, and they have offered courses to over 400,000 parents. Tuition ($40 to $75 per participant) covers instructor fees, meeting room rental, and the support services of the national headquarters office. Since 1974, many PET offerings have been sponsored by community organizations (churches, schools, mental health centers); costs are sometimes paid by the organization and sometimes by class participants. Government and foundation funding has also begun to support some PET efforts. Evaluation of PET has shown positive attitudinal changes in parents and some behavioral change in children, although parents' voluntary participation and ability to pay may be implicated in these findings.

In general, for-profit programs have become a significant, if small, part of the offerings in child care and parent education. They are based primarily on two assumptions: first, that parents want a specific service that is not necessarily tied to a broader or more generally oriented program, and second, that many parents may be willing and able to pay a price for such services that covers the cost and a reasonable profit. Although many are still concerned about the potential conflict of priorities in mixing child care and parent education with a profit-making motive, for-profit programs are growing in number and availability, a sign that many parents are satisfied with the services offered.

Two additional providers of parent education warrant attention. One of these is the health care system.

The Health Care System. Most adults begin their careers as parents within the health care system and stay in that system for pediatric care. A 1975 survey found that 96 percent of all children had some regular source of medical care and that 75 percent of those children were cared for by pediatricians (McInerny, Roghmann, and Sutherland, 1978). Parents seem to turn to pediatricians for at least some childrearing advice; Wright (1979), for example, reported that approximately half of the respondents in a survey of 1,200 mothers sought their pediatrician's advice on matters related to growth and development, discipline and behavior problems, and learning difficulties.

More formal efforts at parent education through the health care system take place in several different ways. Prenatally, the focus is often on preparation for labor and delivery; in the early postpartum days, it is often on infant care. Although there is some evidence that neither of these times is the period of greatest need or motivation for information, they are periods when mothers are at least highly accessible to health care personnel. Greater need and motivation seem to occur during the first few weeks after discharge from the hospital. Only rarely, however, is there a ready delivery mechanism for parent education at that time.

Most health-related parent education occurs during contact between parents and pediatricians, as during routine health supervision and illness care for children. Attempts to incorporate other professionals (psychologists, social workers, nurse practitioners) into pediatricians' group practices have been successful, as has the use of group methods in clinic and community settings. Many of these programs, however, experience difficulty in establishing payment systems sufficient to sustain them.

Although parent education through the health care system is still in an early stage, four areas appear to be especially promising avenues for continued development: preparation for childbirth, short-term postnatal adjustment education for first-time (and perhaps second-time) parents, continuing education for first-time parents extending at least through the toddler period, and consultation for all parents as problems arise and as new behaviors emerge in the developing child.

The Media. Parent education efforts also reach into many homes through the mass media. The Princeton Center for Infancy reports that in the last five years, over 600 books have been published on virtually every aspect of childrearing, a figure indicating that parents are avid consumers of child care information. The demand is also indicated by the sales records of some child care books: Over fifty-nine million copies of the government's *Infant Care* and twenty-two million copies of Dr. Spock's *Baby and Child Care* have been sold. Several magazines devoted exclusively to parent issues have large circulations, and countless articles dealing with parenthood appear in a wide variety of magazines. Audiovisual parent education materials are available in ample supply: Over 100 filmstrip and cassette presentations can be ordered from *Parent's Magazine* alone, and The Parenting Material Information Center (part of the Southwest Educational Development Laboratory in Texas) prints an updated list of over 3,000 parenthood education items available for purchase.

Television has been explored increasingly in recent years as a vehicle for wide dissemination of parent education. These efforts have included such programs as "Look at Me," produced in 1975 by Chicago's WTTV; "Hand-in-Hand," produced jointly by the Hawaii State Department of Education and Kapiolani Hospital in Honolulu; "Feelings," featuring Dr. Lee Salk's approach to understanding young people's emotional states; and "Footsteps," sponsored by the U.S. Office of Education and produced by the Educational Film Center and the University of Maryland. An ambitious project coordinating television presentation, audience participation, written support materials, and local family counseling centers—including an evaluation component—has been developed by the British Broadcasting Company (BBC) in the United Kingdom.

Although mass media transmission of parent education information is increasing at a rapid rate, the impact of such approaches remains largely unexplored. Amidon and Brim (1972) surveyed parents who read child care books and pamphlets and suggested that these materials were not especially influential in childrearing behavior. White (1973) reported that only one of several media studies was experimentally designed, and it found no significant effects. Clearly, if parent education through the media is to be based on a solid foundation, evaluative research measuring outcomes must accompany the effort. This is difficult, however, because even if knowledge or attitude changes are demonstrated as a result of parent exposure to a media program, parents' actual behavior changes remain in question (Amidon and Brim, 1972).

Summary. Child care and parent education programs developed to date in this country represent a diverse and varied undertaking in terms of purpose, sponsorship, and content. What has been made clear in this review is that programs in both child care and parent education have been offered for well over a century in this nation, by myriad private and public sponsors. We also see from this review that the purposes addressed by the programs are many, ranging from the simple and unexamined provision of a service for which there is a perceived demand to the more comprehensive goals of promoting competence in children, opening opportunities for families, and nurturing community through involvement and participation in common purpose (Dunlop, 1980; Florin and Dokecki, 1983). Thus, from our national record of activity in this area, there is historical support for continued pursuit of sensible and wise policies as we work to define the best relationships possible between children, families, and communities.

The Use of Programs

That parents use supplementary child care and parent education provided by a wide variety of sources has been well established. How many families use these services, however, and for what purposes and periods of time, has been the subject of considerable debate and some investigation. We examine these data now with an eye to discerning the degree to which the use of these services is a fact of everyday life for families in this country.

Although there are few empirical data on the family characteristics of parents who use child care and parent education, it seems clear that both services touch the lives of most families. Parental use of nursery schools, kindergartens, center-based daycare, family day homes, parents'-day-out programs, and in-home baby-sitting involves families from all economic, occupational, and ethnic groups, albeit for varying amounts of time. Similarly, families' use of parent education courses in schools, churches, and community organizations, as well as their involvement in buying books on childrearing, watching televised parenting programs, and asking advice of health care providers, indicates the widespread integration of at least some parent education activities into the lives of most families.

Unfortunately, beyond these generalizations and the data incorporated in the previous section, little information on the use of parent education, in particular, is available. There has been some systematic investigation of the use of supplementary child care, however. These studies, although flawed, provide useful data on child care utilization from which some reasonable conclusions may be drawn.

Most preschool children receive most of their care from parents and older siblings. On the other hand, most families use supplementary child care arrangements frequently and regularly enough to be called child care users. The *National Childcare Consumer Study: 1975,* Vol. 1, found that 55 percent of the children under fourteen years of age and two thirds of the children under six (13.3 million) are cared for more than one hour a week by someone other than their parents or siblings. From the perspective of public policy, of course, the most relevant population of families consists of those who use substantial amounts of care—defined as ten or more hours per week—provided by persons other than parents or siblings. The composition of this group and their preferences about care arrangements (familial care or extrafamilial care) are matters that must be understood because of their importance in the child care policy debate. Most families use multiple arrangements to supplement their own care of children, and their reasons for doing so are varied. The reasons include employment, school, and training; concerns about children's development, socialization, and education; time for household maintenance and leisure; and specialized training and care for handicapped children.

Families with younger children use much more child care than the population as a whole (*National Childcare Consumer Study: 1975,* Vol. 2). Families who use substantial amounts of care are characterized by the presence of preschool children, parental employment (both parents, in the case of two-parent families), and single-parenthood. These features of family structure, rather than socioeconomic characteristics, are most strongly associated with substantial use of child care. Income is not a dominant correlate of usage, except to the extent that low incomes are associated with single-parenthood. The absence of teenage siblings is a fourth family structural characteristic associated with the use of extraparental child care; another study found that the presence of a teenage sibling decreased families' utilization of out-of-home care for preschoolers with employed mothers from 60 percent to 30 percent (Shortlidge and Brito, 1977).

Families with young children in which both parents are employed, families in which there is a single parent, and families in which there are no teenage siblings are thus the families who use child care arrangements most heavily. Significantly, these are the populations projected to increase most rapidly in the United States over the next decades.

Families' arrangements for supplemental child care are shown in Table 2. The six types of care most used are in-home care by a relative other than the child's parents or siblings; in-home, nonrelative care; other-home care by a relative; other-home care by a nonrelative; nursery school care; and care in a child care center. Interpretation of the data, unfortunately, is made somewhat difficult by definitional problems. For example, it is not clear whether the other-home categories should be regarded as informal, casual care or family day homes representing relatively stable group programs. Relatives, for example, can and do provide both kinds of care; over half of the day homes surveyed in the National Day Care Home Study (*National Day Care Home Study Final Report*, 1980) served children related to the care giver in stable, monetary small-group arrangements. A second definitional problem is that the terms *nursery school* and *child care center* often are used interchangeably by parents and do not necessarily describe discrete forms of care. Full-time nursery school care is probably comparable to center child care, and many care center users identify their programs as nursery schools. Kindergarten is treated in the study as a separate category, although it is not clear how five-year-olds attending kindergarten were included in aggregating the data. The failure to include enrollment in both kindergarten and other preprimary programs probably produces an undercount of children under six who use group care. Indeed, survey data from the Bureau of the Census indicate that 4.9 million children (almost half of all children aged three to five) were enrolled in preprimary programs in 1975 (Plisko, 1980). These estimates are about twice as high as the 2.4 million estimate derived from the *National Childcare Consumer Study: 1975*, Vol. 2.

As indicated in Table 2, the percentage of the age cohort in care more than ten hours per week represents 31 percent of all children under six, including 28 percent of infants and tod-

Table 2. Child Care Arrangements for Children Under Six Years Old by Hours of Care per Week, 1975: Percent Distribution (Multiple Methods).

Method of Care	0–2 Years Old		3–5 Years Old		Total Substantial Users, 0–5
	10–29 hr/wk	30+ hr/wk	10–29 hr/wk	30+ hr/wk	10+ hr/wk
In home by relative[a]	246,000 (3)[b] 19%	240,000 (3) 20%	302,000 (3) 16%	189,000 (2) 11%	977,000 16%
In home by nonrelative	239,000 (3) 19%	131,000 (1) 11%	340,000 (3) 18%	139,000 (1) 8%	848,000 14%
Other home by relative[a]	403,000 (4) 31%	287,000 (3) 24%	471,000 (4) 25%	347,000 (3) 19%	1,508,000 24%
Other home by nonrelative	285,000 (3) 22%	365,000 (4) 29%	303,000 (3) 16%	394,000 (4) 22%	1,347,500 22%
Nursery school	129,000 (1) 5%	399,000 (4) 11%	399,000 (4) 20%	364,000 (3) 21%	958,000 15%
Child care center	51,000 (1) 3%	95,000 (1) 5%	95,000 (1) 5%	344,000 (3) 19%	531,000 9%
Total	1,280,000 (15) (100%)	1,202,000 (13) (100%)	1,900,000 (18) (100%)	1,777,000 (16) (100%)	6,170,000 (31) (100%)

Notes: Components may not add to totals because of rounding.

Base number of children in U.S. in 1975: 9.1 million 0-2-year-olds + 10.7 million 3-5-year-olds = 19.8 million 0-5-year-olds (National Childcare Consumer Study: 1975, vol. 2, Table IV-9).

a "Relative" means any related person other than the child's parents or siblings.

b Numbers in parentheses are the percent of the age cohort; derived from Bane and others (1979, Table 1).

Source: National Childcare Consumer Study: 1975, vol. 2.

dlers and 34 percent of all preschoolers. The number of children receiving this care is substantial: 6.1 million, including 2.5 million infants and toddlers and 3.6 million preschoolers. Table 2 also indicates a relationship between the number of hours children are in care and the type of program they use. Families of children who are in care full-time (thirty hours or more) use formal arrangements in greater proportions than do families who use less care (ten to twenty-nine hours). The three most formal methods of care—care in a nonrelative's home, nursery school care, and care in a child care center—account for 45 percent of the arrangements made by full-time users for infants and toddlers, and 62 percent of the arrangements made for preschoolers. Among families who use part-time child care, the three most formal methods account for 30 percent of infant and toddler care and 41 percent among preschoolers. Thus, among those labeled "substantial users of child care" (ten or more hours), a total of 1.3 million infants and toddlers and 1.9 million preschoolers receive care in relatively formal settings.

Since the mid 1960s, there has been a dramatic increase in the enrollment of three- to five-year-olds in preschools, an important phenomenon that has largely been overlooked in assessments of both the supply of, and demand for, child care services and parental preferences (Kamerman and Kahn, 1979). Data on preprimary school enrollment of three- to five-year-olds since 1967 are presented in Table 3. The enrollment data show undeviating increases for all ages since 1967, perhaps reflecting an increase in parental preferences for group care. Preprimary enrollment is projected to rise throughout the 1980s, when it will include nearly seven million children between the ages of three and five. Most of the growth in enrollment to date has occurred among the younger age groups, the three- and four-year-olds.

Table 4 presents additional information on preprimary school enrollment for 1978 in relation to mothers' labor force status. Fully one half of the three- to five-year-olds were enrolled in preprimary school: 82 percent of the five-year-olds, 43 percent of the four-year-olds, and 25 percent of the three-year-olds. Fifteen percent of the total age cohort was enrolled all

Table 3. Preprimary School Enrollment of Three- to Five-Year-Olds
by Age Group: 1967–1989 (in Thousands).

Year	Total	3-Year-Olds	4-Year-Olds	5-Year-Olds
		Actual Figures		
1967	3,868	274	871	2,723
1968	3,929	318	911	2,700
1969	3,949	316	879	2,754
1970	4,103	454	1,006	2,643
1971	4,149	438	1,048	2,671
1972	4,230	535	1,120	2,575
1973	4,235	515	1,177	2,543
1974	4,698	684	1,321	2,693
1975	4,955	683	1,418	2,854
1976	4,790	602	1,348	2,840
1977	4,577	645	1,290	2,642
1978	4,584	759	1,313	2,511
		Projected Figures		
1979	4,558	732	1,358	2,468
1980	4,679	778	1,369	2,532
1981	4,770	834	1,427	2,509
1982	4,963	885	1,503	2,575
1983	5,185	948	1,583	2,656
1984	5,481	1,023	1,694	2,764
1985	5,790	1,089	1,786	2,915
1986	6,045	1,128	1,875	3,042
1987	6,274	1,180	1,946	3,148
1988	6,418	1,209	2,007	3,202
1989	6,559	1,255	2,063	3,241

Source: Plisko (1980), Table 5.1, p. 196.

day. Families with both working and nonworking mothers enrolled their children. Children whose mothers work all day were most likely to be enrolled in full-day programs, as might be expected, but about half of all three- to five-year-olds were enrolled, either part of the day or all day, regardless of their mother's employment status. Maternal employment was most clearly associated with preschool enrollment among the three-year-olds. These data lend support to the observation that part-time preprimary programs are often used in combination with other forms of child care to serve the needs of families with employed parents (Bane and others, 1979).

The Census Bureau did not inquire about the child care arrangements or preprimary enrollment of children up to two years of age, despite the fact that the labor force participation of mothers with infants and toddlers is showing rapid growth. While the *National Childcare Consumer Study: 1975*, Vol. 2, found that most children up to two years of age who receive substantial nonparental care were in home settings, a significant portion were cared for in the three more formal settings: 650,000 were in nonrelatives' homes, 528,000 were in nursery schools, and 146,000 were in centers for at least ten hours weekly (Table 2). The *National Day Care Study* (1979) gave a similar estimate for center care: 121,800 children in the two and under age group were enrolled in centers.

Discrepancies between various reports concerning utilization of early childhood education and preprimary programs and the failure of the Census Bureau to collect data on infant and toddler child care are but two features of the knowledge gap concerning child care that induce caution in drawing inferences about parents' preferences for various child care arrangements. Still, the trend in the utilization of group programs by families with three- to five-year-old children may be interpreted as evidence of the confidence that a growing proportion of parents place in center programs.

Data from both the *National Childcare Consumer Study: 1975*, Vol. 2, and the census survey of preprimary school enrollment suggest that there is a suppressed demand for group care and that cost is an important deterrent to utilization. *The National Childcare Consumer Study: 1975*, Vol. 3, includes rich information on parents' attitudes and preferences that has been largely overlooked; most analysts have simply cited the summary findings indicating that 90 percent of the parents were satisfied with their child care arrangements. In fact, the study found that although 90 percent expressed satisfaction, when asked if they would prefer another type of care, 24 percent responded affirmatively. Three quarters of those who preferred another method had children under six. The parents who preferred a change expressed a clear preference for center care (45 percent), with in-home sitters ranked next (30 percent); even

Table 4. Preprimary School Enrollment of Three- to Five-Year-Olds by Age Group and by Labor Force Status of Mother: October 1978.

Characteristics	Total		3-Year-Olds		4-Year-Olds		5-Year-Olds	
	Enrolled	Enrolled All Day	Enrolled	Enrolled All Day	Enrolled	Enrolled All Day	Enrolled	Enrolled All Day
	Number, in Thousands							
Total	4,584	1,403	759	301	1,313	412	2,512	688
With mother in labor force	2,173	892	408	241	609	260	1,156	385
Employed full time	1,309	665	251	189	365	206	693	270
Employed part time	691	161	129	39	180	33	382	90
Unemployed	173	66	27	13	65	28	81	25
With mother not in labor force	2,286	471	319	45	668	137	1,299	289
Keeping house	2,145	418	285	31	631	122	1,229	265
In school	58	34	18	12	15	11	25	10
Other	83	20	16	2	23	4	45	14
No mother present	124	39	32	17	36	8	56	14

Percent of Age Group

Total	50.3	15.4	25.1	10.1	43.4	13.6	82.1	22.5
With mother in labor force	53.0	22.8	29.9	17.7	45.4	19.8	83.2	27.7
Employed full time	53.5	27.2	30.1	22.7	46.2	26.2	84.3	32.9
Employed part time	53.6	12.5	31.1	9.3	42.7	7.7	84.2	19.7
Unemployed	48.0	18.3	23.7	11.8	48.9	20.8	71.7	21.9
With mother not in labor force	47.8	9.8	20.1	2.9	41.6	8.6	81.6	18.1
Keeping house	47.7	9.2	19.3	2.1	41.4	8.0	81.8	17.7
In school	59.2	34.7	a	a	a	a	a	a
Other	44.2	10.6	20.9	2.2	a	a	a	a
No mother present	54.7	17.3	48.5	24.6	46.1	10.2	71.0	17.7

aBase less than 75,000.

Note: Details may not add to totals because of rounding.

Source: Plisko (1980), Table 5.6, p. 206.

parents of children three and under expressed a preference for nursery and center care (45.7 percent) over care at home (34 percent). Child care in a relative's or nonrelative's home—family daycare—was preferred least. The study suggests that there is a solid demand (a projected 1.7 million) by current child care users for nursery or center care. Interpreting the 90 percent "satisfaction" figure to mean that 90 percent of the parents prefer their present mode of care seems simplistic at best; usage is not necessarily synonymous with preference or potential demand (see also Hendrix, 1981).

Parents typically cited child-oriented reasons as the most important reasons for selecting a particular type of care. Although they did not cite cost as a primary factor, it was a consideration to the extent that they observed upper limits on what they were able or willing to spend. A careful reading of data from the *National Childcare Consumer Study: 1975,* Vol. 3, thus leads to the conclusion that parents use child development factors in making choices among various modes of child care and that they are constrained by cost in making their decisions.

The fact that most nursery schools are under private auspices and are rather costly and yet are in increasing use by families with three- to five-year-olds suggests, too, that there is a suppressed demand for these services. Census data on preprimary enrollment indicate that "although the participation rate of three- to five-year-olds in public programs remained fairly constant across family income levels, the rate in nonpublic programs increased substantially from the lowest to the highest income level" (Plisko, 1980). Figure 3, in fact, suggests that parents' ability to pay for private nursery schools is an important determinant of utilization. Like the *National Childcare Consumer Study: 1975,* Vol. 2, then, the census data indicate that cost, rather than preference per se, is probably a major deterrent to utilization of nursery schools and preschools for a large number of families.

The importance of child care to families is indicated in part by the finding that child care is an expensive item in family budgets. *The National Day Care Study* (1978) found, for example, that day care centers for three- to five-year-olds are

Figure 3. Preprimary School Enrollment by Control of
School and Family Income.

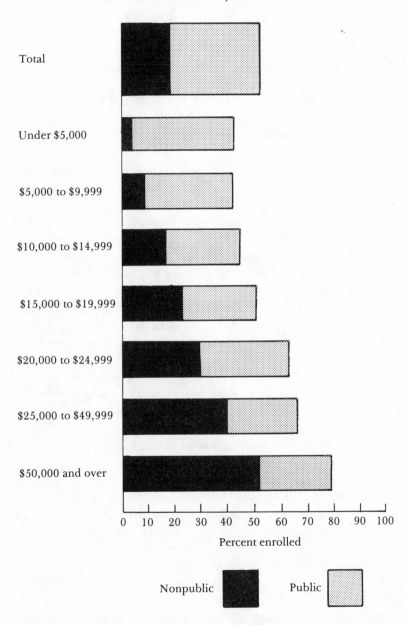

Source: Plisko (1980), Chart 5.8, p. 211.

used by many families who have modest incomes and that those whose incomes are $6,000 or higher pay the full cost of care. Child care was the fourth largest budget item for these families, after food, housing, and taxes, and used 11 percent of their income. The high monetary cost indicated families' need for, and willingness to invest in, child care services, apparently at considerable sacrifice for many.

It is also noteworthy that the *National Childcare Consumer Study: 1975,* Vol. 2, found that the modal age for extrafamilial child care was two years, suggesting that the traditional lower cutoff point of two and a half or three years for entry into many preprimary and child care programs may run counter to the preferences and perceptions of parents concerning their children's (and their own) readiness for supplemental care. The authors of the study suggested three possible explanations for the heavy use of child care for two-year-olds. First, two-year-olds are more likely than three-year-olds to have a working mother (in part because three-year-olds are more likely to have an infant sibling, which tends to preclude their mothers' employment). Second, two-year-olds are more likely to live in a one-parent home than are one-year-olds, and one-parent homes are associated with increased parental need for employment. And third, three-year-olds are slightly more likely than two-year-olds to have a sibling old enough to provide some intrafamilial care. Overall, the entry of so many two-year-olds into the child care system suggests that the continuity of their care may be interrupted if they are not yet eligible for center care.

Summary. The data presented in this section indicate substantial utilization of supplementary child care outside of the family. Group care—offered by a variety of sponsors—is an important source of this supplemental care. The data also indicate that cost probably suppresses the demand for group care. The need for care among two-year-olds may be especially acute, particularly given the number of group programs that do not accept children that young. Patterns of utilization of child care arrangements, coupled with demographic and economic trends described in Chapter Two, indicate the likelihood of an increased need for supplementary, nonparental care, especially group care.

The data substantiating perceived need for parent education are not nearly as abundant as they are in the area of child
care. Beyond recounting a familiar list of children's problems
(for example, academic difficulties, behavioral problems, delin-
quency), rarely is a data-based case made for parent education.
For many, the need is self-evident, and one need not look far
beyond one's own family to perceive it.

Our basic position is that the utility of parent education
is usually but an easy inference away from an understanding of
the fact that parents require knowledge and skill to make appropriate choices and maximize developmental benefits for
their children. Beyond what might be called this prima facie
case for parents' need of knowledge and skill, one may look to
the enduring popularity of books, magazines, and pamphlets
on childrearing, as well as to the growth in parent-oriented media productions, as indicators of perceived need; in addition,
persuasive arguments for the importance of parent education
have been developed recently by Harman and Brim (1980) and
Whitfield (1980).

Information on the variety of programs in both child
care and parent education that are currently available certainly
indicates relatively high levels of family interest in both services.
Data on the use of child care in particular details that level of
interest. It would appear that whatever the sources of child care
and parent education, both have become integral parts of the
social fabric for many families in this country. The increase
brought by the last decades in the availability and use of services
has been accompanied by two significant phenomena: social
concern over the effects of such services, particularly supplementary child care, and scientific efforts to determine the nature and extent of these effects.

The Effects of Participation in Child Care and
Parent Education Programs

Measuring the effects of participation in child care or parent education on children and their families is, of course, a complex undertaking at best. The myriad of programs described earlier gives some indication of the variability among program

offerings in these two areas, and several caveats must be observed here if the findings are to be understood within their proper context (Barnes and Dunlop, 1978).

Attempts to assess effects are complicated first by the difficulty of generalizing from results gleaned in one program to other programs, in light of the wide variety of program sponsors, purposes, and content. In addition, the programs studied tend to be "good" ones—well funded, in the public eye, and willing to subject themselves to research scrutiny. The assessment of effects is also complicated by the choice of methods used to measure the outcomes selected and by the short- or long-term nature of the assessment effort. Research in this area —as is true of most behavioral science—is limited by the appropriateness and sophistication of measures available; in several areas of parent education and child care, measures offer at best loose approximations of the answers being sought. Similarly, many of the questions being asked about child care and parent education imply concern with the long-term effects; but our theoretical, methodological, and logistic capabilities often preclude the possibility of long-term answers.

This review, then, was undertaken with an awareness of these caveats. While the empirical data as a body are far from comprehensive or perfect, they do offer guidance and suggestions that may be of critical importance to the many families in this country who do not have the option of waiting until all the data are in before seeking supplementary help with child care or advice in parent education.

As we delve into the empirical literature on program effects, we find again that the preponderance of information available lies in the area of child care; systematic information on the effects of parent education is quite sparse. Reasons for this are several, but among the most important is the fact that parent education is usually intended to produce change in parent abilities or behaviors as they relate to childrearing. Ascertaining program effects thus often requires observing parents' behavior with their children or—taking a more indirect approach—observing child outcomes assumed to be a result of changes in parent behavior. Efforts in the first area are complicated by the logistic difficulties of observing parents with their children in representative situations at home; efforts in the second suffer from potential weaknesses in the assumption of a causal link between parent behavior and specific child outcomes. For these and other reasons, we have little information as yet about the overall effectiveness of many parent education efforts. That which *is* available however, derived primarily from evaluation of early intervention preschool programs, offers encouragement and guidance for the development of parent education in conjunction with programs for young children. This evidence falls primarily in the area of effects on children's cognitive development and is included in that portion of this section.

The early childhood programs offered by both philanthropic and public sponsors early in the history of child care and parent education in this country were seldom examined for effects. Perhaps because the programs met clear and critical needs, or perhaps because they often served poor families, concern about the effects of supplementary child care did not surface until the 1930s. At that point, scholarly interest in children's development and the effects of their paticipation in nursery schools led to several studies of children in group programs. This interest was spurred in the 1940s and 1950s by research documenting the deleterious effects of institutionalization on children (Dennis and Najarian, 1957; Spitz, 1945) and further theoretical and empirical consideration of the primacy of the mother in the normal development of children (Ainsworth, 1962; Bowlby, 1958, 1964). With the beginning of the early intervention movement in the late 1950s and early 1960s—as well as the War on Poverty's choice of early education as one means of improving the well-being of poor people—interest in the effects of child care and parent education received further impetus, as politicians, scholars, and the public alike sought to discover what the education and care of young children in group programs might produce.

Children's Emotional Development. Perhaps the most pressing question confronting those who have asked about alternative arrangements for the education and care of their children concerns the effect of supplementary care on the emotional at-

tachment between child and parent. There is much popular and
scientific awareness of the importance of the early years in the
development of children's attitudes, values, and cognitive abilities, and it is frequently assumed that those who spend large
amounts of time with the young child will be most influential in
setting the course of the child's present and future development. The critical question for many is whether having someone
other than the parents care for children may replace the parents
as the primary focus of children's emotional attachments and
the primary source of influence in their development.

An early study of the effects of full-day nursery school
attendance on emotional development found only slight differences between group care children and home care children in
measures of emotional adjustment (Glass, 1949). A subsequent
study comparing day nursery children with residential nursery
children found that those in daycare showed no disruption of
the parental relationship, while the children in residential care
showed some significant problems in response to parents' absence and return (Heinicke, 1956). Analysis of several early
studies led Swift (1964, p. 258) to conclude that "the daycare
child maintains his essential relationship with his parents, despite the long day away from home, and is free to participate in
the social and play opportunities afforded by the nursery."

Children's attachment to their mothers became the focal
point of several studies of daycare participation in the 1970s.
Caldwell and others (1970) studied children enrolled in a child
care program aimed primarily at increasing educational stimulation for children from low-income families. They found no differences between center care and home care children's behaviors
toward mothers, nor in the attachment behaviors of the mothers toward their children. Blehar (1974) subsequently found
differences in the attachment patterns of child care and home
care children and suggested that the younger children were
when placed in child care, the more severe the negative consequences of their participation. Two attempts to replicate her
study failed to find these negative consequences, however. Portnoy and Simmons (1978) found no significant differences between child care and home care groups; Moskowitz, Schwarz,

and Corsini (1977) found only one difference, between the male children in the two groups, which they suggested may have been due to differences predating the children's entry into care programs.

Several subsequent studies found that patterns of attachment to mothers among group care children are not significantly different from those of children raised at home. Doyle (1975) found only one difference (amount of time spent looking at strangers), and that difference did not seem to bear negative implications for the development of children in either group. Ragozin (1976) found no significant differences between center care and home care children in attachment or exploratory behaviors. Rubenstein, Howes, and Boyle (1979) found no significant differences between child care and home care groups in behavior toward the mother after separation, children's anxiety during testing, or incidence of specific behavior problems. They did find more complex speech and higher reports of temper tantrums in the child care group. They suggested that the latter finding might reflect either delay in resolving issues of autonomy or more difficulty in mothers' control issues with their children. Overall, they found no decrease in the attachment of group care children to their mothers. Farran and Ramey (1977), looking at group care children only, concluded that the children's attachment bonds to the mothers had formed, despite the children's involvement in group care from early infancy on. Ragozin (1976) found similar evidence of attachment in her group care children.

Dependency behavior in center care and home care children has also been studied. Brookhart and Hoch (1976) found no major differences between children in the two groups, although they did find some differences between males and females. Cornelius and Denney (1975) had similar results and, on the basis of their finding that girls in home care stayed nearer their mothers significantly more often than did boys in home care, suggested that group care children may be less sex-typed in their behaviors than their home care counterparts. Examination of separation protest, another aspect of attachment, has revealed no significant differences between center care and home care infants (Kearsley and others, 1975). The authors suggested that the psychological processes underlying these behaviors were not altered by participation in child care.

Studies of emotional development in general have thus uncovered few effects of participation in child care related to attachment in children ranging in age from three months to five years. Two additional clinically oriented studies (Braun and Caldwell, 1973; Caldwell and Smith, 1970) also found no differences in adjustment between children who had entered child care at twelve to fifteen months and those who had entered later—after three years of age—as rated by psychiatrists. Thus, the child care experiences provided the children in these studies have not been shown to damage children's emotional attachments to their mothers. Overall, the children participating in these group care programs were essentially like their home-reared counterparts. While no emotional advantage for group care has been shown, it is significant that participation in child care does not have negative effects on the aspects of parent-child relations studied.

Children's Social Development. Beyond questions concerning the effects of group care on the child's emotional attachment to the parents, the area of children's social development also looms large. Here, the questions focus primarily on children's behavior while interacting with others: How does the child behave with adults? How does the child get along with other children? Does the child's behavior reflect the parents' values and rearing practices? Here, as with emotional development, there is often fear of parental loss of control over children. The thought that someone else—not the child's parents—might be the primary influence in the child's development represents a profound threat to cultural values that emphasize family autonomy in childrearing. This seems true in spite of the observation that many middle-class parents have long believed that "the opportunity to interact with other children in a controlled setting will result in better social adjustment and the acquisition of social skills" (Swift, 1964, p. 254).

Several studies of nursery school attendance conducted in the 1930s found that children became more socially skilled, outgoing, and independent over the period of their attendance (Swift, 1964). Later studies comparing nursery school and kindergarten participants with children reared at home found improved social adjustment for the attenders or no difference between groups (Allen and Masling, 1957; Bonney and Nicholson, 1958; Swift, 1964). With the coming of early intervention and child care programs in the 1960s and 1970s, attention turned again to examination of relationships between program attendance and children's social development, with particular reference to aspects of children's behavior with adults and their relationships with peers.

Studies examining group care children's relationships with adults have focused generally on the degree to which children's behavior is characterized by cooperation or noncompliance. Schwarz, Strickland, and Krolick (1974) studied a group of children in a preschool, half of whom had been in child care as infants. They found that children with infant daycare experience showed significantly more physically and verbally aggressive behavior toward care givers than did the new entry group and suggested that early entry into child care may have slowed the children's acquisition of some cultural values. However, Macrae and Herbert-Jackson (1975), in a similar study, found no significant differences between groups in aggressive behavior toward adults. They suggested that the discrepant findings of the two studies may have been due to differences in the practices of the programs attended by the children. In offering this suggestion, they highlighted the critical importance of the environment—the program and the expectations established by care givers—in influencing the behavior exhibited by children. Rubenstein, Howes, and Boyle (1979) took a different approach in comparing child care and home care children's behavior toward mothers by observing mother-child interaction in the home. They found that group care children showed significantly more noncompliance toward the mother, specifically when asked by their mothers to complete a boring task (sorting a pile of pegs by color into two boxes). Noting that group care children also showed higher rates of temper tantrums as reported by mothers, the authors suggested that maternal anxiety may have resulted in both permissiveness and overcontrol around the development of autonomy in the group care children. The findings on quality of children's interactions with adults, thus, are mixed: There is evidence indicating that participation in child care is, and is not, related to more aggressive behavior toward care givers and less compliant behavior toward the mother.

Another group of studies compared children's orientation toward adults vis-à-vis peers. Schwarz, Krolick, and Strickland (1973) compared two groups of preschool center care children; one group had had infant group care experience and the other had not. The authors observed the children on their first day in a preschool center and again five weeks later. They found that the early care children showed more social interaction with peers and adults on both occasions. McCutcheon and Calhoun (1976) found that children's interactions with adults decreased significantly during the first month of participation in a preschool center, while their interactions with other children increased. Finkelstein and others (1978), looking at children between the ages of fifteen and thirty months in group care, found that as the children's age increased, their interactions with adults decreased and their interactions with peers increased. Cochran (1977) examined child-adult interactions in a study of Swedish children in group care centers, daycare homes, and "own homes." He found that children in daycare homes and "own homes" had more cognitive-verbal interactions with adults than did children in the centers and that they also received more negative sanctions from adults ("No, No!") than did children in the center settings.

There is some indication in this group of studies, thus, that the earlier the entry into group care, and the longer the time spent in care, the more likely are children to show increasing rates of interaction with peers and decreasing rates of interaction with adults, although Schwarz, Krolick, and Strickland (1973) found increased rates for both peers and adults. Cochran's findings indicate the possibility of qualitative differences in child-adult interaction as related to type of care setting.

Another group of investigators has examined peer relationships in child care programs. In general, these studies have focused on the incidence of aggressive or negative behavior toward peers and on the development of social competence and positive relationships with peers.

Aggressiveness was the focus of attention in four studies. Finkelstein and Wilson (1977) compared the peer interaction of children enrolled in a child care intervention program with that of another group of children, most of whom were receiving home care. They found the behavior of children in both groups to be characterized by friendliness and very low rates of aggressiveness. McCutcheon and Calhoun (1976), looking at group care children only, also found very few instances of aggressive behavior in the children. Schwarz, Krolick, and Strickland (1973), comparing children who had been in group care for different amounts of time, found that children who entered care earlier showed significantly more physical and verbal aggressiveness than was shown by children who entered later. Macrae and Herbert-Jackson (1975), on the other hand, found no significant differences between early and late entry groups. It is possible that characteristics of the settings influenced observed rates of aggressive behavior. McCutcheon and Calhoun, for example, noted that in the program they studied, "aggression is ignored, or if it persists, is punished by time-out. In the few children who did show aggression against others, the behavior was rapidly extinguished, disappearing within the first two to five days" (p. 107). Thus, differences in program orientation and content might well have been influential in producing different rates of aggressive behavior.

Group care children's social competence and positive relations with peers have also been examined. Schwarz, Krolick, and Strickland (1973) found that social interaction scores—measured by nearness to peers and quality of activity with peers—increased for children with and without infant daycare experience over the first five weeks of a preschool group care program. The children with infant care experience, however, had consistently higher scores across the whole period. The authors suggested that "the prior existence of peer attachments among this group probably accounted for the higher levels of peer social interaction" (p. 345). This finding, supported by the research of Freud and Dann (1951) on the growth of mutual support bonds among refugee children, may indicate that children are capable of forming strong attachments to peers at early ages and that these bonds may be helpful in enabling children to adapt successfully to environmental change (such as entry into a new program). In another study, Finkelstein and Wilson (1977) found that children in group care showed a behavior pattern characterized predominantly by friendliness.

Lieberman (1976) looked at children in full-time center care and part-time nursery school care, focusing on the relationships between children's attachment to the mother and their social interaction with peers. She found that children in both groups who showed low anxiety in attachment to the mother had significantly higher scores on social competence with peers than did children who showed higher anxiety in attachment. When anxiety was held constant, there were no significant differences between the child care and nursery school children in social competence. Interpreting the findings, Lieberman suggested that security of attachment and prior exposure to peers may be more influential than preschool attendance in the development of social competence.

Three other studies pertinent to this area assessed social competence as related to age of entry into child care. Raph and others (1968), using observations of children's social interactions, found no significant difference between children who had been in care programs for one to three years and others of the same age who had been in for a very short time. Largman (1975) found no significant differences in social competence between children who had entered group care before the age of two, children who entered between two and three years, and children who entered between three and four years. In accord with these findings, Resch and others (1977) found no significant differences in the play behavior and social interaction of children who had been in care from three to eighteen months of age.

In general, then, the children in group care studied in these reports reflected high levels of positive social attachment to peers, social competence with peers, and friendliness. There are indications that several environmental factors may be more influential in the development of positive peer relations than simple involvement in child care; among these factors are a history of relationships with peers, relatively secure attachment to parents, and appropriate types and numbers of objects in the care environment for play. These children also revealed a pattern of less attentiveness to adults than might be expected of similarly aged children reared only at home. This may represent the earlier manifestation of a developmentally normal pattern among young children, a pattern that traditionally coincides with the age of school entry. Environmental expectations may also play a role, however, as care giver and parent behavior is usually significant in influencing young children's behavior.

Children's Cognitive Development. Just as the effects of group care on children's emotional and social development have concerned parents and policy makers, so too have the effects of child care on cognitive development in young children. The concern grows largely out of public and scientific awareness of the importance of the early years of life in the development of cognitive abilities and structures. It also grows out of an awareness that environmental factors—the stimulation and responsiveness provided by people, events, and objects in the environment—play a significant role in the development of children's intellectual abilities.

Until the 1960s, most professionals and most parents who used preschool programs such as nursery school, kindergarten, and daycare for their children assumed that participation in the programs had beneficial effects on children's cognitive development. These assumptions were usually based on informal observations, however, because studies of nursery school care in the 1930s and 1940s generally revealed a mixed pattern of findings, some studies reflecting gains in measured intelligence, others finding no effects (Swift, 1964). Swift concluded cautiously that "the possibility that certain nursery programs can contribute to increase in mental functioning . . . is not ruled out" (p. 254).

In the late 1950s and early 1960s, the confluence of several developments in the sociopolitical arena and in the field of psychology led increasing numbers of people to look beyond these cautious conclusions to new programs of early childhood education as potentially influential in increasing the cognitive abilities of many of the nation's children (see, for example, Bloom, 1964; Hunt, 1961). Leading this effort were several programs of early intervention that included full-day care and education for children, as well as various kinds of educational programs for their parents. From these programs emerged Head Start, a major and comprehensive social action program aimed at reducing educational disadvantage in poor children (Zigler and Anderson, 1979). Thus, in the 1960s and 1970s, programs providing care and education for young children expanded from their established base in kindergartens, nursery schools, and some daycare programs to include early intervention preschool programs, Head Start, and an increasing number of specifically educational child care programs. And the question most frequently asked of these programs was, Does the program enhance participating children's cognitive development?

Many observers were persuaded by an early examination of Head Start (Westinghouse Learning Corporation, 1969) that while there were some cognitive gains from participation, the gains were likely to "wash out" soon after the children entered elementary school, leaving them no better off for having had the intervention experience. This pessimism was disputed, however, by several researchers who focused on the effects of specific early intervention programs. Gray and Klaus (1970), for example, spoke of their "cautious optimism" based on findings of positive program effects after intervention ceased. Caldwell and Smith (1970) found increases in developmental scores across two years of participation in a program that included daycare; although the children's scores dropped once they left the program and entered elementary school, their scores continued to be higher than a group of matched control children who had not participated in the program. Caldwell and others (1970) also found that aspects of the home environment were significantly related to the cognitive performance of home care children but were not so related for children in the group care

program. They concluded that involvement in the program miti-
gated the negative effects of low levels of home stimulation on
children's cognitive development. Robinson and Robinson
(1971) found that infants in an early intervention care program
had significantly higher developmental scores than their home
care counterparts; when they assessed the children again at two
and a half and at four and a half years, their findings led them
to suggest that participation in the program had had a major impact in preventing a decline in intelligence test scores among
disadvantaged children.

Later studies affirmed these findings. Fowler and Kahn
(1975) found that children who had entered group care before
twelve months of age showed "modest gains" in IQ scores by
eighteen to twenty-nine months. The gains had evened out by
the time the children were thirty-six to forty-three months of
age, but the fact that their scores during the latter period were
still within the normal range (104 to 108) was considered important, given the frequent finding that the measured IQ of
many low-SES children in home care declines after the age of
two. Doyle (1975) found that children in a center care program
for about seven months showed mildly advanced developmental performance when compared with a home care group.
Resch and others (1977) found that children who had been in a
center care program from infancy on had significantly higher intelligence scores than did similar children who entered the center care program at the age of three; Ramey and Smith (1977)
found that group care children showed significantly higher cognitive performances than a home care comparison group did at
ages six and eighteen months. Thus, there is considerable evidence drawn from studies of several child care and education
programs that children's participation in programs of high quality can have a significant and positive effect on cognitive development, particularly in children from disadvantaged homes.

At least two additional systematic efforts were under way
during the 1970s, however, in an effort to examine comprehen-
sively the overall and long-term cognitive effects of children's
participation in programs of early intervention. Bronfenbrenner
(1974) conducted a major review of twelve programs and drew

several conclusions. First, participating children showed significant cognitive gains during the first year of involvement in the program. Second, within one to two years after completing the program, most children had begun to decline in cognitive gains; by the third to fourth year after completion, their measured cognitive abilities had returned to control group levels. Third, there was evidence to indicate that the decline could be offset by the continuation of intervention programs into the elementary school (the sharpest declines in cognitive gains were registered when children entered regular elementary school). This aspect of Bronfenbrenner's review indicated that while participation in early care and education programs clearly had positive short-term effects on children's cognitive development, these effects did not extend into later years if subsequent schooling was "regular" (that is, if there were no efforts to continue intervention focused on cognitive development).

Further light was shed on these observations in 1977 when the Consortium for Longitudinal Studies reported finding long-term positive effects of participation in early intervention programs. Taking behavioral indicators of cognitive performance, the consortium found that children who had participated in early intervention programs as preschoolers, when compared with control group children, were at a significant advantage in several areas of school performance (Lazar and others, 1977). Participating children showed significantly lower rates of retention in grade level throughout elementary school, significantly lower rates of placement in special education classes, and significantly higher rates of graduation from high school before the age of eighteen (Lazar and others, 1977; Lazar, 1980). The consortium studies suggested that even if measured intelligence gains declined as children progressed in elementary school, behavioral manifestations of cognitive ability and attitude indicated important and positive effects of program participation.

These findings were significant, for they suggested some of the potential long-term benefits of participation in well-designed early childhood programs of care and education. They went beyond the several studies establishing that at a minimum, no harm comes to children's cognitive abilities from participating in child care (Cochran, 1977; Kagan, Kearsley, and Zelazo, 1977; Rubenstein, Pedersen, and Yarrow, 1977; Winett and others, 1977). Similarly, they went beyond the several studies cited earlier that found short-term positive gains in children's measured intelligence. They established a basis for asserting the importance of good child care in cognitive development, and, when taken together with other literature, they formed a basis for establishing guidelines necessary to the development of care programs that are most likely to have long-term positive effects.

One important element of that "other" literature is focused on the effects of parent involvement in early childhood programs. Although this body of evidence is limited in many ways, it allows the assertion that parents' involvement in their children's preschool programs enhances positive results.

While many of the early intervention preschool efforts of the 1960s were characterized by the absence of serious attention to the role of parents, that situation quickly changed. Indeed, the suggestions of several researchers—who had long viewed the home environment provided by the family as the single most important influence on the social and intellectual development of children (for example, Bloom, 1964; Hunt, 1961)— were put into use as policy makers and program developers alike struggled to respond to the early negative findings on intervention programs such as Head Start (for example, Westinghouse Learning Corporation, 1969). While some have asserted that the shift of focus in many early childhood programs to include parents was a politically motivated evasion of responsibility for the alleged failure of compensatory education—and a classic instance of blaming the victim (Schlossman, 1978)—the psychological base for including parents was strong. Ainsworth (1975), for example, suggested that improving the child's home conditions through parent involvement and parent education would lead to the creation of a more beneficial environment for the child long after the early childhood program was over. Palmer (1977) suggested that involving parents, attending to them individually as is frequently done in parent education efforts, simply makes intervention effects for children longer and more intense, as the parent continues to be "invested" in his or her role in the child's ongoing progress. Whatever the motivating factors, parents' involvement in their young children's group experiences seems clearly to improve and extend the positive effects on cognitive development in particular.

Lazar and Chapman (1972) found that parent programs focusing on mothers as primary agents of intervention had a higher frequency of immediate positive cognitive effects on children than did programs focusing primarily on the child. Other reviews at about the same time supported findings of a notable correlation between high parent involvement and positive outcomes for children's cognitive development (Biber, 1970; Mann, Harrell, and Hurt, 1977; MIDCO Educational Associates, 1972; White, 1973). Bronfenbrenner (1974, p. 55), based on an extensive review of early childhood programs, concluded that "the involvement of the child's family as an active participant is critical to the success of any intervention program." He went on to observe that "without such family involvement, any effects of intervention, at least in the cognitive sphere, appear to erode fairly rapidly once the program ends. In contrast, the involvement of parents as partners in the enterprise provides an ongoing system which can reinforce the effects of the program while it is in operation and help to sustain them after the program ends" (pp. 251-252). Bronfenbrenner also cautioned about the possibility of negative effects associated with failure to involve parents. Schaefer's (1977) work added further information about the need to attend to appropriate forms of parent involvement.

The Consortium for Longitudinal Studies (Lazar and others, 1977; Lazar, 1980) also found that parent participation contributed to positive, long-term program effects on children. Of further interest in their findings was the fact that parents themselves reported very positive attitudes toward the programs. Weikart (in press) estimated that these interventions, in part because of the effects of involving parents, were quite cost-beneficial. Further evidence on the positive effects of parent participation came from a review of the effects of ESEA Title I programs for young children. Keesling and Melaragno (in press) found that child performance in ESEA schools where parents participated in the classroom was better than the performance of similar children whose parents were not so involved.

Overall, this body of literature on child care in relation to children's intellectual development points to the positive effects of children's participation in good group programs, particularly when supplemented by parents' involvement. That the focus of attention in this body of research since the 1960s has been on lower-income families means that we are limited in the conclusions that may be drawn directly for all families. At a minimum, we know from both early studies of nursery school and more recent studies of early care and education that children's cognitive development is not harmed by participation in good programs. It seems quite likely, given the cautious conclusions drawn in early studies and the results of more recent research, that all children benefit from such participation. Certainly, the continued and increasing use of preprimary education by middle-class families supports this view. It is probable, however, that the cognitive effects of participation will always be most noticeable in children whose home situation is not able to offer the developmentally appropriate stimulation available in good group programs. While measurable cognitive effects may range from slight (for children from homes that are highly nurturant, stimulating, and appropriately challenging) to moderate and significant (for children from families less able—for whatever reasons—to provide such an environment), the potential of well-designed group care to benefit the cognitive development of young children has been established.

Summary. Taken as a body, the studies of the effects of child care and parent education programs indicate that children's participation in group care programs of good quality is associated with several outcomes. First, children in group care and home care are essentially similar in emotional development, particularly in terms of attachment to the mother. Second, children's social development shows some effects related to participation in group programs. Children who have been in group care as preschoolers, particularly if they have been in care from an early age, tend to be somewhat less adult-oriented and somewhat more peer-oriented than are similar children who have received care only at home. Participation in group programs seems to promote relatively high levels of attachment to peers, social competence with peers, and friendly behavior. Further, it is likely that social effects vary with different teaching orientations and program values as communicated through teacher behavior. Third, and perhaps most important from an educational perspective, participation in group care of good quality appears to have positive effects on children's cognitive development. This seems especially true of children from disadvantaged backgrounds. The positive relationship between participation in group programs and cognitive development is enhanced particularly when parents are involved in their child's program or in a complementary parent education program.

That there are overall positive effects of participation in good group care programs for young children is evident. Equally evident and critically important, however, is the qualifier attached to the group care programs from which these findings have emerged: they were *good* programs. The qualities of good care and parent education, while defying simple description, go beyond the simply intuitive (for example, good care is dependent on caring—even loving—adults who do a "good" job, and good parent education is dependent on competent teachers). In the final section, we examine the literature with an eye to determining some of the specific organizational and personal characteristics found in high-quality programs of child care and parent education.

Guidelines for Program Development

If we assume, as a matter of national policy, that communities as expressed through governments have a significant role to play in strengthening families and enhancing parents' abilities to rear their children well, it becomes important to look to the literature for guidelines to be used in implementing this responsibility. In this section, we offer suggestions derived from the literature for a policy approach to child care and parent education that meets the needs of children, families, and communities; we focus specifically on identifying characteristics associated with quality.

We look first to deriving guidelines for institutional arrangements for child care and parent education; in doing so, we preface specific aspects of our analyses in Chapters Six and Seven and our recommendations in Chapter Eight. Then we examine the literature for guidance on the issue of optimal parent-program relations. Here we build on the conclusion of the previous section that program effects for children are more positive and pronounced when parents are involved. Finally, we look to the literature on program effects for the development of guidelines concerning optimal relations between children and care givers in child care programs.

Institutional Arrangements. Some of the most heated debate in child care and parent education in the United States has been sparked by strong differences of opinion as to the appropriateness of different institutions and institutional arrangements as primary providers of service. At a basic level, the debate centers on the question, Who should and who shall control the goals, content, and process of child care and parent education? For those concerned with empowering and enabling parents to make wise choices that contribute to the healthy development of their children, themselves, and their families, the question becomes, What institutions or organizations, or combinations thereof, are most likely to support parents as competent decision makers and informed mediators of their children's experiences?

In both child care and parent education, as we have seen, institutional and organizational sponsors of service are numerous, ranging from wholly private and individual sources to highly structured organizations, such as industries, churches, and the public schools. In a thoughtful review of programs in the United States and other countries, Robinson and others (1979) specified some of the advantages and disadvantages of large, centralized institutional systems.

The advantages of large organizations as sponsors of child care and parent education are several. First, if well run and attentive to the needs for expertise and training, they minimize the possibilities of local groups "reinventing the wheel," allowing them instead to draw on organizational resources for program development, personnel training, and problem solving in the day-to-day questions that routinely emerge in most programs. Second, they tend to encourage planning rather than a haphazard approach to program content and activities, thus enhancing the probability of well-designed, sequential curricula. Third, they are usually able to ensure some level of program quality across varied locations, thus giving consumers general and readily available information about program content, independent of extensive investigation on the part of parents. Fourth, they sometimes enable coordinated programs of research. This may be of less importance to parents than are other program characteristics, but it can be of particular social relevance in value-laden and relatively untested areas of policy endeavor such as child care and parent education. Finally, large organizations permit the application of "principles of modern management and collective bargaining" (Robinson and others, 1979, p. 125), thus presumably increasing administrative efficiency and the satisfaction and competence of staff.

Large systems, however, have several disadvantages as well. They may foster rigidity, stifle creativity, and fall victim to inertia, thus negating many of the benefits brought about by access to expanded resources and the encouragement of systematic planning. Just as they permit the rapid transmission of new information, so, too, do they permit the rapid transmission of mistakes. One of the most telling criticisms, however, may be that large organizations often make local initiative impossible. Granted that local initiative may be seen as a liability rather than a strength, our value position in this project treats the initiative and purposes of communities with respect, particularly when those purposes are consistent with the enhancement of human development. Thus, tendencies to stifle local initiative would be seen in our value scheme as a serious detriment. The concern becomes more serious when taken in the light of Robinson and others' observation that "the more diverse the country and its population, the more difficult it is to adapt a centralized system to local conditions" (p. 125).

Robinson and her colleagues went on to address the advantages of a decentralized system, primarily the opportunity for both consumer control and the initiation of improvements and innovations in service. As for disadvantages, however, decentralized systems may make planning difficult, if not impossible; they may suffer from "insufficient quality control" (p. 126); and they may be somewhat isolated from news of success and improvements in other programs.

In child and parent education programs, it would likely be optimal if institutional sponsors were centralized or coordinated to the extent that they encourage planning; facilitate the transmission of information, knowledge, and other resources; ensure some acceptable and basic level of quality; and not only permit, but value, consumer involvement and shared control, as well as creativity and local response to local need. Optimal levels of decentralization would allow for clear orientation toward, and respect for, the varying needs and preferences of participating parents and the local community as a whole.

In the United States, the debate concerning institutional sponsorship has centered in the last decade primarily on the question, Should the public schools or a variety of other institutions assume prime sponsorship of child care and parent education? Public schools have come to the fore perhaps because they already serve children (and, to some extent, parents) and have a well-organized constituent component in teachers, many of whom have vested both energy and time in promoting the potential role of schools as the primary sponsor of early childhood care and education. Other large institutions, such as churches and employers—perhaps because they do not have the care and education of children or parents as a central focus—have not emerged as primary contenders for institutional sponsorship of either child care or parent education, although both have certainly been involved in providing such services. Profit-making organizations developed particularly for the purpose of providing child care might have entered as major contenders for sponsorship, but the frequent suspicion of those who link child care and parent education with profit making and the political realities of being a relatively new industry have led profit-making organizations to present themselves not as the best and presumably prime provider, but rather as one of several provider options that ought to be available to parents.

The American Federation of Teachers (AFT) (1976) issued a position paper on the public schools as primary providers
of child care that addressed many of the centralization-decen-
tralization issues described by Robinson and others (1979). The
paper specified that public schools should be designated as a primary sponsor of child care programs primarily because the field
of child care suffers from problems that professional teachers in
established systems could remedy (for example, inadequate and
poor services, untrained staff, and confusion growing from an
uncoordinated federal support and delivery system). The AFT
noted that the public schools are capable of both addressing
these problems and offering other benefits as well. In relation to
the problems, the AFT saw the public schools as being in a position to ensure quality and compliance with regulations through
the existing centralized bureaucracy. In addition, it asserted
that use of the public schools would "naturally guarantee democratic control of programs," ensure a major role for parental
choice, allow for variability in approach within schools, increase
the accessibility of daycare to many parents, and offer a free
and universally available early childhood and daycare system—a
goal that will remain elusive as long as the administration of
these services remains fragmented and confusing" (American
Federation of Teachers, 1976, p. 14).

Perhaps anticipating the critics, the report went on to
specify some of the ways in which schools would have to
change to achieve realization of these benefits. Schools would
have to do several things: develop flexibility in regard to the
administration of various programs; take care not to press their
new early childhood and daycare programs into a school format; develop certification standards specifically for teachers of
preschool children; and learn to address the special needs of different ethnic and language groups. Interestingly, the changes
specified reflected attempts to remedy some of the disadvantages of centralized delivery systems noted by Robinson and
others (1979).

While few have disagreed with the changes recommended
by the AFT as prerequisite to the designation of the public
schools as a primary or sole provider of child care and parent

education services, some have questioned whether a major institution of any kind is capable of the kind of change called for in the AFT report. Levine (1978), for example, who reviewed a small sample of public schools that sponsored child care programs, concluded that neither the public schools nor any other organization should be promoted as sole sponsors of child care. He suggested rather that "cooperatives," combining public schools with groups of parents, offered the best solution. Such a model would utilize some of the advantages of the public school system, such as facilities, but would add the major advantages of private, nonprofit groups, such as greater possibilities for parent involvement and control and more flexibility in administration and staffing.

Galinsky and Hooks's (1977) examination of child care programs indicates that the designation of a particular model of institutional sponsorship may not be as important, however, as the ability of any models selected to support administrative characteristics linked to high-quality programs. Across all of the programs they reviewed—representing twelve types of sponsorship—they found qualities of program leadership transcending specific institutional arrangements. For example, the administrators of their exemplary programs all believed in their programs, selected strong staff people with whom they could work well, allowed their staffs a large measure of independence, saw themselves as "taking care" of their staffs, and encouraged their care givers to work in pairs, providing some relief from the intensive demands of the job periodically throughout the day. Galinsky and Hooks's findings suggest that qualities of program leaders, whatever the specific form of sponsorship, are very significant variables in determining program success. While their examination included only programs of child care, it is safe to assume that some of the qualities they identified—belief in the program, strong staff, good working relations, independence for individual staff members' creativity and decision making, concern about the well-being of staff—would also characterize the leadership of successful parent education programs.

One of the implications of Galinsky and Hooks's findings, of course, is that institutional arrangements and sponsorship are not as important as the qualities of individuals who give leadership to programs. While we believe this to be the case—and believe that ultimately it is the characteristics of individual providers and consumers coming together in any child care or parent education program that are most significant in determining program quality and outcomes—we also believe that the institutional framework and goals within which individuals work have a substantial impact not only on what is encouraged in any program but also on what is permitted. Attention to that framework is critically important, then, as we seek to develop policies enhancing family and community abilities to raise the next generation of children with competence and a sense of caring.

The Role of Parents. Equal in importance to the institutional arrangements derived for the implementation of child care and parent education policy are the guidelines to be developed for the role of parents. Our values reveal our predispositions here: We believe that parents should be strong partners in a collaborative, interdependent relationship with professionals who staff any child care and parent education programs created by the implementation of policy (see, for example, Dokecki, 1977).

In developing policies responsive to families' child care and parent education needs, the choices concerning the participatory role of parents assume major importance. The parental role cannot be ignored in child care, regardless of the specific arrangements that are made, because of the indispensable contribution parents make to their children's early development (Bronfenbrenner, 1974; Fein, 1980). Neither can their role be ignored in parent education, since the nature of parents' participation as adult learners influences program effectiveness (Knox, 1977).

Guidelines for parent participation, or the relationship between parents and professionals, emerge in part out of the history of such relationships. At one level, the professions—particularly the helping professions such as education, medicine, law, psychiatry, psychology, and social work—have been severely criticized (for example, Bledstein, 1978) for the tendency of professionals to create dependency (Donzelot, 1979) or ignore the wishes and needs of those whom they ostensibly serve. Those who have attempted to develop policies to improve professional services for families and children have been branded by critics in the last decade as dishonest and dangerous (Donzelot, 1979; Farber and Lewis, 1975; Schlossman, 1976, 1978; Ravitch, 1980), and a hands-off, noninterventionist stance has become increasingly popular. While the concerns raised by these critics strike a legitimate and important chord, we believe with Joffe (1977) that "a one-dimensional view of the social services" is inappropriate: "It is true that services can undermine individuals' authority and self-confidence; yet services can help promote new manifestations of these same qualities in other individuals. It is also true that services can be used to oppress politically powerless groups; yet, at the same time, involvement with services can be a profoundly politicizing experience. And given that the politics of family life is one of the major political issues of our time, we must recognize—and make use of—the progressive role that services can play in the painful struggle for more satisfactory family forms" (Joffe, 1977, p. 60). The "progressive role that services can play" involves important issues of participation and collaborative relationships, ideas receiving the support even of staunch critics of traditional professional roles (Lasch, 1980).

At another level, guidelines for the role of parents may be derived from the history of child and family policy specifically. Fein (1980) has demonstrated that at least since the seventeenth century, there has been a tension between the idea of the *informed parent* and the idea of the *informed professional* in efforts to establish the proper relationship and assignment of responsibility regarding childrearing between parents and institutions of the broader society. To emphasize the informed parent is to believe that parents have the primary responsibility for rearing their children and have, or should be helped to develop, the knowledge and skill necessary to exercise this responsibility. An emphasis on the informed professional gives individuals outside the family the prime responsibility for influencing the course of child development, with the assumption that they know better than parents what is good for family life and child development. Fein indicated that in different historical periods, this tension has been resolved by placing different amounts of emphasis on one or the other pole; at no time—not even in the highly participatory 1960s and early 1970s—has the tension been resolved exclusively in favor of the parent or the professional. It is important, thus, that we not draw the issue in either/or terms but conceive it as a matter of relative emphasis. In the areas of child care and parent education the question becomes, What are the most appropriate degrees and forms of parent involvement? To find the answer, we look first to the guidelines offered by the standards developed for existing programs.

In Head Start, there has been a tension from the outset between parent participation, which has "often combined home economics education, training in childrearing techniques, and encouraging parents to be 'teachers' in the home," and parent control, which has usually taken the form of advisory and policy-making activities (Valentine and Stark, 1979, p. 297). A deficit model theory is said to support parent participation, while a social institutional or structural theory of poverty supports parent control. Early in its history, Head Start adopted a parent policy wherein parent advisory committees were to promote maximum feasible participation. The parent coordinator staff position was developed subsequently to promote parent involvement, and by 1970, "the right of citizens' advisory groups to approve or disapprove the appointment of Head Start directors and staff was firmly established" (Valentine and Stark, 1979, p. 305). In 1975, federal guidelines laid out four aspects of parent involvement. At a first level, "parent participation" included decision making related to program content, working and volunteering in classrooms, planning parent education, and receiving home visits from professional staff. At a second level, "parenting education" provided opportunities for parents to learn more about child development and childrearing skills. At a third level, parents, administrators, and staff shared open channels of communication. At a fourth level, program administrators developed ways for parents to affect other community institutions. In spite of these guidelines, Valentine and Stark (1979) opined that parent involvement in Head Start for the most part remained in the traditional arenas of educational programs and participatory decision making, rather than branching out to political organizing. In spite of its shortcomings, however, parent involvement in Head Start produced notable effects, among them the following: The more intensive the parents' involvement, the more noticeable were the children's gains; when parents perceived themselves in the role of the child's most important teacher, the effects on children's intellectual development were stronger; and parents' employment as child care workers in the programs seemed to have beneficial effects on the children's cognitive development (Fein, 1980).

Another major set of policies governing parent involvement in early childhood programs appears in the Federal Interagency Day Care Requirements (FIDCR), originated in 1968 and revised in 1980 to guide the implementation of programs funded under a variety of federal auspices.* Section VII of the 1968 FIDCR specified several requirements related to parent involvement (U.S. Department of Health, Education, and Welfare, Office of Child Development, Federal Panel on Early Childhood, 1968, pp. 14-15):

1. Opportunities must be provided parents at times convenient to them to work with the program and, whenever possible, observe their children in the daycare facility.
2. Parents must have the opportunity to become involved themselves in the making of decisions concerning the nature and operation of the daycare facility.

*The 1968 FIDCR applied to childcare programs authorized by Title IV of the Social Security Act, Part A and Part B; Title I, ESEA (requirements were subject to the discretion of the state and local education agencies administering the federal funds); the Manpower Development Training Act; the Economic Opportunity Act, including Titles I, II, III (Part B), and Title V (Part B). Programs included in the 1980 FIDCR were the childcare components of the Social Security Act, including Titles IV-A, IV-B, IV-C, and Title XX; the Mental Retardation Facilities and Community Mental Health Centers Construction Act of 1963; the Developmental Disabilities Services and Facilities Construction Act of 1970; and the Developmentally Disabled Assistance and Bill of Rights Act of 1975. Title I of ESEA was omitted from the 1980 list.

3. Whenever an agency (that is, an operating or
    an administering agency) provides daycare for
    forty or more children, there must be a policy
    advisory committee or its equivalent at the ad-
    ministrative level, where most decisions are
    made [decisions on the kinds of programs to be
    operated, the hiring of staff, the budgeting of
    funds, and the submission of applications to
    funding agencies]. The committee member-
    ship should include not less than 50 percent
    parents or parent representatives, selected by
    the parents themselves in a democratic fash-
    ion. Other members should include represen-
    tatives of professional organizations or individ-
    uals who have particular knowledge or skills in
    children's and family programs.
4. Policy advisory committees [a formal means
    for involving parents in decisions about the
    program will vary, depending upon the admin-
    istering agencies and facilities involved; they]
    must perform productive functions, including,
    but not limited to:
    a. Assisting the development of the programs
        and approving applications for funding.
    b. Participating in the nomination and selec-
        tion of the program director at the operat-
        ing and/or administering level.
    c. Advising in the recruitment and selection
        of staff and volunteers.
    d. Initiating suggestions and ideas for pro-
        gram improvements.
    e. Serving as a channel for hearing complaints
        about the program.
    f. Assisting in organizing activities for par-
        ents.
    g. Assuming a degree of responsibility for
        encouraging parents' participation in the
        program.

Fein (1976) criticized the requirements with particular reference to the fact that they were applicable only to programs
using federal funds directly for child care services (thus ignoring
such indirect funding mechanisms as tax-exempt statuses, tax
deductions, and tax credits); she also criticized the difficulty of

accountability, since it was not clear how "administering agencies" were to be designated. She made several recommendations for revision of the requirements, including the following: Parent participation should be mandatory where federal funds are directly used for child care; major disbursal points in distributing federal funds should be identified so that "administering agencies" can be well identified; the requirement of parent participatin on decision-making bodies should be maintained in full; and parents should be participants in an advisory capacity at the national level of decision making.

The 1980 FIDCR, replacing the 1968 version, contained several requirements for parent involvement in child care, specifying that programs were to "(1) Provide parents with opportunities to observe the center and to discuss their children's needs before enrollment; (2) Offer parents unlimited access to the daycare center to observe their children; (3) Regularly offer parents opportunities to meet with care givers to discuss their children's needs; (4) Regularly exchange information with parents about their children and the daycare program; (5) Offer parents, individually and as a group, meaningful opportunities to participate in general program policy making; and (6) Provide parents, upon request, any monitoring reports or evaluations of the center prepared by and received from federal, state, or local authorities" (U.S. Department of Health, Education, and Welfare, Office of the Secretary, 1980, p. 17882). The 1980 FIDCR specified that state agencies administering funds should provide information and technical assistance to child care centers on involving parents and should offer parents a choice in child care facilities whenever administratively feasible. Subsequent comments by administration officials on the meaning of participation and the degree of discretion to be allowed in implementing the parent participation requirement indicated that the parent involvement policy of the new requirements was weaker than either the 1968 FIDCR or Fein's (1976) recommendations for revisions.

The new requirements were based in part on a survey of parent involvement literature by the U.S. Department of Health, Education and Welfare, Office of the Assistant Secretary for Planning and Evaluation (1978), which reported several findings: low levels of actual parent participation in decision making; low levels of parental desire to participate in policy making (Fein, 1980, however, disputed this finding); moderate parent participation in parent education endeavors; a frequent claim by parents that daycare centers can be a source of information on childrearing; positive effects in the social-affective domain for parents and children when parents participate as learners and decision makers in programs; and some debate on the causal influence of participation in policy making on parents and children. These findings constituted much of the data base on which the parent participation portions of the new requirements were based. Many political factors were involved, however, not the least of which was the allegation that high costs, in time and money, are necessary to achieve high levels of parent involvement.

Title I of ESEA has also incorporated parent participation. From the early recommendation that all Title I programs have advisory councils, there was a move in 1970 to require such councils. In 1974, Title I was amended to provide for the involvement of parents in planning, implementing, and evaluating programs. The amendments also required that local education authorities establish parent advisory committees and that the advisory councils have a majority of members from among the parents of children served and be composed of members selected by parents (Hightower, 1977). Hightower noted, however, that these guidelines have been subject to a wide variety of interpretation and modes of implementation, rendering their effectiveness difficult to ascertain and somewhat dubious.

Guidelines for participation also emerge in the broader literature on models of parent-professional relations. Some of these models have been implemented and others have not; all, however, offer information useful in guiding optimal parent involvement in child care and parent education.

Hill-Scott (1977) suggested a ladder of parent participation in which parents move upward from nonparticipation to degrees of tokenism and, finally, to degrees of real citizen power. Low involvement is characterized by staff-generated activities such as public information campaigns, demonstration procedures, and listening to public suggestions. Moderate involvement is characterized by a great deal of interaction between professionals and the community through techniques such as citizen advisory committees, establishment of decentralized program locations, use of advocates, and employment of community people. Acknowledging that higher levels of participation are difficult to achieve and presumably costly in time and money, Hill-Scott nonetheless urged their achievement. She concluded that "No one group—parents, citizens, or professionals in child care—had the complete or total right to decide policies for families and children. Our goal should be to establish dialogue among the parties" (Hill-Scott, 1977, p. 27). Techniques at low, moderate, and high levels should be used, where appropriate, with the goal of operating at the highest feasible participatory level; however, neither the parent nor the professional should ever be completely excluded.

Gordon (reported by Leler, in press) suggested three ways of conceptualizing participation: the parent or family impact model, in which the school influences the parent; the school or agency impact model, in which the parent influences the school; and the community impact model, in which parents, the school, and the community influence one another. Gordon preferred the community impact model for early childhood programs and saw it as comprising multiple possible roles for parents: program volunteer, paid staff member, educator of the child at home, audience member, program decision maker, and adult learner.

Leler (in press) also presented a scheme for conceptualizing levels of parent involvement in education originally described by Schickendanz (1977). Low parent involvement entails "parental activities that do not challenge the expertise of the teacher or the decision-making power of the school" (Schickendanz, 1977, p. 332). A second level entails parent participation in the classroom, in such roles as classroom observer and aide. At the highest level of involvement, parents teach their own children and make educational policy decisions. At this level, teachers help parents develop knowledge and skill once thought to be the exclusive province of the professional; also at this level, there is a sharing and collaboration between parent and professional in forms similar to Gordon's community impact model and Hill-Scott's dialogue approach.

Moroney (1980), analyzing professional-family relations in the areas of mental retardation, mental illness, and physical handicaps, developed a fourfold typology of professionals' attitudes toward the family: Families are viewed as part of the problem; families are viewed as resources for the professional to use in treating the problem; families are viewed as part of the treatment team; and families are viewed as needing resources in their own right. These four professional viewpoints can be seen as moving from an informed professional focus to an increasing emphasis on the informed parent. The last two views, in fact, seem to embody enabling and empowerment principles, with a decided developmental (as opposed to pathological) orientation. Although we have not focused on the specific problems investigated by Moroney, his scheme is relevant to child care and parent education.

We believe that *shared responsibility*, which characterizes the last two options in Moroney's typology, should be carefully considered in developing policy specifications in child care and parent education. However, such shared responsibility—developmental rather than pathological in orientation and closer to the notion of the informed parent than to the notion of the informed professional—will require a reorientation of the typical practice of most professionals. As stated by Moroney (1980, p. 152), "To successfully implement such an initiative, professionals would begin by asking the care givers [parents] what services or resources would enable them to continue as care givers [parents] and then provide them. What professionals think is beneficial becomes secondary, and requests from family members [parents] are not to be translated by the professional into services which agencies are organized to provide or services which the professional believes are important."

Using the information reviewed thus far, we identify the primary importance of the notion implicit or explicit in the work of several authors (Fein, 1980; Galinsky and Hooks, 1977; Gordon, 1977, 1979; Lambie, Bond, and Weikart, 1975; Moroney, 1980; Roberts and Dokecki, 1980): the idea of shared responsibility between professionals and parents. The sources cited here all point out the importance of professionals who have knowledge and resources to bring to a situation and who are imbued with a respect for the knowledge and resources that parents bring to the process of defining needs and developing solutions. Given social values in the United States (Dunlop, 1980) and our project's values focused on the promotion of community and the development of children, parents, and families, a model of shared responsibility between providers and parents seems to be of great potential worth. There is a caution to be observed in a shared responsibility model, however. Robinson and others (1979, p. 144) noted that participants in such a model—rather than sharing responsibility and knowledge related to desired outcomes—may become "equally timid caretakers who are not convinced that what they are doing is right, unambiguous, and urgent." To prevent such an outcome and encourage the optimum in the model of shared responsibility, individual providers of child care and parent education should have several attributes: knowledge and expertise concerning the child and parent needs the program addresses; skill in supporting the knowledge and expertise of parents; and the ability to share power related to the meeting of parent and child needs.

Reasons for promoting a model of shared responsibility are several, not the least of which is the increased likelihood that programs will meet participant needs and participants will gain experience in decision-making and power-sharing processes. In addition, there are reasons related to simple practicality and effectiveness. Fein and Clarke-Stewart (1973, p. 176) observed, with particular reference to parent involvement in child care programs, that parents generally have the best idea as to the specific programs that their children will find "most compatible and helpful." Galinsky and Hooks (1977) noted further that one characteristic of the effective programs they observed was an "alliance" between parents and providers within which parents and professionals respected each other, knew they had important things to learn from each other, and knew that they shared a common concern for "their" children. In fact, Galinsky and Hooks observed that the key criterion for parents in selecting programs for their children was usually the parents' perception that the program "felt right"—that it respected and reflected parental goals and values.

In spite of the apparent importance of mutual respect and communication between providers and parents, however, there is evidence that these qualities appear infrequently in many programs. While the providers observed by Galinsky and Hooks (1977) were characterized by strong professional identification and strong intentions to have their centers function as extended families for participants, other observers have reported less optimistic findings. Powell (1977), for example, found a disturbing lack of communication between parents and providers in his sample of twenty daycare programs in a large urban area, and Levine (1978) found that of the public school daycare programs he examined, those with the greatest degree of integration into the school system had the lowest level of formally structured parental input into the program. Powell (1979) subsequently noted work by Lortie (1975) indicating that teachers in schools considered parents to be "good parents" if they observed the teachers' rules and "avoided intervention in classroom affairs" (Powell, 1979, p. 16). Specific attention to means of enabling both providers and parents to participate in a model of shared responsibility is thus clearly warranted.

Given the political histories described, as well as the lack of comprehensive and well-tested guidelines to be found anywhere in the literature, it is clear that the task of developing optimal parent-professional relations will not be easy. But upon its resolution ride many of the chances for successful implementation of community-responsive policy options in child care and parent education.

Provider Relations with Children in Child Care. In programs of child care especially, it is critical that staff have certain abilities and characteristics if children and parents are to realize the maximum benefits from participation. Several research reviews indicate clearly that better child outcomes are associated with certain care giver characteristics and certain qualities of care giver–child relationships (Barnes and Dunlop, 1978; Belsky and Steinberg, 1978; Bronfenbrenner, 1978; Galinsky and

Hooks, 1977; Kilmer, 1979). Some of the qualities are related to conditions that the institutional sponsor allows or encourages, and others are related primarily to care givers as individuals.

Institutions as providers are implicated heavily in care giver–child relations in at least four ways: in requiring a care giver–child ratio that allows for an optimal amount of child-adult and child-peer interaction; in providing adequate space, appropriate health conditions, toys, and equipment to enable good child-adult and child-peer interactions; in requiring and enabling care giver training that supports the skills and personal qualities needed for optimal child-adult and child-peer interactions within the child care setting; and in providing the salary levels necessary to maintain provider morale and stability within the program.

Within the context permitted and encouraged by the institution-as-provider, individual care givers also must have personal skills and qualities if optimal outcomes—in the promotion of community and the promotion of human development in children—are to be accomplished. Care givers should be able, first, to initiate and maintain a productive and communicative relationship with the child's parents, focusing particularly on parents' wishes and goals, program goals, and the child's progress. Second, care givers should be able to plan meaningful and developmentally appropriate activities for children within the context of a generally sequenced curriculum. Third, care givers should be able to communicate clearly and effectively with children, in a manner that both enhances children's skills and communicates the care giver's respect and concern for the children. Fourth, the care giver should be able to establish clear and reasonable discipline and control and should be able to help children develop skills in self-discipline as well. Finally, and perhaps underlying all of the other points, care givers should feel good about children and the children's families; they should enjoy working with them and should communicate this fact, for they are indeed sharing both community and parental responsibility for the rearing of caring and competent individuals. Ultimately, the characteristics of *good* care, as we have used the term

throughout our consideration of child care programs and research, are to be found in these few critically important qualities of care givers and sponsoring agencies.

Conclusions

The mass of child and parent education data that we have
considered in this chapter—related to the goals, content, and
sponsorship of programs; the use of programs; the effects of
participation in programs; and guidelines to be used in developing programs—constitutes the informational foundation for our
analysis of various policy options. We have analyzed these data
with an intent to ascertain the "state of the art" in child care
and parent education and with the further intent of gaining a
rich and well-informed perspective from which to understand
the usefulness of the various policy options that have been suggested for child care and parent education in the service of
strengthened families. The findings presented in this chapter do
not, in themselves, lead to particular policy conclusions, nor do
they speak explicitly to the wisdom of pursuing either a human
capital or a human development rationale for public attention
to child care and parent education. They are of great importance, however, as we combine them with our values criteria in
analyzing the wisdom of several major policy directions. It is to
the definition and analysis of these policy options that we turn
in the next chapters.

FIVE

○I○I○I○I○I○I○I○I○I○I○I○I○I○I○I○I○I○I○I○I○I○I○I○I○

Assessing Options
for Serving Families

A full array of policy options in child care and parent education may be derived in several ways. We have chosen to draw on varied sources in defining the range of possibilities that we believe must be considered in developing resources for child care and parent education in the interests of strengthened families. Our sources have included the legislative history of child care and parent education in the United States; the political advocacy and opposition generated by proposed policies and programs; and the experience of Western European nations. Analysis of these sources has led us to delineate five major policy options that we believe warrant serious attention.

In describing each option, we attempt first to establish that it represents a programmatic approach to the problems of child care and parent education that reasonable people have supported or could support. Arguments for each option are presented to establish its credibility; they are cited to help make clear what the option is, not to establish its advantages over other options. Arguments against an option are also sometimes cited, but usually only for the purpose of showing that someone thought the option sufficiently likely to gain support to be worthy of opposition.

We then turn in each instance to the values implicit in the options. As discussed in Chapter Three, we believe that the analytic process, although often appearing objective—given customary emphases on such instrumental considerations as coverage, cost, comprehensiveness, and feasibility—frequently has a highly intuitive and value-laden component that may go unstated, perhaps even unrecognized, by the individual policy maker, scholar, research group, or commission. Thus, we analyze each option with reference to the values we have specified in Chapter Three, those we have identified as most significant to the strengthening of families and communities. The value analysis becomes more specific as we move through the various options, which themselves become more detailed. Even so, variation in the applicability of the criteria is to be expected. For options that have simply been proposed or tried on a very limited scale, detailed analysis is difficult; for options that are well established and have been tested in many programmatic settings over time, more complete analyses are possible.

We present the five major options as groupings of strategies that are more clearly defined than any "real-world" solution to issues in child care and parent education is likely to be. In reality, we would expect a mixture of policies. Nonetheless, we believe that each of these specific options warrants careful consideration on its own merits because each has been presented as a serious offering by persons concerned with the development of a humane and balanced response to the sometimes conflicting needs of children, parents, families, and the society as a whole. The five options include the following:

Option 1:   Do nothing new; take no new government action and accept the status quo; assume that problems will work themselves out on the basis of existing public programs and private initiatives.

Option 2:   Build a comprehensive national family policy and include child care and parent education as two of its constituent elements.

Option 3:   Provide flexibility, especially in the workplace, to make it possible for families to care more fully for their own children.

Option 4:   Provide resources for families to obtain child care and parent education services of their choice on the open market.

Option 5:   Provide child care and parent education services directly as a responsibility of government (federal, state, or local).

As will become clear, our values have led us to choose one of these options as most desirable, even while we assert the usefulness and viability of some of the others. In this chapter, we analyze the first four options. In the following two chapters, we examine the fifth option as it has been implemented at both the national and state levels.

Option 1: Do Nothing New; Accept the Status Quo

To do little or nothing new, to accept the status quo, to make a restrained response to the demands for child care and parent education, is a reasonable option that must be weighed seriously. The reformer's urge to do something needs to be resisted until the case for that "something," whatever it is, has been well made. The potential for making a mistake, for spending resources unwisely, is simply too great. A number of responsible people have endorsed the "do nothing new" option. Their reasons are diverse, and we present them with the observation that the arguments are discrete and not cumulative.

First, it is argued that the status quo in policy making not only enjoys an advantage but *should* enjoy an advantage. There is no need for change unless a convincing case can be made for change, and the burden of proof should lie with the advocates of a new course rather than with those who are content with things the way they are. This is an essentially and classically conservative position, one asserting the social usefulness of maintaining present structures and practice unless clear and compelling rationales for alteration can be developed.

Second, it is asserted that the "problem" of child care (not necessarily including the issue of parent education) is of minor importance or has already been solved. This line of reasoning assumes that parents are able to make whatever arrangements they need for child care and that they are essentially content with those arrangements. Only professionals who stand to gain from new programs, this line of reasoning goes, are pressing to alter current conditions. We interpret Woolsey (1977, pp. 129, 145) as espousing this position when she argued that what we need is "some modest tinkering at the margin of the system. Information services to enable parents more efficiently to make their own arrangements would be welcomed; flexible work hours and allowing leave to care for sick children would help a number of families. But such changes hold no utopian promise. . . . Such a view relegates daycare to that most undignified of political categories: a secondary issue."

A similar position was advanced by Steiner (1976), who argued that a humane society should help "the unlucky" and suggested that the best way to do this is through time-limited categorical programs addressed to the specific, well-recognized needs of those who are seriously disadvantaged. No great benefits are to be expected; it is simply the decent thing to do. The needs of children other than the "unlucky," it is assumed, are adequately and appropriately met without any organized and intentional social intervention.

A third line of argument here asserts that we should do nothing because nothing works. This point of view gained many adherents following the presidency of Lyndon Johnson. Early evaluations of some social programs (Head Start and Title I of ESEA, for example) provided data that seemed to support this pessimistic position, but the anti-Washington sentiment appeared to have been informed by issues antecedent to and transcending any empirical data; indeed, the main source of opposition seemed to spring from ideological considerations only tangentially related to specific aspects of the programs themselves. Subsequent research has found some early intervention efforts reasonably effective and perhaps even cost-efficient, but these data are likely to have little impact on ideological bases of this position.

A fourth rationale here asserts that we should do nothing about child care and parent education because such concerns are not the proper responsibility of government in a democracy.

This is essentially the argument advanced by President Nixon in vetoing the Comprehensive Child Development Act of 1971 (although interestingly, Nixon did not push for dismantlement of child care programs already in place). A related argument with comparable immediate consequences but different strategic implications has been a centerpiece of the Reagan administration, namely, that social and educational services are state, not federal, responsibilities. While states may elect to provide universal child care and parent education services if they wish, it is argued that these are not appropriate concerns of the federal government.

Overall, this "do nothing" option—if we take into account the varied lines of argument it embodies—has its persuasive advocates. The restrained-response version of the argument, detailed perhaps most eloquently by Steiner (1976), appeals to many as particularly well reasoned. Nonetheless, this course of action is starkly antithetical to the evidence and arguments accumulated in the course of our study of the problem. We believe that the data do add up to a need for national attention to child care and parent education (for example, increasing numbers of parents use these services, there is evidence of a suppressed demand for group care and for help with the care of very young children, and there are increasing numbers of families with two parents employed—all of which imply a continued increase in demand for these services). Perhaps even more important, however, is that the "do nothing" option is antithetical to our values. It does not, for example, elevate quality of services offered to children and their families to a level of acknowledged social responsibility. And our valuing of both competence and caring in the present and future generations certainly implies the importance of quality as an issue of critical public concern.

Policy makers, especially those who may not have ready access to the results of research on the effectiveness of social programs, should be particularly wary of the argument "Do nothing because nothing works." For example, evidence is now available, contrary to earlier and widely publicized negative assessments of child development and parent education programs, that quality early childhood programs comparable to Head Start have enduring beneficial effects; and in another example, ESEA Title I has been found to be achieving its objectives as defined by legislation. One lesson learned by social scientists from this experience is that it simply takes a number of years to get social, health, and educational programs working well in our large and diverse federation of states. Members of the Congress, faced with early negative findings, were more farsighted than the critics and continued appropriations to the programs. Their patience, undoubtedly fueled by political considerations, has subsequently been vindicated by research.

At the present time, child care and parent education are relatively dormant issues on the national political agenda. However, we note that a number of states (California and Minnesota, for example, whose programs we describe in detail in Chapter Seven) have forged ahead in mounting child care and parent education programs. Furthermore, it seems likely that a new constituency—composed in part of citizens intending to combine childrearing with careers—will be pressing for more adequate child care arrangements and parent involvement in the years immediately ahead. Government support of child care and parent education in the past has often been identified with welfare objectives (breaking the poverty cycle, teaching parents how to teach their children, enabling mothers on welfare to get jobs). The new constituency will cast the problem in a much broader perspective, which will probably include equity for women, family needs emerging from the demands of employment, and, perhaps, a concern for the competence and caring capacity of the new generation.

In our effort to analyze this option, we were hard pressed to find persuasive arguments in its favor. The affirmative arguments seem to boil down to three: child care exists only for the convenience of parents, and parents are satisfied with the arrangements they have been able to make; child care and parent education do not have demonstrable positive effects and therefore have no claim on public resources; and how children are reared is entirely a family matter and any intrusion by the larger society (except in circumstances of neglect or abuse) is an expression of a philosophy alien to American traditions and there-

fore unworthy of consideration. The first two arguments, however, are contradicted by evidence presented in Chapters Two
and Four. The third argument is a matter of value (or perhaps
political expediency), which seems to us to be starkly at vari-
ance with the commitments to social well-being that have been
a proud hallmark of our nation in its most enlightened periods.
We do not, of course, recommend casual intrusion into family
life. We do believe strongly in the reciprocal benefits that accrue
to families and communities when both assume some shared responsibilities for the well-being of the other.

   We therefore find option 1 unacceptable. Our main argument against the option is that the nation simply cannot afford
not to invest in sustaining families in their arduous task of rearing each new generation. We believe this is so partly because it is
the decent thing to do, partly because research has supported
the effectiveness of well-designed programs in supporting family
tasks, and partly because of the values we have placed on the
social good that accrues from the nurturance of caring and competent citizens.

Option 2: Build a National Family Policy

   The United States does not have a comprehensive family
policy, although many countries do. Several countries with
strong democratic traditions, in fact, have family policies explicitly articulated to advance the national purpose; included in this
group are Canada, Denmark, France, and Sweden. Great Britain
and West Germany, in a pattern similar to that of the United
States, have varied components of child and family services in
place, but have refrained from developing an explicit and comprehensive policy.

   Those who propose the development of a national family
policy argue that it simply makes good sense, in terms of the
general social good and efficiency, to do so. Indeed, several contemporary political leaders (among them John Brademas, Jim-
my Carter, Walter Mondale, and Joseph Califano) have at various times asserted the wisdom of examining family policy as a
whole in order to arrive at recommendations that will overcome

the deficiencies of our currently scattered and categorical efforts to meet disparate family and social needs. Even a brief
examination of existing child care and parent education programs and policies, as described, for example, in Chapters Four
and Six, reveals that these particular family needs are normally
addressed categorically, as if they had little or no relationship to
other family needs or a broad pattern of social goals.

Several scholars and government councils have come
forth to suggest the wisdom and potential efficacy of developing a national family policy in the United States. The National
Research Council's Advisory Committee on Child Development,
for example, recommended the development of a comprehensive national policy for children and families (National Academy
of Sciences, 1976). The committee, composed of nationally recognized scholars, politicians, and service providers, proposed
"specific policies and programs of economic resources, health
and health care, child care, special services, and the delivery of
services" (p. 3). The committee also recommended the expansion of research efforts in these areas as a means of improving
the knowledge base on which policies are built. The Carnegie
Council on Children followed with a recommendation for a national program, a "broad, integrated, explicit family policy" in
the interests of children's well-being (Keniston and the Carnegie
Council on Children, 1977, p. 216). Others, individual scholars
such as Kahn (1980), have also argued the wisdom of a broadly
based, well-integrated, and comprehensive approach to the development of policies meeting the needs of families in this nation.

The recommendation of a comprehensive national policy
for families and children must be taken seriously; this is attested
to not only by the support it has received but also by the opposition it has generated. Steiner (1976, p. 255), for example,
counseled a much more limited national agenda: "It may develop that private families really are not equipped to meet most
children's needs. . . . Unless and until that case is made more
persuasively than it has been, however, a children's policy will be
successful enough if it concentrates on ways to compensate
demonstrably unlucky children whose bodies or minds are sick
or whose families are unstable or in poverty." Later, Steiner

(1981) concluded that national family policy is simply not feasible. Consensus on such a policy, he argued, is virtually impossible because of our nation's commitment to pluralism and the reality of interest group politics. Value clashes over issues such as abortion, divorce, and women's rights guarantee that consensus will not be reached and strongly suggest from the outset that the quest for an overarching family policy is futile.

The Washington-based Family Impact Seminar also took a position opposing the development of a national family policy. Arguing from the belief that a family policy would "work to impose a single set of standards for family life," Sidney Johnson, Director of the Seminar, went on to observe that development of such a policy would suggest "that there is some comprehensive national solution to the problems facing American families. This concept directly contradicts our respect for the personal, private, sensitive, and unique qualities of family life. It also ignores the diversity and pluralism among American families that are both facts of life and sources of national strength" (Johnson, 1980, p. 19). Johnson went on to propose that "a variety of policies be made more sensitive and responsive to the needs and aspirations of American families" through means such as new legislation, if necessary, innovative private initiatives, and family impact analysis (p. 19).

The good sense of this statement can hardly be argued, but one can appropriately question the assumption that a national family policy would have to be a monolithic policy. A sensible national family policy, its proponents argue, would of necessity be complex, embracing a wide variety of programs that are now developed independently without consideration of their interactions or effects, especially with respect to the family. Further, a national policy could explicitly embrace the values of pluralism, privacy, and other traditional goals of American family life. Indeed, one of the first steps in constructing a family policy might well be to develop a national consensus on the criteria to be used in deciding its dimensions and assessing its worth (see, for example, Rice, 1977).

Whatever the arguments surrounding the development of a national family policy, it seems to be in almost total political

eclipse at the present time. The most recent such effort in the
early 1970s, the Mondale-Brademas Child and Family Services
Act, suffered a stunning defeat by a grass-roots campaign apparently sparked by fundamentalist groups that saw in the proposed legislation a government effort to take childrearing responsibilities away from the family. Its final defeat coincided
with a growing national focus on economic recovery and increased military strength, thus consigning concerns for social,
educational, and health programs to a clearly secondary position. For the present, at least, the issue of a national family
policy seems politically dead.

But the concept retains an intrinsic validity that will likely work to ensure its revival when, and if, the development of
human resources once again becomes a major concern of the
nation. Effective human resource development demands attention to hundreds of interrelated issues: care for the aged, tax
policies, child care, employment opportunities, housing subsidies, care of chronically ill and handicapped family members,
aid to the poor, and on and on and on. Such issues, whether we
acknowledge it explicitly or not, are parts of a dynamic and interrelated system; actions on any particular issue often reverber-
ate throughout the whole. In making hundreds of separate legislative decisions affecting families directly or indirectly, we
arrive at a family policy by default, as many observers have
pointed out.

A sensible family policy for the United States seems best
understood as complex, embracing a wide variety of programs
and regulations that have been developed to date without serious consideration of their potentially contradictory and negative impacts on families. Movement in this direction would require a dynamic process of inquiry, especially into the values
that inform the making of policy. This process has begun in the
work of the Advisory Committee on Child Development of the
National Academy of Sciences, the Carnegie Council on Children, the Family Impact Seminar, the White House Conference
on Families, and a number of individual scholars. The concept
of family impact analysis, which was transformed by the Family
Impact Seminar from an abstract concept to a powerful operational instrument for assessing the significance of legislation for

family life, is highly commendable, perhaps an essential step in the direction of establishing a national consensus concerning the relationship between communities, families, parents, and children.

The development of a national family policy might well allow a sensible shift in focus of responsibility for programs affecting children, parents, and families from the federal government to the states and local communities. In the slow and arduous process of building national consensus on the most desirable relationship between the family and the state, we have in our federated structure an opportunity to observe fifty forums for debate and experimentation with various approaches. However, much depends on how the states respond to such an opportunity and what responsibility the federal government takes in making a genuinely decentralized system work. Decentralization, as we observed in Chapter Four, may simply increase confusion, lack of coordination, duplication and maldistribution of services, and the proliferation of competing bureaucracies, while decreasing available funds and services to families who need them. If the federal government takes responsibility for providing technical assistance to the states as needed and ensures the dissemination of information resulting from the fifty experiments made possible by the devolution of authority and funds from Washington to the states, then perhaps a national policy would in fact allow for more local community control of the pattern and content of response to family needs.

An appropriate and sensible national family policy could well enhance and strengthen the values of human development and community. The dynamic process of inquiry necessary to clarify values and understand the consequences and interactions of the necessary pieces of the family policy mosaic is far from complete, however; in fact, it has probably just begun.

Option 3: Provide Flexibility to Families

Even if one agrees that out-of-home child care and comprehensive approaches to parent involvement and education are essential features of a modern, industrial society, public policies in the United States today must clearly and properly be based on the continuing central role of families in childrearing. Even the most enthusiastic advocate of a comprehensive, publically supported family services system in this nation is quite likely to emphasize that such a program should only *supplement* and enrich families' abilities to do their tasks well. One of the values on which we appear to have some national consensus, in fact, is the importance of competent and capable families.

There are multiple means to the goal of strong families, of course, and one of those means asserts the importance of giving families more flexibility as they work to integrate the various demands of contemporary life into their everyday functioning. This position downplays public responsibility for making programs available to meet family needs and assumes instead that support for families—and the family functions of child care and parent education—is best offered by enhancing the range of options that may be selected by families to maximize their own direct role in child care.

Most Americans believe that the family is the best institution for rearing children, and most Americans who have children put their beliefs into practice. When young children *are* taken outside of the home for care, they are most frequently placed with a neighbor or relative, who may care for several children in a family daycare home. Most parents, thus, provide most of their own children's care and many parents appear to prefer keeping their young children's care as familylike as possible.

Proponents of the flexibility option often suggest that optimal arrangements for the care of young children, especially infants and toddlers, call for relationships between the child and the care giver that can best be provided in the family. This is not to say that it is impossible to devise out-of-family care that meets the child's need for nourishment, comfort, security, stimulation, and identification with caring adults, but only that such arrangements may be difficult to accomplish, especially when high-quality child care services are in short supply.

Proponents of the flexibility option also suggest that parents can probably deploy their own time in child care with more assurance of quality and stability in relationships than is possible when they try to arrange for care outside of the family. Furthermore, attachments between the very young child and the adult care giver are mutually reinforcing, so that parents who are unable to spend quality time, particularly with their infants and toddlers, may themselves be deprived. The importance of predictable, nurturing relationships with stable care givers has been underscored by Fein and Clarke-Stewart (1973) and also by Bronfenbrenner (1978, pp. 767, 787), who observed: "In order to develop, a child needs the enduring, irrational involvement of one or more adults in care and joint activity with the child. . . . The development of an irrational, mutual, emotional attachment takes even more occasions, even more time, and, if the attachment is to be mutual, it not only takes somebody to be there, it takes the *same* somebody."

The argument for parents providing the major part of the care of their own children is most persuasive with respect to infants and toddlers (suggesting, in part, that there may need to be two child care policies, one for very young children and another for preschoolers and older children). Older preschoolers, of course, from the age of two and a half years on, generally need regular opportunities to learn social skills in relationship to other children and need, as well, opportunities to develop relationships with other care givers. Such opportunities initiate the process of gaining independence, a process that speeds up at school age and culminates in late adolescence and early adulthood. Various group care opportunities are thus developmentally warranted for older preschoolers. (A sharp age demarcation is not implied here, of course; individual differences—in children's development, in family configurations, and in parental preferences—indicate that children will vary substantially in their readiness for various experiences.)

For younger preschoolers, however, some advocates of flexibility argue that it is particularly important to have high-quality care given by continuous care givers. Preferably these care givers would be the mother and/or father, assisted when necessary by another family member, a dependable neighbor, or a qualified child care provider in a high-quality day home or center with stable personnel and a limited number of other children. Perhaps some combination of these arrangements may be indicated; however, goes the argument, one or both parents should be expected and enabled to invest substantial amounts of personal time on a predictable basis to give the child a good start in life. Especially to be avoided are various slipshod, pillar-to-post arrangements for infants and toddlers that may ensue from the absence of an adequate child care system or from individual and community failure to appreciate the importance of continuous, loving care.

In advocating family care for young children, the proponents of flexibility do not necessarily see the family as possessing some mystical quality that is good for children. Rather, the suggestion made is that the things that are good for young children can best be supplied in familylike arrangements. Further, biological parents are not necessarily better care givers than unrelated adults who are willing to make a parentlike commitment. But the bearing of children, it is argued, may create a presumption of a commitment to caring for children in ways appropriate to their developmental needs. Although it is not always possible (for a variety of personal, economic, and employment reasons) for all parents to take full-time, direct responsibility for the care of infants and toddlers in the family, the familylike model may be useful in helping parents define criteria for appropriate substitute care.

In any event, argue the proponents of flexibility, more families should be enabled to spend more of their own time caring for their young children, especially their infants and toddlers, without undue economic or employment penalty. This simply makes sense, so the line of reasoning goes, for the children, their parents, and the community as a whole. For example, providing care for preschoolers has been suggested as a way of helping single mothers with young children get off welfare and into employment. The economic benefits to this arrangement, argue the proponents of flexibility, are minimal; it often costs more to provide care than low-income mothers can possibly earn, and it makes no sense in these circumstances to pay strangers for child care. The child is probably better off with the mother, and the mother would likely be better off financially if the money paid out to a care program were paid to her directly, perhaps in recognition of her own child care functions. To increase her own skills, the money might be linked, for example, to regular participation in a parent education program.

A policy focusing on flexibility as a means of encouraging child care in the family is not without its disadvantages, however. Some families clearly need external services and support, rather than flexibility, if they are to raise their children well. This is evidenced in extreme circumstances by child neglect, but another more prevalent example here is the large group of single parents who find it impossible to care for their children because of the need to work. A further objection arises from the observation that it is usually the mother in two-parent families who stays at home; this implies that a policy of flexibility might have the effect of discouraging women's employment and career development. Further, if a mother who wants to work has sole responsibility for child care, with little relief or opportunity for personal and career development, the quality of her care may suffer (Dunlop, 1981; Hoffman, 1974). Thus, any argument for flexibility based on the role of the family in child care must take into account how men and women will negotiate their roles and functions within the family. Providing family flexibility can too easily translate into restricting the choice and freedom of one parent; therefore, the parental child-caring role and the possibility of true choice by women would seem to be indispensable for a just and effective flexibility option.

Considering the preferences of many parents and the need of young children for steady nurturing relationships, how might public policy be shaped to make it possible to provide more child care in the family? This question immediately turns our attention toward the world of work, for the option of flexibility almost automatically requires the development of new accommodations between work and family life.

Kamerman (1980, p. 12) observed that "work and family life can no longer be viewed as separate domains." She went on to assert that the central question in family policy has become "What is to be the nature of the relationship between work and family life, when most adults, regardless of gender, are increas-

ingly likely to be in the labor force during the same years that
they are at the peak of their childbearing and their childrearing
responsibilities? What should be the role of government in addressing this issue?" That the workplace profoundly affects the
character of family life has been well established (Kanter,
1977), as has the observation that to date, when family and
work needs conflict, they are "almost always settled in favor of
the job" (Keniston and the Carnegie Council on Children, 1977,
p. 122). Nonetheless, several specific means of increasing the
accommodation of the workplace to the demands of family responsibilities have been developed in our own nation and in several other countries. We will now review several of these specific
flexibility options.

Flexible Working Hours. Under flexible hours work plans
(flexitime)—widely established in Western Europe, Japan, and
Canada, and growing in acceptance in the United States—employees decide when and how long they will work each day so
long as the total amount of work in a week or two adds up to a
required total. The flexibility thus achieved can make it possible for mothers and fathers to share in child care responsibilities
and to take care of periodic special needs, such as visiting the
pediatrician. Although flexitime is not easily adapted to some
kinds of work situations (such as those involving assembly
lines), where it has been used, it has been successful: Productivity increases, morale is improved, and turnover, absenteeism,
and overtime decline (Keniston and the Carnegie Council on
Children, 1977).

Flexitime was initiated by a large German industrial firm
two decades ago as a measure to relieve traffic congestion. Not
only did the traffic situation improve, but 65 percent of the employees also reported that working conditions were much better
under the flexitime system. The most frequently mentioned advantage of the system was that it offered a better balance between
work and private life. The company concluded that increased
productivity and lower absenteeism produced a substantial cost
saving (Wade, 1973). Employees using flexitime in a chemical
company in Switzerland were surveyed by Racki (1975), who
found that 35 percent of the workers used the flexitime system

to spend more time with their families. Ninety-five percent of the employees were in favor of flexitime, and the largest single group, 45 percent, were especially pleased with it for the impact it had on their private lives. A study of an American firm revealed the same worker preference for flexitime and noted that attending to personal matters was the most frequently mentioned alternate use of time (Golembiewski and Hiles, 1977). The U.S. Geological Survey initiated flexitime in the mid 1970s with comparable results (Mueller and Cole, 1977).

The crucial issue, from our perspective, is the effect of flexitime on family life. Does it actually ease family burdens and make it possible for mothers and fathers to spend more quality time with their children? Bohen and Viveros-Long (1981), who studied employees of the U.S. Maritime Administration who had been using flexitime for one year, concluded that enthusiasm for flexitime must be muted considerably. For example, they found that the employees most helped by the flexitime program "were those with the fewest work-family conflicts, namely, those without children" (p. 192). They concluded that "complicated and unresolved value questions, both about men's and women's roles and about the relative importance of work and a family, underlie the ambiguous expectations for, and effects of, flexitime. Minor changes in the formal conditions of work (like scheduling) will not significantly affect the family variables measured in this study (like sharing of family work). More substantial structural changes, as well as shifts in values and expectations about people's participation both in work and a family must occur first." The authors were meticulous in pointing out the limitations of their study (it involved only one agency; the program had been in place for only a year; it was done in a large metropolitan area) and observed that flexitime might well work better in smaller cities and might also work better once it has been in place for a longer time. Nonetheless, their observations constitute a major contribution and temper vigorous enthusiasm for flexitime by the hard realities of data carefully collected and interpreted with good judgment.

Leave for Childbearing and Childrearing. In the United States, the concept of maternity leave for pregnancy and childbirth has been reasonably well established. However, the provisions for compensation and job security are grossly inadequate, as is the period of time usually thought appropriate for taking leave to have and care for an infant.

In several European countries, satisfactory plans have been operating for a number of years. The leave pattern varies from country to country, from a minimum of three months in Denmark and several other countries to a maximum of three years in Hungary. The average leave is from six months to one year. Usually, the mother (and the father in countries where the benefit can be shared) is assured of her (or his) position, with full protection of seniority, benefits, and other entitlements, much as veterans were protected after World War II in the United States. Provisions are usually made for continuing subsidized payments to the mother or father during childbearing and childrearing leaves; these are variously financed as health insurance benefits, unemployment compensation, or a special parental leave allowance. Specific plans vary from country to country. Hungary, for example, has a plan designed to encourage mothers to care for their own children until the age of three. After termination of parental leave, the mother is guaranteed 40 percent of her wage until the child is three, with full assurance of her position, seniority, and benefit entitlements when she returns to her job. In Sweden, parents may take seven months of leave and are guaranteed 90 percent compensation and continuation of benefits and job seniority. Parental leave may be divided between mother and father in any way they wish. Although reports indicate that men seldom take advantage of the opportunity, the plan is relatively new and it does establish an expectation that fathers may appropriately be involved in child care, which could lead to improved child care, an enriched experience for the father, and greater mutual support between mother and father. Public opinion polls in Sweden show leave for the birth of a child to be the most appreciated benefit in a nation that has a large number of social programs aimed at improving the quality of life.

The needs of sick children may constitute a major problem for workplace-family relations. While many employers in the United States provide a certain informal flexibility to permit a mother or father to attend at least briefly to a child who is ill, the lack of formal arrangements makes taking such leave uncomfortable if not actually unwise. Most Western European countries have a definite allowance of time (comparable to sick leave for the employee in the United States) for sick child care. Apparently, this arrangement is much appreciated, since it relieves some of the anxiety generated by strongly competing demands for parents' time. In some countries, health or social services departments provide child minders for such occasions.

The percentage of compensation, duration of leave time, and job security are among the many factors that must be dealt with in using leave policies to provide flexibility to families in performing their childrearing functions. And while it may appear at first glance that the measures also share the attribute of not costing money, this implication is not intended. All of them entail costs that must be covered. A major problem with this policy approach, as is true of other flexibility options, is the paucity of specific information on how they actually operate or would operate in the United States.

Part-Time Jobs. The availability of part-time jobs with appropriate compensation and benefits might enhance the ability of parents to provide more quality care for children in the family. For example, a father or mother might work part-time while a child is enrolled in a half-day preschool or kindergarten. At present, however, employers may be at a disadvantage in using part-time workers, and part-time work is usually associated with low pay, few or no benefits, little security, and few opportunities for career advancement. These drawbacks may be especially critical to families with young children, where the need for the benefits of full-time employment may be acute.

A variation in the part-time job arrangement is job sharing, in which two people share one job, each approximately half-time, with schedules worked out to their convenience. This arrangement has been tried in a number of places in recent years, but we know of no evaluation of its effects on work and family life. Some participants in job sharing, however, have reported satisfaction with the arrangement, mentioning that it allows them to spend more time with their children (Keniston and the Carnegie Council on Children, 1977).

Evaluation of the Flexibility Option

Several manifestations of the flexibility option have thus been tried in the United States or are suggested by the experience of other countries. The advantages and disadvantages of this major option, as implied in the positions of its advocates and opponents, have been given here. We now turn to an evaluation of this option from the perspective of our values criteria.

Does the Policy Enhance Community? In general, providing flexibility for working parents to care for their own children measures up reasonably well on the criterion of community enhancement. Perhaps the single greatest benefit that could derive from these measures would be a narrowing of the now enormous gap in the United States between the workplace and the family (Kanter, 1977). In the place that is most important to their own (and the nation's) economic well-being, most parents now have little authority with respect to matters pertaining to their families. Rubin (1976), in her poignant and depressing book, *Worlds of Pain,* pictures the dehumanizing effects of the workplace on the family life of the blue-collar worker. Experiences of other nations where management has been attentive to family needs and the experiences of enlightened companies in the United States make it clear that the disjunction between work and family is not only harmful to families but to the workplace as well. Use of the several flexibility measures could enhance the situation of all workers, whether they are parents or not. They could dramatize the common benefits to be derived from a policy motivated primarily by concerns for the rearing of children and the strengthening of families. The one potential exception to the general community benefit accruing from the flexibility option lies in the provision of extended leaves for childbearing and childrearing with little reduction in income and an assured position with no loss of seniority. Implementation of this specific measure could diminish community by creating resentments on the part of workers who do not plan to have children or older workers who are past childrearing years. The future security of all workers, however, is likely to depend on the quality of children's experiences, and this realization (that the security of all citizens past retirement will depend on the competence and caring of the younger generation) may mute this criticism.

None of the specific flexibility options would be means-tested, thus avoiding an invidious comparison between the haves and have-nots and removing the necessity of humiliating inquiry into the economic condition of families. *All* families, indeed all employees, would enjoy the benefits of the policy, thus eliminating a source of community discord.

All three of the White House Conferences on Families that met in 1980 had as a priority their concern with diminishing stresses between the workplace and the family. While narrowing the gap between work and home would contribute substantially to the enhancement of community, it would be a mistake to assume that the several formal arrangements for increasing job flexibility discussed in this section would completely solve the problem. What seems required above all is a changed attitude on the part of employers toward families, a recognition of the interdependence of home and workplace, and increased responsiveness on the part of employers to family needs.

Does the Policy Strengthen Families? Whether or not the flexibility option strengthens families is difficult to answer because there have been relatively few studies of families functioning as units in relationship to the larger society. The little evidence that we do have indicates that flexibility options may in fact be related to increased family tensions (see, for example, Bohen and Viveros-Long, 1981). Adjusting the circumstances of work without accompanying adjustments in the roles of family members, particularly the roles of mothers and fathers, may increase pressures on mothers and increase both marital and family strain.

All of the arrangements to augment child care resources by providing flexibility in the workplace appear to demand a fundamental realignment of the roles of women and men. For example, job sharing for the purpose of making it possible for

mother and father to share equally in childrearing assumes not
only that men are willing to change long-established and highly
elaborated attitudes about what is "manly" but that they will
also acquire skills not now normally taught to males in the process of growing up. Since children learn role models in part
from parents and other adults, the process of realignment needs
to begin in childhood. It is reported that in Sweden, for example, which has an advanced national family policy with the
equality of sexes as a centerpiece, men seldom take advantage
of the generous childrearing leaves provided to both mother and
father. Some say that it simply takes a long time for social
change to occur; others observe that men can recognize a gruel-
ing job when they see one and stay away from it. Nonetheless,
it seems a reasonable hypothesis that efforts to adjust the requirements of the workplace to the requirements of families
would enrich the quality of our national life and strengthen
families in the process.

The discussion thus far has concentrated on two-parent
families. Some of these observations apply to single-parent families, and some do not. For many single parents, especially wom-
en, much depends on the availability of resources other than
those produced by a job. When private resources (for example,
gifts from parents, generous child support) are available, part-
time work, shared jobs, and other flexibility measures may be
highly useful. But full-time work is often a necessity, particularly considering that families headed by single women have substantially lower incomes than any other type of family. Flexitime may afford modest relief to single-parent families, and
leaves to care for a sick child can be a great boon. However, on
the whole, it would seem that a policy of providing flexibility
to enable parents to take care of their own children is more likely to help two-parent families than single-parent families.

We know of no studies of the problem, but we cannot
foresee how the provision of flexibility in job arrangements
would lead to an increased intrusion into family life. There may
be a need for a somewhat more elaborate accounting for time
on the job, but we can see no need for any intrusion into privacy attendant upon this option. However, it is important to re-

call that in a day when industries and families were closely linked, as in the textile mills of the North and the South, there was an extraordinary amount of employer control over families, including employer determinations of where employees might live, where they could buy goods, how they must dress, and so on. In reexamining the relationships between workplace and family, care must be exercised to avoid the reinstatement of such practices in a modern idiom.

Does the Policy Enable Parents to Do Their Job Well? In considering whether a policy enables parents to do their job well, we are really asking if a policy makes available to parents the time, energy, satisfaction, knowledge, and resources needed to do their job well. The several arrangements for providing flexibility differ with regard to these specifics.

Flexible work schedules provide convenience, and that is all. They do not make additional time available. The employee must work just as many hours in a designated period as on a fixed schedule, but he or she has options for the disposition of time within prescribed limits. There is evidence that employees like the plan and that it improves morale. But the high hopes once held that flexitime would reduce stress on families have been muted, although additional studies of the plan clearly are needed before firm conclusions can be reached.

Part-time jobs and shared jobs would obviously make available to parents time that could be used for childrearing; and presumably a reduced work load would free up an equivalent amount of energy that could be invested in families and children. Certainly, many families would welcome an increase in the number of available part-time jobs and greater ease of access to them. In many circumstances, part-time employment, particularly if it included greater access to benefits, would enable parents to do a better job than would otherwise be possible. But there are clear trade-offs. Part-time jobs reduce family resources, not only in total income but also in rates of compensation, opportunities for advancement, and availability of benefits that are often essential for family security. Families most in need of the time freed up by part-time employment are often the families who can least afford it. Finally, in two-parent families, it is usually the mother who is expected to accept part-time employment. While this is a choice preferred by some women, for many it is a choice dictated by tradition and economic inequities (women generally earn less than men) rather than by preference.

It appears that none of the proposed arrangements to provide flexibility would promote shared responsibility among parents and service providers, including professionals, which is one of the specifications of the criterion concerned with enabling parents to do their job well. Further, none accords attention to parents' needs for knowledge in relation to childrearing (in fact, parent education is virtually ignored in the flexibility option), thereby causing it to fall short on this aspect of the criterion as well.

Does the Policy Enhance Individual Development and Protect the Rights of Individual Members of the Family? In regard to individual development and individual rights, the flexibility options are somewhat lacking, largely because of the probability that they will be "paid for" mostly by women and it is likely that the benefits will not be shared equally in two-parent families until there is a fundamental revision of private and public attitudes toward equality of opportunity for women and men. For women who want to make their primary investment in caring for children and who have resources to do so either personally or through the husband's earnings, an opportunity to work part-time may be an ideal arrangement, especially after the child is ready to benefit from group experiences. Certainly, the proposed extended leave at childbirth for mothers, sharable with the fathers, could be a great help to both women and men who are employed and have a child. For single parents, women and men, flexible working hours could provide some convenience; for most, however, part-time and shared jobs would probably be impossible from an economic perspective.

If and when increased job flexibility indeed makes it possible for mothers *and* fathers to spend more time with their own children, the greatest beneficiaries will be the children themselves. The policies then will quite conceivably make possible the irrational commitment of quality time by a limited number of care givers that Bronfenbrenner (1978) posits as essential for the well-rounded development of a child.

Conclusions. The various proposals for modulating work arrangements and providing flexibility so that parents can take care of their own young children or increase the proportion of time that they can devote to their children deserve thoughtful consideration by policy makers. Children, especially in the earliest weeks and months of life and up to the age of two or three, benefit from constancy of care by a limited number of loving and responsive adults. Parents—mothers *and* fathers—deserve a choice in how they rear their children, including the choice of taking major direct responsibility for their care, particularly in the early years. Flexibility options might well be pursued in an effort to find ways through which women and men can give first priority to their young children without incurring penalties in the workplace.

Overall, however, the flexibility option yields mixed results when viewed from the perspective of our value framework. It has great potential for enhancing community; it may or may not strengthen families, depending on the way male-female roles and rights are construed; it may be of some, but limited, help in enabling parents to do their job well; and it could certainly benefit children, but again, issues of gender equality cloud its different effects on individual members of the family.

Option 4: Provide Resources to Families

Freedom of choice is a highly cherished value of people everywhere, and opportunity for its exercise is deeply rooted in the American ethos. Even though circumstances may lead more frequently to its abridgement than to its fulfillment, and although it has been more valued at some times in history than at others, it remains a defining aspiration of many democratic societies. Thus, one attractive option for the provision of child care and parent education services is to put into the hands of parents resources that would enable them to choose the kinds of supplementary services they prefer. The Carnegie Council on

Children, for example, took the position that the best way to strengthen families is to be sure that parents have the resources needed to obtain for their children the kinds of services they judge to be appropriate (Keniston and the Carnegie Council on Children, 1977). Yet another reason for suggesting the option of providing resources to families, revered if not always exercised in the American tradition, is that our economic system works best when people can choose among competitive products. Not only do people get what they want, the position goes, but steady and unrelenting pressure is put on producers to supply and improve their products. That this system has its limitations is reasonably well recognized, but it enjoys unquestioning support in some quarters and generally widespread support in the population. In the provision of child care and parent education services, freedom of choice can be enhanced by such mechanisms as income supports, children's allowances, vouchers, and tax credits. The voucher and tax credit mechanisms receive somewhat more attention in this section than do income supports and children's allowances, since they can be targeted explicitly to child care and parent education.

Income Supports. Various proposals to reform the patchwork income support system have been made over the last several decades. The most notable recent proposal is that of the Carnegie Council on Children (Keniston and the Carnegie Council on Children, 1977). Complementing the income support recommendation of the National Academy of Sciences (1976), the council opted for a plan that provides strong incentives to work, including especially the elimination of abrupt loss of benefits as a result of modest increases in income; contains adequate safeguards against abuse (for example, capable adults should work if they are not caring for dependents); guarantees a minimum income equal to 40 percent of the median for families of a given size, which, if coupled with a program of job supports, would put virtually all families above one half the median income; and gives the parent responsible for childrearing a true choice about going out to work or staying at home to work. It is important to emphasize that the Carnegie Council did not recommend income supports alone; the formulation assumes a program of nearly full to full emloyment.

The council suggested a "credit income tax" system in which "virtually all deductions, exemptions, and shelters would be eliminated. All earnings and property income would be subject to a fixed tax rate—that is, everyone would pay a flat percent (the same regardless of income). But every man, woman, and child in the country would be entitled to a tax credit, money they would receive if they had no other source of support. For the poor, this would be a tax in reverse—a payment made to them instead of taken from them. Since tax credits would offset taxes at low income levels, the effective rate of tax in the overall tax structure would increase as a family's income got larger" (Keniston and the Carnegie Council on Children, 1977, p. 105). Table 5 illustrates how the Carnegie Council credit income tax

Table 5. The Carnegie Council on Children's Recommendation for a Credit Income Tax: An Illustration for a Family of Four.

1 Initial Income	2 Tax Liability (50% of Column 1)	3 Net Credit or Income Tax ($6,000 Minus Column 2)	4 Final Income (Column 1 Plus Credit or Minus Tax)	5 Effective Tax Rate
$ 0	$ 0	$ 6,000 Credit	$ 6,000	—
$ 3,000	$ 1,500	$ 4,500 Credit	$ 7,500	—
$ 6,000	$ 3,000	$ 3,000 Credit	$ 9,000	—
$ 9,000	$ 4,500	$ 1,500 Credit	$10,500	—
$12,000	$ 6,000	$ 0	$12,000	0
$15,000	$ 7,500	$ 1,500 Tax	$13,500	10%
$21,000	$10,500	$ 4,500 Tax	$16,500	21.4%
$30,000	$15,000	$ 9,000 Tax	$21,000	30%
$50,000	$25,000	$19,000 Tax	$31,000	38%

Source: Keniston and the Carnegie Council on Children, 1977, p. 107, Table 1.

plan would work; other variations are possible, of course. While the cost to the federal government would be between $40 billion and $50 billion, that much is currently invested in assistance programs, many of which would be eliminated. The main burden of the plan would be borne by citizens in the upper 25 to 30 percent of the income distribution. The plan provides resources for the whole family and for all kinds of needs; indeed, families without children would benefit.

Currently, supports to low-income families who maintain households for at least one child are provided through the tax structure in the form of a refundable earned income credit. Originally enacted to partially offset the increase in Social Security taxes, the credit acts as a work incentive for families as incomes rise from zero to $6,000. The earned income tax credit is limited to families' *earned* income and is gradually phased out as family incomes rise from $6,000 to $10,000. The refundable nature of the credit sets an important precedent in that the credit is available regardless of tax liability and for the last several years has been available throughout the year in the form of advanced earned income credits to families whose income was insufficient to require income tax withholding.

Although the earned income credit is imperfect in a number of respects—notably its failure to account for the number of children in a family—it illustrates that it is possible to provide transfer payments that are tied to the needs of children. It is to three such options—children's allowances, vouchers, and income tax credits—that we now turn.

Children's Allowances. A very direct way to recognize and partially compensate for the economic burden of children on families is the payment of a direct public allowance for each child. The children's allowance system was initiated in France in the 1930s and has spread throughout the world since that time. Today, sixty-six countries provide such an allowance. The United States, in fact, is the only developed nation that does not directly recognize the added cost to all families of childbearing and childrearing.

Generally, the plans provide an allowance for each child from birth to a fixed age, usually eighteen, and the allowance normally goes to all families with children, thus eliminating demeaning certification requirements and their attendant bureaucracies. In France and other countries, allocation starts after the first child and sometimes increases for families with handicapped children or with several children; sometimes the allocation increases with the age of the child. In most Western European countries, the benefits range from $300 to $600 per year per child, a not inconsiderable amount, especially for poor people, and the allowance is sometimes tax-free, an important provision. The allowance usually adds from 5 to 10 percent to median family incomes.

Although child allowances have been advocated in the past as a means of encouraging women to have babies to ensure an adequate supply of workers (or, in some instances, soldiers), they seem to have had little effect on the fertility of populations. Those who fear that children's allowances would cause a new baby boom can find no support for their concern in the experience of other countries; those who want to stimulate population growth will have to discover some other means of achieving this objective. Children's allowances commend themselves not for puposes of population control but for recognition of the contribution that parents make to the society by rearing children and for recognition of the fact that rearing children brings added costs to families, including the cost of child care. Berger (1979, p. 14) elaborated on these reasons, arguing that

> to assure in practice, and not only in rhetoric, respect for the great variety of American life-styles, for their widely varying perceptions and goals, as well as for the distinctive structures in which they are embedded, and yet to be responsive to the different needs of families and their children, some thought of child allowance seems to be indicated. This mechanism, in my opinion, would resolve most of the controversies around the national day-care debate. A child allowance would allow individual families the widest possible choice in arranging for the care of their small children. The varied forms of care should include the option for the individual parent (father or mother) to stay home during the crucial period of infancy and early childhood or longer, as well as arrangements such as "grand parenting," care by extended family members or neighborhood groups, full-time, even hourly arrangements at drop-in centers, as well as existing and to-be-established governmental centers of any size.

The need to allow for the expense of raising children has long been recognized in this country, not in the form of children's allowances, but in the tax code, in the form of an exemption for dependent children. The personal exemptions for all family members are designed to free from taxation the income needed to maintain a minimum standard of living and to differentiate tax liability according to family size. However, each personal exemption is of much greater value to persons with high incomes than to persons with low incomes, because the marginal tax rate rises with income. For example, in 1981, the value of the exemption was zero for low-income people, $140 at the income level at which people begin paying taxes, and $700 at the level of upper-income taxpayers (Weeks, 1980).

Because the value of the exemption varies inversely with income, from time to time various changes have been proposed. One proposal had been to substitute fixed tax credits for personal exemptions, which would differentiate the tax burden according to family size and would treat families at all income levels equally. Others have suggested that the personal exemptions be withdrawn gradually as income increases, since they are not needed in middle and upper classes to protect a minimum standard of living. This arrangement, called a vanishing exemption, has been used in some Commonwealth countries.

While these proposals would reduce taxable income to allow for the cost of raising children, they do not include *payment* of a children's allowance through the tax system. The latter concept, refundability, implemented partially through an earned income credit, would have to be joined with the personal exemptions for the income tax system to provide a children's allowance for *all* families, those who pay taxes and those who do not.

A variant of the children's allowance is the constant attendance allowance provided in some countries to families with a severely handicapped, infirm, or otherwise incapacitated member. The allowance, paid to the family, acknowledges the fact that it is often extremely difficult to provide care for dependent members and at the same time maintain an adequate income. The response in the United States has largely been to provide out-of-home care in daycare or residential programs for handicapped dependents. However, the cost of out-of-home care is great, and there is some evidence to suggest that families frequently are willing to assume directly a substantial part of the burden of care. Moroney (1980, p. 159) concluded that in Great Britain the allowance often makes "a real difference in the family's financial status; less measurable but in the view of the program designers as important, families were told in a tangible way that their efforts were recognized, that they were not ignored."

Vouchers. Resources could also be provided to families for child care and parent education in the form of vouchers. Demand-side subsidies such as vouchers and tax credits at times have strong political appeal and warrant somewhat detailed description, although to date their use in providing child care and parent education has been confined mainly to experiments and demonstrations.

Voucher proposals take many forms. Defined broadly, a voucher is a means for granting an individual the right to purchase a good or service. The voucher might be a certificate, such as food stamps, that is redeemable for goods; or it might be a promise to pay, as conveyed by the Medicaid card, which is presented to the doctor or hospital of choice. The GI bill provided vouchers, in effect, for education following World War II. Vouchers may be unregulated or regulated. Both food stamps and Medicaid are examples of the latter; food stamps can be spent only for specified products and Medicaid payments cover some types of medical services but not others. Examples of mostly unregulated vouchers are the child care expense allowance for persons receiving Aid to Families with Dependent Children (AFDC) and the reimbursement for child care expenses incurred by participants in the Work Incentive (WIN) program; both programs have no regulations regarding type of reimbursable care. Most voucher proposals for child care and parent education, however, include provisions for regulation. For example, the Santa Clara County (California) pilot study of an experimental child care voucher program provided that participants could choose child care services with any licensed provider of out-of-home care.

A great deal has been written about the use of vouchers

for elementary and secondary education, and some of the analysis is pertinent to child care and parent education. There are important differences, however, which should be noted at the outset. First, in contrast to child care, the right to a free public education has been viewed as an entitlement, and there is a consensus regarding the universal need for the service. Second, the means for delivery of elementary and secondary education are already in place; the educational enterprise is generally run by well-organized professionals. Control is vested locally, but there is surprising uniformity in the content of education, spawned in part by standards imposed by accrediting associations. A voucher system in education thus would be grafted onto the existing public school structure. In contrast, the present system of child care services is pluralistic and highly decentralized; professionals in the field are not well organized. A system of vouchers for child care would therefore have to be created almost anew.

Proponents argue that vouchers would stimulate competition among providers, promote diversity in the types of care, encourage innovation, facilitate the mixing of children from various socioeconomic groups (since cost would not be a barrier), and enable parents to choose the type of education or care that they believe is most suitable for their children. Detractors argue that cost competition could lead to a reduction in quality and that parents might not be able to make appropriate choices, especially in an imperfect market.

Among the most eloquent and persuasive advocates of a voucher system for education are Coons and Sugarman (1978, pp. 15-16), whose analysis of schools can be extended by analogy to child care: "We hold no loftier objective than this: experimentation with systems that increase family choice. . . . The grant to families that we propose would come in the form of a scholarship that would be limited to something defined as 'school.' What could qualify as school might be very diverse, but it would still be limited to education. . . . Indeed, even if one wanted eventually to divert public school spending to day-care, child health care, or even to general income redistribution, providing educational subsidies would be a strategically sensible first step." The value commitments underlying their position were made clear: pluralism and diversity; maximization of choice for parents, and for children when old enough; reduction of inequities in educational opportunities between families with means and those without; adherence to certain standards of performance; and, above all, experimentation with various means of financing and improving education.

A number of mechanisms are possible for implementing a voucher system: Each child could receive a scholarship or voucher of equal value; larger vouchers could be given to poorer families; vouchers could be adjusted to variable costs of educational programs; or vouchers could promote variability in quality of schools, rather than uniformity, by allowing schools to charge tuition within a wide range, with either the family or the state making up the difference over a uniform voucher payment. Coons and Sugarman diminished familiar arguments against voucher plans by imposing limitations (for example, vouchers could not be used to purchase education in schools that segregate by race) and by providing for information and counseling services to overcome the disadvantage a voucher system might impose on less well-educated and less confident people.

The strength of the argument for vouchers can be assessed in part by its opposition. Edelman (1974, p. 72) expressed several reservations, asserting that vouchers "reinforce existing patterns of class and racial segregation. They put the cart before the horse. What is there to buy? Who's going to get served? Start-up costs to build and begin daycare programs are high; where will community groups and the poor get the funds to do this if government has withdrawn? Until there are more good services available, I'm not clear that giving individuals money means much."

Two experiments with vouchers, one involving schools and the other child care, have provided some information on the results of implementing a voucher system. One, patterned after the regulated compensatory voucher plan developed for the Office of Economic Opportunity by Jencks and his associates, was tested during a five-year period in a small school district in Alum Rock, California (Cohen and Farrar, 1977; Doyle,

1977). The plan included the following controls: no participating school could charge more than the value of the voucher; any participating school had to accept all applicants, eliminating racial or social-class discrimination; overapplied schools could select (and deselect) only by lot; while all children received basic vouchers, poor children were given "bonus" or compensatory vouchers, both to make them "attractive" to schools and to provide additional resources for their education; a parent-student information system was to be established; and a school evaluation system was required, a "truth in packaging" device for participants (Doyle, 1977).

The school system, a low-income, kindergarten through eighth-grade district with substantial Mexican-American and black minorities, was eager to secure assistance for implementing a decentralization plan. Federal monies provided operational and evaluation support and funding was also offered by state and local sources. During the period 1972–1977, the experiment was gradually extended from six to all of the district's twenty-one schools. The plan was modified somewhat during this period, but the compensatory feature was kept intact. In the first year of the experiment, over half the children were eligible for compensatory vouchers.

This market experiment was imperfect in a number of important respects: No private schools were included (none was in existence at the beginning of the plan, and new entrants were not encouraged); teachers were guaranteed jobs if displaced from voucher schools; students were guaranteed the right to attend neighborhood schools; teachers were not rewarded if they succeeded in attracting additional students to their programs (in fact, it was necessary to place a cap on enrollment in certain successful schools); and so on. Despite these limitations, considerable change took place in the schools, most notably in greater diversity of curriculum, such as bilingual programs and mini-schools with special emphases. Notable as well was the increased independence of teachers. In fact, teachers, not parents, seemed to gain the most power from the changes. Parents did not use vouchers to influence what went on in the classroom, but teachers did use their increased flexibility in education design. All things being equal, parents seemed to prefer neighborhood schools; but they indicated a willingness to transfer their children to other schools to attend desired programs.

A limited child care voucher program was authorized by the California legislature in 1973 and implemented in Santa Clara County between July 1975 and July 1977. Parents of all children under fifteen were eligible for a subsidy (within certain maximum allowable rates per hour), which ranged from 100 percent of costs for low-income families to 20 percent for families with high incomes (Stoddard, 1978). Parental employment was not required for participation in the voucher program; thus, all families were eligible. Reimbursable care included both full-day and part-day care by any *licensed* provider of out-of-home care; specifically excluded were in-home care and private schooling for kindergarten or elementary grades. An information and referral system was also included in the project. Results of the program indicated that families used program content as the most important factor in choosing particular child care arrangements. Families subsidized by the pilot study used more child care per week on the average than the general population did (California State Department of Education, 1978).

The short-term nature of the study and subsidy did not provide enough incentive for the establishment of new child care programs of the types having major start-up costs. Thus, during the two-year period, there was no change in the number of child care centers. There was a 35 percent increase in the number of licensed family day homes, however. Stoddard (1978) suggested that unlicensed family day homes may have become licensed so as to be eligible for the subsidies. She also suggested that there must be an adequate supply of child care at the local level, that entry by new providers into the system should be facilitated as part of the design of a voucher system, and that for the market effect to be realized, "the system should be implemented at a scale adequate to ensure consumer impact on the overall supply system" (p. 153).

The purpose of the pilot study included asessment of the effectiveness and efficiency of a delivery system in which parents had a choice in selecting specific child care programs. While the study was still under way, the California state legislature established an Alternative Child Care Program (ACCP), which had as one component a vendor-voucher payment program and the purpose of which was to provide a broad range of choices for parents and to address unmet needs in geographical areas throughout the state. Under the vendor-voucher payment program of ACCP, once a child was determined eligible (according to income), the benefit followed the child from one type of care to another as the child's needs or family's preferences changed. The gradual expansion of the program could be viewed as an outgrowth of the Santa Clara County pilot study. In a sample month, March 1979, twenty-five child care agencies operated vendor-voucher payment systems that served approximately 4,800 children; of these children, 47 percent were enrolled in centers, 37 percent were enrolled in family day homes, and 26 percent were cared for in their own homes (California State Department of Education, 1979).

The potential variety of modes of care available in a voucher system was demonstrated by the Palo Alto Community Child Care (PACCC) voucher plan, which included a Montessori school, after-school center programs, two infant programs, day-care homes, a traditional nursery school, and parent-run centers. Parents chose preferred programs with the assistance of a PACCC information and referral worker. To participate in the PACCC plan, child care providers had to meet standards regarding program, staffing, equipment, nutrition, and salaries; the facility had to be open to parents and PACCC staff; and the program was required to follow a nondiscrimination policy. The program director observed: "The voucher system is an excellent way to get services in the hands of the people who need them. You don't have any start-up costs, and if you have existing services, you can plug them together. Then you can use any extra money for start-up where it's needed. But [to maintain quality and help the system work] you can't have a voucher system without support services" (quoted in Majteles, 1979, pp. 18-21).

The critical issue in successfully implementing a voucher plan appears to be the range and availability of existing services. This issue is also important in providing resources for child care through the tax mechanism.

Tax Credits. The tax credit for child and dependent care expenses can be viewed as a means for providing resources to parents for care of their children. However, from its inception in 1954, the benefit for child care (an itemized deduction until 1976) was viewed primarily as a cost of earning income, not as a transfer program or entitlement. Originally, the benefit was available only to single-parent families in which the mother was compelled to work by economic necessity. Various rationales were offered for the deduction: Child care expenses were necessary to conduct business; defrayal of child care expenses was justifiable for mothers who were compelled to work; and tax benefits would assist welfare mothers in seeking employment. Congress strayed from the original rationale (defrayal of work-related child care expenses) in 1971 when it broadened the deduction to include household expenses; the new rationale was to provide jobs to unemployed household workers.

Although successive changes in the tax code expanded taxpayer eligibility, by the mid 1970s there was considerable pressure to correct various anomalies in the law; in particular, Congress was concerned that low-income families were not eligible for the benefit because of the requirement to itemize. Considerable discussion ensued regarding how best to extend the benefit to low-income families, and the deduction was changed to a credit in 1976 in accordance with the popular view that deductions favored taxpayers in the higher marginal tax brackets, whereas credits provided tax relief more or less equally to all income brackets (U.S. Congress, Joint Committee on Internal Revenue Taxation, 1976). The new credit did not produce its intended effect, however.

Successive changes in the tax code expanded taxpayer eligibility, removed income limitations, increased the ages of eligible children, removed the requirement that the taxpayer itemize deductions (1976), and lifted most constraints on hiring relatives as care givers (1979). Thus, the credit is now available to all families who work, pay income tax, and can afford to pay for child care. Families have the widest possible choice of mode of care. In 1982, the tax credit allowed parents to subtract from their income tax (within certain limits) up to 30 percent of expenses incurred for child care. Taxpayers could report a maximum of $2,400 in expenses for the care of one child; for two or more children, the maximum allowable expenses were $4,800. The percentage of child care expenses parents could take as a credit was dependent on their income and ranged from 30 percent for families with incomes below $10,000 (a maximum credit of $720 for one child) to 20 percent for families with incomes of $28,000 or more (a maximum credit of $480 per child).

An important issue for public policy, however, is a determination of who benefits from the tax credit. The change from itemized deduction to tax credit in 1976 did not help the lowest-income groups as had been anticipated. Paradoxically, those gaining the most from the change were households with incomes above $20,000 because the income ceiling (which had been in effect with respect to the itemized deduction) was removed (see Table 8). In addition, other changes in the tax law—the replacement of the standard deduction by an increased zero bracket amount and increased personal exemptions, effective 1977—reduced the amount subject to tax for many low-income families. Taxpayers who owe no income tax thus derive no benefit from the credit. More important, since the amount of the credit is computed as a percentage of child care expenditures, larger benefits are available to those who can afford to pay more for child care. Congress did not anticipate the implications of this relationship between ability to pay and tax benefit. A further consideration is the psychological barrier for some families to filing the required 1040 (so called "long form") and supplementary form 2441 to claim the tax credit. In addition, providers of less expensive or unlicensed care may be reluctant to report their income, a fact that may effectively preclude parents who use their services from taking advantage of the credit.

The number of families claiming the child care benefit has increased steadily from 1.7 million in 1976 (the first year of the credit) to an estimated 4.0 million in 1981. Table 6 shows the revenue loss and average benefit for the period 1975–1980. The total revenue loss ($792 million in 1979) associated with the tax expenditure has increased more rapidly than originally projected—even though the average benefit has increased

Table 6. Estimated Revenue Cost of Child Care Deduction/Credit
and Average Deduction/Credit.

	Total Revenue Cost (millions)	Average Credit
1975	$275	$165.00 (deduction)
1976	458	172.00
1977	521	181.00
1978	632	190.00
1979	792	206.00
1980	919	228.00

Sources: Internal Revenue Service, 1979, 1980, 1981, 1982, 1983.

only slightly—because of the large increase in numbers of persons claiming the credit, especially among those with incomes greater than $20,000.

The average credit varies somewhat across income groups. For example, the data in Table 7 show a gradual rise in average

Table 7. Average Tax Credit for Households Claiming Child Care Credit by Size of Adjusted Gross Income.

Adjusted Gross Income	1976	1977	1978	1979	1980
Total	$190	$181	$172	$206	$228
$1–$4,999	109	128	81	75	133
$5,000–$9,999	161	163	175	167	212
$10,000–$14,999	149	162	175	191	224
$15,000–$19,999	156	160	178	198	207
$20,000–$29,999	196	191	189	205	211
$30,000–$49,999	230	236	229	232	253
$50,000 or more	333	329	309	311	313

Sources: Internal Revenue Service, 1979, 1980, 1981, 1982, 1983.
Note: All figures are rounded.

benefit for groups between $5,000 and 30,000. However, taxpayers with less than $5,000 annual income have significantly lower average benefits, whereas taxpayers with incomes above $30,000 show substantially higher average benefits.

For public policy considerations, perhaps the most important index is the distribution of tax expenditures among various income groups. The distribution of tax benefits has moved steadily away from low-income groups to higher-income groups, as shown in Table 8. This movement is partially attrib-

Table 8. Distribution of Revenue Loss for Child Care Deduction/Credit by Size of Adjusted Gross Income.

Adjusted Gross Income	1972[a] Deduction	1975[b] Deduction	1976[c] Credit	1978[d] Credit	1979[e] Credit	1980[f] Credit
$1–$4,999	1.3%	.3%	.6%	.2%	.1%	.0%
$5,000–$9,999	23.6	19.0	12.8	9.9	6.9	3.1
$10,000–$14,999	39.7	35.0	19.5	14.4	13.4	14.4
$15,000–$19,999	30.3	37.3	24.2	19.2	17.5	13.7
$20,000–$29,999	4.9	7.6	33.0	35.9	35.1	32.7
$30,000–$49,000		.7	8.3	17.6	23.3	30.6
$50,000 or more		.03	1.5	2.8	3.8	5.9

[a] Derived from unpublished estimates of U.S. Congress, Joint Committee on Internal Revenue Taxation, September 23, 1974, and Internal Revenue Service, *Statistics of Income—1972: Individual Income Tax Returns* (1974). Income limitation: deduction phased out after $18,000.

[b] Data derived from Internal Revenue Service, *Statistics of Income—1975: Individual Income Tax Returns* (1978). Income limitation: deduction phased out after $35,000.

[c] Data derived from Internal Revenue Service, *Statistics of Income—1976: Individual Income Tax Returns* (1979). No income limitation for credit.

[d] Data derived from Internal Revenue Service, *Statistics of Income—1978: Individual Income Tax Returns* (1981). No income limitation for credit.

[e] Data derived from Internal Revenue Service, *Statistics of Income—1979: Individual Income Tax Returns* (1982). No income limitation for credit.

[f] Data derived from Internal Revenue Service, *Statistics of Income—1980: Individual Income Tax Returns* (1983). No income limitation for credit.

utable to the upward trend in personal income; a more important explanation, however, is found in the changes in the tax laws described earlier. For example, in 1976 only 37 percent of the taxpayers claiming the child care credit had incomes below $15,000 (the Internal Revenue Service (IRS) data category approximating median income), and these taxpayers received only 33 percent of the total tax expenditures. Applications of the poverty level yardstick suggests that the tax credit is of little use to the group below the poverty level. Applying IRS statistics to taxpayers with incomes of less than $6,000 yields the following: A mere 3 percent of taxpayers claiming the child care credit had incomes below the poverty level; they received 2 percent of the total tax expenditures for the child care credit (Weeks, 1980).

Concurrent with the gradual expansion of the child care tax benefit has been increasing attention to the general issue of achieving public policy objectives by indirect spending through tax mechanisms. Congress has become interested in knowing the extent to which various activities are subsidized by tax expenditures; and since the passage of the Congressional Budget Act of 1974, a listing of tax expenditures is required in the budget. Tax expenditures are revenue losses attributable to the provisions of federal tax laws that allow special exclusions, exemptions, or deductions from gross income or that provide special credits, preferential tax rates, or deferrals of tax liability. Thus, tax expenditures are means by which the government pursues public policy objectives, and they can be viewed as alternatives to direct expenditures.

Proponents of this indirect tax mechanism of funding make several arguments: Tax incentives encourage the private sector to participate in social programs; they are simple to administer; they involve less government supervision; and they promote private decision making. Those who do not favor tax incentives argue that they permit windfalls by paying taxpayers for doing what they would do anyway, that they are inequitable because they are worth more to high-income taxpayers than to low-income taxpayers, that they distort the marketplace by affecting the allocation of resources, that they push the tax rates higher by reducing the tax base, and that the appearance of loopholes undermines public confidence in the system. Stanley Surrey, Assistant Secretary for Tax Policy in the Treasury Department, was critical of the use of tax expenditures to pursue social policies that, in his view, could be accomplished more effectively through direct programs (Surrey, 1973). The political acceptability of tax expenditures draws from conservatives who favor tax expenditures as a means of reducing government involvement and from liberals who see tax expenditures as the only politically expedient way to achieve enactment of programs to address social problems. The current proposals for change in the credit reflect this combination of rationales.

Current proposals for change are to be taken seriously because the credit for child care reaches more children indirectly than all the direct program expenditures combined. A study done by the IRS for tax year 1977 showed that on 2.9 million returns, credit was claimed for care provided for 4.4 million children under fifteen (or for disabled adult dependents), at a cost of $119 per individual (Internal Revenue Service, 1980). Applying the same ratio, one can project that benefits claimed on an estimated 3.8 million returns for 1979 reached 5.7 million children or other dependents. We do not know what proportion of these children are under six years of age, nor do we know what kind of care is being subsidized by the credit. Since the benefit was not viewed as a child care program, no attempt to introduce requirements regarding standards for care programs eligible for the credit was made until 1981. The proposals for change should be looked at carefully also because of the size of the federal investment (an estimated $1 billion in 1981), a substantial amount when compared with other direct program costs.

For some time and from various sources have come proposals either to increase the percentage of allowable expenses or to make the credit refundable, that is, to allow the credit to families who pay no income tax. Even when the first tax credit was being debated in 1976, Senator Edward Kennedy proposed that the credit be made refundable and that an income limitation for eligibility be retained to contain costs. Using projections by the Joint Committee on Taxation for the costs associated with expanding the credit to 35 or 50 percent and for making the credit refundable, Weeks (1980) noted that increasing the percentage of allowable expenditures, while greatly increasing the costs, does not significantly change the distribution of benefits across income groups and that making the credit refundable changes the distribution slightly by allocating a somewhat larger portion of the benefits to income groups below $15,000.

The tax credit for child care was expanded in 1982 to provide a 30 percent *nonrefundable* credit to families with incomes below $10,000. The legislation provides that the credit be reduced by 1 percent for each additional $2,000 of income, so that families with incomes above $28,000 would receive credit for 20 percent of child care expenses. The maximum expenses for the credit were increased from $2,000 to $2,400 for the care of one child and from $4,000 to $4,800 for the care of two or more children. In theory, the maximum credit allowable for a low-income family for the care of one child is $720; this plan makes the unlikely assumption that a family earning less than $10,000 can afford to pay $2,400 for child care.

Both refundability and advance payment of the refundable portion were considered and dropped in the course of passing the 1982 legislation. The House of Representatives opposed refundability because the refundable portion appeared in the budget as an appropriation, rather than as a revenue loss. The Treasury Department did not support the concept because of difficulties of administration and the precedent established for income transfers through the tax system.

Although the additional benefits in the 1982 legislation were modest, the introduction of a sliding scale concept represented a significant philosophical change and reflected the objective—even if not fully realized—of many senators to increase benefits to families who need them. Another important addition was the requirement, promoted by Senator Alan Cranston, that all providers who care for more than six children—in centers and family day homes—must comply with state and local laws and regulations. Child care advocates supported this concept instead of one involving federal regulations, which they felt would jeopardize the passage of the bill. The concept of compliance with state and local laws was argued as a states' rights issue, namely, that the federal government should not allocate money to child care programs that violate local law.

Taken together, these two concepts—sliding scale credit and compliance with state and local regulations—represent a shift in the underlying purpose of the credit. Originally viewed as a tax benefit recognizing the cost of earning income, the credit is gradually coming to be viewed as a means of subsidiz-

ing child care through market mechanisms by providing resources to parents. The new provisions have altered the terms of
the debate somewhat by recognizing the greater needs of low-
income families and by acknowledging that the credit should
subsidize care that meets certain standards. Child care advocates
will likely continue to press for an increased percentage on a
sliding scale, for refundability, and eventually for advance payment (which will be the most difficult to achieve), all three of
which are necessary if the credit is to function as a market
mechanism.

The tax credit, as presently structured and implemented,
is imperfect as a market mechanism for reasons that go beyond
the credit itself. Certain elements required for the successful implementation of a market subsidy are absent: full information
to consumers about the choices available to them; competition,
which implies an adequate supply of child care of high quality
and diverse modes; and full access to that supply of services. We
do not know the extent to which economic incentives influence
a parent's choice of care. To the extent that a 50 percent refundable credit would increase a parent's net wage, the increase
in disposable income might influence choice of care and reduce
some of the barriers to access, assuming that services are available.

Several conclusions can be drawn regarding the tax credit. First, it is of greatest benefit to families with incomes above
the median, but is of little use to the several million children
under the age of six who live in families with working parents
who are not eligible to claim the credit because they owe no income tax or because they can afford to pay very little for child
care. Second, because the benefit is pegged at 30 percent of *actual* expenditures by low-income families for child care, the
credit does not purchase very much care. Few families with incomes between the poverty and median income levels can
afford expenditures that allow them to receive the maximum
credit for which they are eligible. For upper-income two-earner
families, the credit does reduce the tax burden associated with a
second wage earner. Third, although the total cost of the tax
benefit in 1976 (and the cost per child) was modest when com-

pared with other direct expenditure programs, the total cost of
the program (although not the benefit per child) is rising rapidly
owing to increased numbers of taxpayers claiming the credit.
We cannot draw conclusions about the effectiveness of the tax
expenditure until more is known about the type of care being
subsidized, the ages of the children served, and whether full-
time or part-time employment is being subsidized.

Evaluation of the Resources Option. As we have shown,
there are several strategies focused on providing families with
resources that can be used at the discretion of parents to obtain
goods and services, including child care and parent education. In
two of the approaches, income supports and children's allowances, there are usually no formal restrictions on the purposes
for which the resources may be spent, although there is the
clear intent that the resources be used in the interest of children
and families. The other two approaches, vouchers and tax credits, are intended to increase families' resources specifically for
the purchase of child care services. Our values analysis reveals
several strengths and shortcomings in this option.

Does the Policy Enhance Community? Each of the specific resource options reflects, in one way or another, a commitment to the redistribution of income in the interest of either
the economically disadvantaged or families with children. Thus,
they require for their support in the first place a fairly strong
commitment to community, and it is at least possible that they
could, in turn, contribute to an enhanced sense of common purpose within a community.

The income support plan proposed by the Carnegie Council on Children, which would replace the present welfare and income tax structure with a uniform credit income tax, would
allocate a basic level of support to all adults and children. The
other three resource options—tax credits, children's allowances,
and vouchers—transfer resources from citizens in general to
those who are parents. The rationales for this transfer usually
involve, at least implicitly, a view of parents as serving the community by rearing the next generation of citizens. In many
ways, these several strategies for providing resources to parents
so that they can obtain child care and parent education are an

ideal expression of community commitment. Indeed, viewed from a distance, they would seem to effect an elegant balance among commitments to liberty, equality, and fraternity. Parents are left free to make their own choices; the poor can be provided more equitable treatment than they might otherwise receive; and the schemes could draw from and contribute to a sense of community, national and local. Unrestrained by the reality principle or by an appreciation of the size, diversity, and political complexity of our nation, one could imagine the emergence in the United States of resource redistribution plans such as those evaluated in this section. The experience of some European nations, for example, reveals the achievement of a reasonable level of equity in income distribution while approaching or even surpassing the United States in per capita productivity and income.

A closer look at these several means for making child care and parent education available to families, however, suggests why they are not likely to contribute to the building of community. The national plan for redressing inequities in resource availability proposed by the Carnegie Council should likely be regarded as establishing some kind of distant ideal: Its immediate relevance must be judged as limited, in part because its implementation is dependent on the achievement of full employment, a possibility that seems remote. And in spite of a considerable investment in making the plan known to members of Congress, there has yet to be a hearing on its merits. Children's allowances, another resource option, have been standard policy in many nations, including our neighbor Canada, but the idea has never been popular in our own country. Vouchers could possibly be used to promote community, but only if accompanied by adequate information and referral systems and other provisions to ensure that all members of the community have equal access to their use. Experience in California demonstrates that at least some voucher programs have been well used by low-income families, single-parent families, ethnic minorities, and rural populations (California State Department of Education, 1979). The tax credit plan, as it currently operates, is paradoxical in the context of community building because two thirds of the tax expenditure is distributed to families with incomes above the median; at present the tax credit is useful only to families who have sufficiently high incomes to generate a tax obligation and who can afford to pay the large portion (80 percent) of child care expenses that is not reimbursed. Although the change from a 20 percent credit to a 30 percent credit for low-income families effective in 1982 represents a symbolic recognition of the greater needs of these families, the change will have little impact on the poorest families who still can ill afford the expenditures that would enable them to receive the maximum credit for which they are theoretically eligible; without a refundability provision, the increased credit is of little use to families who have little or no tax liability.

As a group, these approaches to providing resources present challenges to the larger community's interest in the quality of child care paid for with public funds. Legislation and regulations governing vouchers and tax credits could be designed to require that public monies be spent for child care that meets prescribed standards—such as the regulations for the use of vouchers in California and more recent requirements for the use of the federal tax credit—but income supports and children's allowances would not lend themselves to achieving this objective.

Does the Policy Strengthen Families? It seems highly probable that the income support option, coupled with a full-employment policy, would strengthen families. It would remove some of the present incentives that appear to encourage the breakup of poor families and discourage remarriage. It should provide for all families a minimum level of resources needed for effective functioning. Children's allowances would presumably work in the same direction but would be available only to families with children. The provision of resources through vouchers and tax credits for the specific purposes of obtaining child care and parent education, insofar as they are designed to meet specific family needs, could also contribute to the strengthening of families.

The resources option, however, appears to offer no particular advantage for improving the quality of intrafamily systems or the effectiveness of the linkage function between the family and other social institutions. To the extent that the child care arrangements families may obtain also provide high-quality parent education (formal and informal), parents could be enabled to enhance the effectiveness of the family as a unit.

There is no inherent reason that programs designed to provide resources to families could not also be designed to protect the family from unwarranted intrusion. In fact, the Carnegie Council proposal for income supports, as well as the provisions of the tax credit to partially offset the cost of child care (especially if made refundable), would eliminate the need for multiple certifications of eligibility and intrusions into family life, because they link entitlements to the tax system. This is the general pattern that has been developed in several European nations over the years to operate social programs with minimum abridgement of family privacy.

Does the Policy Enable Parents to Do Their Job Well? We have suggested earlier that parents need five things to do their job well: time, energy, satisfaction, knowledge, and resources. The approaches considered here are, by definition, resource-producing arrangements. If the resources are used wisely to obtain needed services efficiently, then it is reasonable to expect that increased availability of time, energy, and satisfaction would follow, at least in some measure. If use of the resources were linked to parent education, some increase in parents' knowledge might also be expected.

There is nothing inherent in these resource-producing plans that promotes shared responsibility between parents and professional service providers. However, the plans that are amenable to regulation (vouchers and tax credits particularly) could require several shared-responsibility provisions, for example, that parents have full information about and access to the program at any time, that parents participate in the making of policy, and that, in some circumstances, parents have an opportunity to participate directly in program operations. Further, if parents have adequate information about a program, they can "vote with their feet"; that is, they can take their children out of programs that do not involve parents and put them into programs that do, if they so choose.

All of these strategies have the important attribute of allowing parents substantial freedom of choice in the expenditure of resources. Income supports and children's allowances ordinarily are not restricted with regard to goods and services that may be purchased, although there is a clear expectation that children will benefit. Vouchers and tax credits can not only be limited to the purchase of child care or parent education but can also be controlled so that public funds would not be used to support programs that discriminate on the basis of race, religion, or other nonfunctional criteria or that fail to meet minimum requirements for the provision of quality service. It should be possible through use of the resources option to achieve considerable freedom of choice for parents while adequately protecting the public interest.

Does the Policy Enhance Individual Development and Protect the Rights of Individual Members of the Family? Many authorities agree that the neglect and abuse of individual family members are associated with family stress: with deprivation, with alienation and isolation, with certain high-risk situations such as single-parenthood, with the absence of adequate social and support services, and with the general breakdown of community. Of the several specific resource options, the Carnegie Council's recommendation of income supports plus a full-employment policy appears most likely to relieve the stresses associated with neglect and abuse in families. The other plans may provide some indirect assistance, but there would seem to be no compelling reason to believe that they would contribute significantly to the solution of this particular aspect of individual protection and enhancement.

Beyond the protection of family members from harm, however, it seems likely that child care and parent education programs made available to families through provision of resouces—if they meet minimum standards of quality, including standards of parental involvement—would enhance individual opportunity for self-realization and the development of competence in the new generation.

Resources: In Summary. The concept of providing resources—through income supports, children's allowances, vouchers, or tax credits—to enable parents to purchase care in the marketplace is attractive, especially in its provision of maximum choice to parents and its potential for promoting diverse forms of care. There is reason to believe that the values of community and human development could be enhanced in some measure by the strategies within this option. However, for mechanisms such as vouchers and tax credits to express successfully a national commitment to creating a competent and caring society, there must be careful attention to safeguards against the imperfections of the market.

At least three issues are central to the effective implementation of market mechanisms in the interest of families, service providers, and the community at large: Families must have adequate information so that they can make informed choices; the supply of services must be adequate and reasonably responsive to demand; and families must have access to available services. We expand briefly upon the conditions under which provision of resources must be implemented if human development and community values are to be enhanced, so that policy makers may be mindful of their importance should the nation move more decisively toward the adoption of all or portions of this option.

First, for market mechanisms to work well, parents must have adequate information and they must have the competence and confidence to use it well. They must have information about what services are available, what standards they meet, and their location, cost, and conditions of use. Having selected a service, parents must know how well the provider is performing. Parents should have free access to observe the child care facility's day-to-day operations both before and after selecting the provider; as Nelson (1977) suggests, operation in a "fishbowl" is a significant means of enhancing quality. Implementation of observation must take place in the context of knowing that parents' ability to assess quality of care takes skill and time. Child care information and referral services are another means for assisting families in finding appropriate child care. Estimating that approximately 6,400 public and private organizations provide child care information and referral to families in various ethnic and income groups, it has been suggested that information and referral organizations facilitate a balance of supply and demand by providing parents with information on how to select child care. Further, the information and referral agencies may affect the quality of care by training care givers and by encouraging unlicensed facilities to undertake changes needed to obtain licensing.

Second, there must be a supply of services responsive to the particular needs of families and children. Vouchers, tax credits, income supports, children's allowances, and similar mechanisms address only the demand side of the market. In theory, the demand will stimulate the requisite supply. In fact, however, social institutions are not always as automatically responsive as theory implies. An adequate supply of child care services is essential to ensure that the market produces care of high quality and diverse modes; it is also essential if parents are to be empowered to help shape the child care environment. Some suggest that the way to ensure that a supply of good services matches demand is to direct public support *not* to core services but rather to information and referral services, to training of child care providers, to toy-lending libraries, to assistance with licensing and administration, and to start-up grants for new entrants. Some states are already providing some of these supports to consumers and providers. Such suggestions imply, of course, decreased emphasis on the resource provision option.

There is substantial debate about the role of regulation in ensuring quality of care. Some argue for a strong regulatory role by government, asserting that any provider who receives public assistance, including the indirect assistance resulting from the provision of resources to parents, should meet at least minimum standards. Others, however, advocate a minimum regulatory role and argue that quality of care will improve with an increase in supply of services and competition fostered by government support of market mechanisms. Congress appears to have recognized the value of government standards by providing in the 1981 revision of the child care tax credit that most group care must meet state and local regulations.

Third, families must have access to available services. As mentioned previously, access requires the development of a referral system to assist parents in matching the needs of their children with the services available. Beyond that, however, access requires that parents have the financial resources to purchase the chosen care. We can assume that very poor families will require a high level of subsidy, although other parents can contribute to payment on a sliding scale basis. The prospect of integrating poor and nonpoor children in the same care facilities is one of the most attractive features of the option of providing resources to families. If all families are to have access to good-quality care, some means must be found to ensure nondiscriminatory admissions practices on the part of providers who accept public subsidy and to provide assistance in obtaining services for hard-to-place children. A final issue related to access is that of parent participation once a program has been chosen and the development of shared responsibility between parent and provider.

It is not certain that a subsidy for demand alone, through the provision of resources, will create conditions optimal for the development of child care services. For the market to work well in the interests of families and providers, it is necessary that systematic attention be given to the supply of services as well. There has been lively debate between proponents of resources strategy and those of services strategy for mitigating poverty in the United States. We would agree with the Carnegie Council on Children that an income or resource strategy is a basic need for the strengthening of communities and families. However, a strategy that provides only resources to meet the child care and parent education needs of American families has inherent limitations if the overarching goal is to ensure that the resources are directed not only to limited, private purposes but to the nation's common interest as well.

Conclusions

We have considered the four major policy options that have been discussed and implemented in this and several other countries. The *do-nothing* option we reject wholeheartedly; although we applaud some of its rationales (caution and care in the creation of social interventions), we find it contrary to both the evidence and our values. The *national family policy* option we find intriguing, particularly for its promise of a thoughtful and integrated approach to the multiple needs of families. While it could be designed to meet our values criteria quite well, we are persuaded that for the time being its political unpopularity renders the necessary background work, action and analysis most difficult and its implementation therefore a far distant goal. Further, while a national family policy may establish a valuable framework, it does not necessarily define fully the contents of specific approaches to meeting the needs of families. Thus, we have found other, programmatically oriented options more useful.

The *flexibility* option holds a great deal of promise for improving critical relationships between the workplace and employees and, in some of its specific manifestations, appears to improve employees' ability to attend to the multiple demands of their lives. While it warrants serious attention for the possibilities of increasing parents' abilities to care well for their own young children, the evidence to date that it does in fact do so is scant. The flexibility option meets some of our values criteria well but falls short on others. As a primary national policy, it is confounded further by the fact that most of the flexibility it offers is likely to fall to women, who—if traditional patterns are not altered—will continue to bear major (or full-time) responsibility for the parental role while "working in" employment responsibilities on the side.

The *resources* option also holds significant promise for improving families' capacities to perform their functions well. Although some of its specific manifestations, such as income supports, seem improbable as candidates for implementation in this country in spite of their meritorious foundations, other of its manifestations, most notably tax credits, are presently in a full and complex state of implementation. This set of options meets some of our values criteria well but presents serious difficulties in regard to others. Most notably, the resources strategies —as they have been implemented—do not address issues of the supply or quality of services offered to families. They rest large-

ly on the market assumptions that supplies of service will follow
demand and that all consumers are informed in a manner that
will enable appropriate choices. The evidence and logic contra-
dict both of these assumptions in the area of child care and parent education, however. The data indicate a presently suppressed
demand for service, and other conditions related to the notion
of informed consumers pertain as well; for example, many
adults are not well informed about the components of good
care for children, many parents do not have good access to information about program availability, and, in child care, parents
make choices not for themselves but for their children as direct
consumers of service. Our analyses of these four major options
thus lead us to a fifth: the provision of services to parents and
children. It is to a detailed analysis of this last policy option that
we turn in the next two chapters.

SIX

Providing Services
Directly to Families

The provision of services to support various family needs has a long and complex history in our nation. In fact, service provision is the one option—among the several discussed in this volume—with which we have had the most extensive national experience. Beginning at first under private auspices and later funded increasingly by government sources, our varied approaches to service provision have resulted from a mix of rationales and purposes (Dunlop, 1978, 1980). These varied approaches have expressed several facets of our national life: the changing values, needs, and life-styles of families; broadbased social, economic, and technological trends; the results of scholarship on child and family development; and our collective experience over many decades with service provision of several types.

From the early 1960s to the late 1970s, direct government involvement in child care and parent education services expanded dramatically, as was true in many sectors. Of the many federally supported child care and parent education service programs that were developed extensively during this period, the largest included Title I of ESEA, Head Start, and Title XX of the Social Security Act. In addition, a major federal initiative

to create a comprehensive child and family services program was
proposed, but never enacted, in a series of bills throughout the
1970s. In this chapter, we attempt to capture the nation's experience in supporting child care and parent education programs
by giving a relatively detailed review of these major federal initiatives.* We then turn in Chapter Seven to a similarly extensive
review of two substantial state initiatives in these areas.

The child care and parent education programs analyzed
here represent three distinct models. ESEA Title I is squarely
positioned in the public schools. It provides remedial education
services for children from preschool through high school, with
the heaviest concentration in the elementary grades. Apart from
the school lunch program, it constitutes the single largest federal contribution to the public schools. Head Start is a comprehensive child care program for preschool children embracing
concerns for health, nutrition, cognitive development, and social skills. Essentially a community-based program, it requires
substantial parental participation. About one third of the Head
Start units are in the public schools. Title XX of the Social Security Act (now the Social Services Block Grant, enacted in the
Omnibus Budget Reconciliation Act of 1981) is not a program
per se, but a block grant funding mechanism providing resources
to the states to plan and fund various social services, including
child care and parent education. Finally, the comprehensive
child and family services proposals in the 1970s envisioned, in
their early stages, several family services based on the Head
Start idea of comprehensive, locally controlled programs; in the
later versions, they resembled Title XX's funding mechanism
approach.

ESEA Title I, Head Start, and Title XX are similar in that
they are directed to poor families. However, they differ in
stated goals, professional and bureaucratic auspices, intergovern-

*These programs constitute only part of the federal government's
direct support of child care and parent education services, but they are the
largest (in terms of expenditures and population reached) and they have
had the most significant influence on program development. (See U.S.
Congress, Congressional Budget Office, 1978, pp. 24-26, for a chart listing
these and other federal programs.)

mental relations, and several program elements. In the area of goals, ESEA Title I emphasizes remediation of the academic deficits of economically and educationally disadvantaged children, and it provides general financial support to the public schools. Head Start focuses on children's development as the common concern binding the interests of people in poor communities and combines goals of children's academic school readiness and social competence, community development, and the political empowerment of poor people. Title XX explicitly emphasizes enabling welfare families to become economically self-sufficient. The programs it funds tend to stress comprehensive child and family support. The ill-fated child and family services proposals of the 1970s expressed, in subsequent forms, the broader goals of Head Start and then the narrower goals of Title XX.

The bureaucratic, administrative, and professional auspices of ESEA Title I are the federal, state, and local education agencies. Head Start, the product of child development specialists and psychologists, has been affiliated from an early time with the poverty program bureaucracy and various community agencies. Title XX has been identified administratively with welfare bureaucracies and social work professionals, although the direct service providers have tended to have some child development training. The child and family services proposals, in their early versions, attempted to merge the child development, social services, and early childhood education traditions bureaucratically and professionally.

The intergovernmental relationship between the federal government, state and local government agencies, and community-based sponsors varies among the programs. ESEA Title I calls for shared responsibilities among the federal, state, and local education agencies, with local school districts and individual schools having considerable leeway in designing the services they offer. The Head Start federal agency bypasses state and local governments, funding programs through community action agencies, schools, and single-purpose, nonprofit organizations. Title XX, originally neither a purely categorical program nor a pure block grant, was converted to a block grant in 1981.

Federal funds are allocated to the state agency, which in turn
provides services directly or contracts for services with other
state agencies, local governments, and local voluntary organizations. The categorical child and family services initiatives shifted
over the years from the Head Start to the Title XX model, emphasizing direct allocation from the federal government to local
organizations in the early version and a federal-state relationship
in the last bill.

The program elements also vary. ESEA Title I encompasses a wide variety of regular and special classroom services, in
groups and for individual children, in both regular and special
classroom settings. Head Start emphasizes center-based group
programs for children but has generated a large variety of home-
based programs, parent- and family-based interventions, and
follow-up programs in the elementary grades. Comprehensive
health and nutrition for children, as well as parent participation,
are also Head Start hallmarks. Title XX has funded child care
and parent education programs primarily in centers, but family
day homes, group homes, parent training and counseling, information and referral, and other program models have also been
funded; supplemental health, nutrition, and social work services
are often included. The categorical child and family services
proposals envisioned a comprehensive array of service options,
similar to Head Start's, in its first version, but later focused on
child care per se.

Trends in the early 1980s indicated that increased responsibilities for the detailed planning of child care and parent education programs were being shifted to the states. As financial resources from the federal government were reduced, so too were
federal regulations. This has meant that state administrators and
legislators, as well as public interest groups concerned with children and families, will need to have a much deeper understanding of service programs—and the values underlying various approaches to child care and parent education—than was necessary
when both funds and regulations were supplied by Washington.
In a sense, the number of policy shapers and makers who require an understanding of child care and parent education is increasing fiftyfold.

For this reason, and because of our nationally extensive

experience in providing services, we have carried out the description and value analysis of the federal service programs in greater detail than was given for the four major options described in the previous chapter. We describe each of the service programs separately, reviewing their legislative and political origins, program features, effects, and costs. We then analyze the programs as a group in light of our community and human development values.

Elementary and Secondary Education Act, Title I

A law entitled "the Elementary and Secondary Education Act" would seem to have little relevance to either child care or parent education. In reality, however, ESEA Title I has been a major source of federal funding for educational programs for children under the age of six, serving more young children than Head Start. ESEA was first passed in 1965 and has been frequently amended, most extensively in 1978, making the program difficult to describe in some respects. However, none of the amendments, not even those of 1978, changed the character or the intent of the legislation in any significant way. We therefore describe ESEA Title I as it evolved from 1965 to 1978.

Title I of ESEA was designed "to strengthen and improve educational quality and educational opportunities in the nation's elementary and secondary schools," emphasizing the development of programs for children who are poor, handicapped, neglected, delinquent, migrant, and Indian (U.S. Congress, 1978). ESEA Title I programs are administered by state and local school districts, following guidelines prescribed by the federal Department of Education. Federal funds are allocated to states on the basis of a formula reflecting the state's expenditure for education and the number of poor children served. Although the legislation restricts expenditures to programs for children of five years of age or older, in practice, school systems—exercising the considerable autonomy they enjoy under the act—support programs for younger children. Approximately 8 percent of Title I funds support preschool and kindergarten programs.

ESEA Title I funds are used for a variety of purposes reflecting a great diversity of program plans across the nation; they are used to support salaries of special teachers (excluding the payment of salaries to regular teachers), bonuses to teachers working in designated project areas, the training of teachers, the purchase of equipment, program planning and evaluation, and, in special circumstances, the construction and renovation of facilities. Early education programs under ESEA Title I are generally strong in individualization of programming and involvement of parents. They tend to place greater emphasis on basic academic skills than do most early education programs. Overall, ESEA has been recognized as landmark legislation, bringing the federal government decisively into the public education system of the country.

Under ESEA Title I the federal Department of Education allocates funds through the states to local school districts in the form of formula grants related to the state's per-pupil expenditure and population of low-income children. Specifically, the formula provides that for each school-age child from a low-income family (as determined by family AFDC eligibility and free-lunch eligibility), the local school district is entitled to a federal grant worth a certain percentage of the average per-pupil expenditure in the state. Within a school district, monies are allocated to schools also on the basis of number of low-income children. Within the schools, students are selected to receive ESEA Title I services on the basis of *educational* need. Thus, at the point of application, Title I can be used to provide services without regard to the socioeconomic status of a child's family.

National figures on the number of preschool children served through ESEA Title I are unclear and conflicting. This is in part due to different definitions of the term *preschool children*. Some sources define it as all children under six; others define it as kindergarten children. Though the law authorizes serving only children between the ages of five and seventeen, reports show that children as young as three participate in ESEA Title I programs; the Congressional Budget Office in fact reported that 367,000 preschoolers (ages three, four, and five) participated in Title I programs in fiscal year 1977.

Standards for determining who shall participate in ESEA

Title I early education programs vary from state to state, and even from locality to locality within states. Methods of assessment appropriate for older children involving academic achievement tests are not suitable for preschoolers and first graders. As a result, many different criteria are used, including low scores on general aptitude tests, teacher judgments, the presence of an older sibling who is or was in an ESEA Title I program, parents who have less than a high school education, inability to communicate in English, and the judgment of parents, with different local education agencies using various combinations of these. Apparently, most local education agencies attempt to conform with ESEA Title I requirements for identifying eligible preschool children, but the state of the art of assessing development in early childhood makes this task extraordinarily difficult.

Early childhood programs under ESEA Title I can be divided into three levels: prekindergarten (serving three- and four-year-olds mostly), kindergarten (serving five-year-olds mostly), and first-grade programs (serving six-year-olds mostly). Prekindergarten programs tend to stress the general development of the child, although they are not without emphasis on the development of academic readiness, usually broadly defined but often including language arts, reading, and mathematics (see also Yurchak and Bryk, 1979). Parent education and parent participation are carried out in two contexts: center-based programs and home-based programs. Most center programs meet for two and a half to three hours a day, although there are some full-day programs. In home-based programs, teachers or home visitors visit with the parents and children about once a week, usually for about an hour. The objective is to engage the child in interesting activities and then to teach the parent, usually the mother, how to become involved in the education of the child. Frequently, one of the purposes of home-based programs is to give the parent specific new teaching skills. In some instances, home-based and center-based programs are combined.

Most early childhood education programs under ESEA Title I are well equipped with a wide variety of materials and instructional aids. Adults working in the programs have a range of qualifications and perform such roles as teachers, teachers' aides, resource people, and home visitors. Everywhere individualization of programming is stressed, sometimes to achieve the well-rounded development of the child but more often to ensure the acquisition of early and basic academic skills.

Early evaluations of ESEA Title I, including its management and effectiveness, led to dispiriting conclusions. The program was widely reported to be an administrative fiasco. The then Office of Education was said to be "pusillanimous" (McLaughlin, 1975) in its management of the law; administrative guidelines were described as confused and confusing; state educational authorities and local educational authorities were accused of shamelessly diverting ESEA Title I funds from the poor to the affluent or treating ESEA Title I monies as general federal aid to education. The program was regarded, in some quarters at least, as but another attempt to solve a problem by throwing money at it. Further problems came when early evaluations indicated that the programs did not make any difference in the performance of poor children; they simply did not work (Westinghouse Learning Corporation, 1969). Other studies showed that gains made during the school year were lost in the summer months.

The criticism of ESEA Title I management and results notwithstanding, the program continued to have political appeal. Congress continued to vote funds for it, increasing appropriations from $959 million in 1965 to $2.7 billion in 1978, thus making ESEA the largest federal education effort at the elementary and secondary levels. In 1974, Congress charged the National Institute of Education (NIE) with the responsibility of evaluating ESEA Title I and appropriated $15 million for the purpose. The results of a carefully planned and executed national study that followed were much more affirmative than had been the results of early evaluations. The study addressed six questions, whose outcomes we summarize here (National Institute of Education, 1978).

Do ESEA Title I Funds Go to Economically and Educationally Disadvantaged Children? One of the principal purposes of ESEA Title I was to direct federal education funds to economically disadvantaged children and to schools serving high concentrations of low-income children. It has frequently been asserted that these funds, in fact, are diverted to support services for children not in economic need, and there is some evidence that this occurs. However, such diversion as may occur is not great and is not altogether contrary to the intent of Congress, which was to give assistance to schools serving large numbers of economically disadvantaged children. Regulations permit giving assistance to children on the basis of educational need rather than economic status. Perhaps even more important, the study found that ESEA Title I funds tend to go largely for instructional purposes. Approximately two thirds of every Title I dollar is spent on additional educational programs at the local level, a figure that far exceeds other federal and state programs.

Do States Use ESEA Title I Monies as General Aid to Education? The intent of Congress was that ESEA Title I monies would supplement state and local education funds. They were to be spent over and above funds normally provided through state and local sources. Since education budgets are always strained, there may be great temptation for local districts to use ESEA Title I monies to replace state or local funds and to use the money thus saved to support other programs. There is evidence that ESEA Title I is used as a source of fungible monies. Remedying this deficiency is difficult, however, for several reasons, among them the following: Dealing with fifty states, 14,000 school districts, and innumerable classrooms is intrinsically a complex business; the intent of Congress is not altogether clear insofar as ESEA Title I is seen variously as limited to the economically disadvantaged and then as more broadly construed general aid to education; finally, the Department of Education was internally split on its role in an area where local autonomy is traditional. The 1978 amendments to ESEA strengthened the hand of the Department in monitoring the expenditure of funds.

Could Achievement Test Scores Be Used to Allocate ESEA Title I Funds? Congress asked the NIE to address this question specifically, thus revealing the divided opinion in Congress about the purpose of ESEA Title I: whether it is intended primarily for *economically* or *educationally* disadvantaged children. The advocates of a formula based on achievement test scores argued that compensatory education programs should provide services to children who have educational deficits, and they argued further that the poverty criterion is a poor proxy for educational underachievement. The proponents of the poverty criterion, on the other hand, argued that the purposes of ESEA Title I are broader than providing assistance to low-achieving students. In the spirit of the 1960s, with its emphasis on equality of opportunity, they argued that poverty and academic underachievement are closely linked and further that ESEA Title I should provide assistance not only to poor children but also to schools that serve large numbers of poor children. The NIE concluded that funds could be allocated on the basis of achievement test scores but that the costs of doing so would be substantial.

Is the Legal Framework of ESEA Title I Clear and Consistent and Are Federal Regulations Adequate to Ensure Compliance with the Law? The legal framework for administering ESEA Title I was found consistent with the law and within itself. However, the regulations were evaluated as extremely complicated and obtuse. The 1978 ESEA amendments, responsive to these criticisms, required the Department of Education to prepare an ESEA Title I policy manual, to make explicit the basis for the approval of state applications, and to report biannually to Congress on enforcement of Title I.

Are Parents Effectively Involved in ESEA Title I Programs? Although the federal mandate for parent involvement seems clear, there has been great variety in the degree of commitment, effort, and implementation among the states. Where commitment is high among ESEA Title I personnel, parent involvement programs have flourished in both participation and education activities. While almost every preschool program has a parent education component, parents' involvement tends to drop off rapidly as children approach first grade. By the time children reach kindergarten, the antiparent attitude characteristic of many public schools begins to manifest itself. The teacher becomes more dominant than in earlier programs, and, perhaps sensing this change in attitude, parents begin to withdraw. By first grade parental involvement is quite formal, usually limited to activities on the required parent advisory councils.

Do ESEA Title I Programs Work; Do They Help Economically and Educationally Disadvantaged Children Improve Their Academic Performance? As already noted, early evaluation studies yielded disappointing results; they focused primarily on educational gains and generally showed no effects, leading Rivlin (1971, p. 83) to observe that the studies "added to the layman's impression that compensatory education doesn't work and led some to believe that 'there is nothing we can do through education that will help poor children.' "

The NIE collected data during the period 1976–1977 to assess the academic gains of first- and third-grade students receiving ESEA Title I services. The study involved over 400 first- and third-grade classrooms in fourteen school districts. First graders recorded average gains of twelve months or twelve percentile points in reading and eleven months or fourteen percentile points in mathematics. The third graders made average gains of seven months or nine percentile points in reading and twelve months or seventeen percentile points in mathematics. These achievement gains were described by the NIE as "extremely encouraging."

To ascertain whether or not students in Title I programs would lose these impressive academic gains, a follow-up study was carried out on a representative sample of 3,000 students from twenty-seven schools in seven of the fourteen original districts. Students who had been tested in 1976–1977 were retested on reading and mathematics tests in September or early October of the following school year. The results led the NIE to the conclusion that students in compensatory education could maintain impressive gains over the calendar year.

Thus, contrary to early assertions, it can be stated with confidence that children in ESEA Title I compensatory education programs have benefited substantially from the experience. Not all the problems of providing compensatory instructional services have been solved by any means, but it is clear that "school districts can create the conditions necessary to make compensatory instruction services effective" (National Institute of Education, 1978, p. 10). Information regarding more recent evaluations confirm these earlier findings (see, for example, Edmonds, 1981).

Conclusions: ESEA Title I. For the first five years of the program, ESEA received major criticisms related to implementation and effectiveness. Most of these problems appear to have been reasonably well solved (particularly as compared with any other highly decentralized federal program), although there remains a fairly strong tension between advocates of centralization and advocates of decentralization. The Department of Education has been polarized on the issue from time to time, thus reducing the effectiveness of federal oversight of state and local ESEA operations. On the other hand, Congress has consistently strengthened the hand of the Department of Education by amendments to the 1965 legislation to improve accounting procedures, require technical assistance to local units, and carry out the major, nationwide evaluation of the program just discussed.

Some critics have faulted ESEA from the outset because it intruded the federal government so deeply and extensively into education, an endeavor viewed by many as the virtually exclusive prerogative of state and local government. For others, however, this intrusion was viewed as serving the value of equality, and, as we have seen, despite ESEA's focus on low-income groups, the value of community has also been served. ESEA Title I has several major weaknesses, however: It has not been concerned with strengthening families; it has had long-standing problems in implementing parent involvement, although the situation is better in its early childhood programs; and it lacks comprehensiveness, particularly in relation to children's health and related educational problems. Also, ESEA Title I does not concern itself with working parents' child care needs; parent education, beyond some attempts at parent involvement, has clearly not been an emphasis of the program.

In sum, ESEA was not designed specifically to address the concerns of our project, the strengthening of families through child care and parent education. Given its prevalence and general success, however, it may be a source of significant learning about public school involvement in child care and parent education.

Head Start

The War on Poverty of the 1960s was fought on many fronts. When President Lyndon Johnson signed the Economic Opportunity Act of 1964, he enacted a law that was to eliminate "the paradox of poverty in the midst of plenty ... by opening to everyone the opportunity for education and training, the opportunity of work, and the opportunity to live in decency and dignity" (U.S. Congress, 1964). Although the initial act did not make reference to Project Head Start as such, it provided the statutory authority for educational programs aimed at increasing the school and career chances of low-income children. The act's general approach opened the door to the growing number of educators, psychologists, and social reformers who helped the Johnson administration believe that real reform and redistribution were possible if the right educational and developmental programs were put into place (Mallory, 1979). Narrow academic goals for such programs were soon broadened by these advisers to include comprehensive child and family support in the areas of social competence, health, nutrition, and parent participation. The new purposes incorporated a blend of cognitive skill building through environmental intervention and rejected earlier beliefs in fixed inherited intelligence.

In early 1965, a planning committee established seven objectives for a preschool program for low-income children to be known as Head Start (Cooke, 1965). The objectives were to improve the child's physical health; to foster the child's emotional and social development through self-discipline, curiosity, spontaneity, and self-confidence; to improve the verbal skills; to foster the child's mental abilities, especially conceptual and verbal skills; to foster the child's self-confidence; to strengthen the child's family relationships and enable the family to better meet the child's needs; to develop positive attitudes toward society in the child and family and improve society's ability to work with the poor in solving problems; and to increase the sense of dignity and self-worth of the child and family.

Within six months of the committee's recommendations, 65 percent of the counties in the United States had requested operating funds and Head Start programs had begun in 40 percent of all counties (Smith and Bissell, 1970). Most initial projects ran for eight weeks during the summer prior to young children's entrance into public schools. These projects—and those that followed—emphasized community development, swift implementation, and nonprofessional staff. The lack of centralized management and the pressure of rapid development produced great variety in the programs, which differed in length of program, length of program day, the experience and training of teachers, and pupil-teacher ratios. It was not until the fall of 1968, over three years after the program's initiation, that Head Start could be called a stable and fully implemented program (Datta, McHale, and Mitchell, no date).

From 1965 to 1970, summer Head Start programs outnumbered full-year programs by two to one. During 1968–1969, 216,700 children were enrolled in full-year projects, and 1969 summer projects enrolled 446,000 children. In the fall of 1969, summer projects were given the option of converting to full-year status, and the subsequent 1969–1970 full-year projects enrolled 262,900 children, a 22 percent increase over the previous year (*Project Head Start, 1969–1970: A Descriptive Report of Programs and Participants,* 1972). That shift continued, and by 1978, only 161 of 1,400 grantees were operating summer programs only (U.S. Congress, Senate Committee on Human Resources, 1978). One fourth of the full-year programs were operated by public schools and one half were operated by community action agencies. By 1970, 45 percent of the Head Start children were in the program for a second year, and two thirds of all Head Start families had previously participated in the project through one or more children. The largest ethnic group served was blacks, followed by Caucasians, then Mexican-Americans (*Project Head Start, 1969–1970,* 1972); these figures also represent the current status of Head Start.

During the 1970s, Head Start legislative activity centered

on five policy issues: expansion of the target population, charging fees for services, serving handicapped children, the allocation formula, and moving Head Start administration into the federal education bureaucracy. A brief overview of these activities gives the flavor of the development of Head Start in this period.

A controversial fee schedule to enable children above the poverty line to participate in Head Start was established by Congress in 1972, only to be repealed two years later. Grantees resisted the movement toward fees, since only one fifth of the poverty-eligible families were enrolled at the time (U.S. Congress, House Committee on Education and Labor, 1972); further, there was reluctance to impose fees on the many families above the poverty guidelines who were already receiving free services (General Accounting Office, 1975).

Another issue, the 1972 mandate to set aside 10 percent of Head Start's national enrollment for handicapped children, generated substantial controversy about labeling and classifying children. In addition, many people pointed to the difficulty of monitoring a national quota. In response to the criticism, the 1974 Head Start amendments shifted the 10 percent national figure to a percentage based on state-level enrollments (LaVor and Harvey, 1976).

In yet another area of controversy, Head Start, from its inception, had funded eligible program sponsors (including schools, community action agencies, and single-purpose, nonprofit agencies) through competitive grants. This process produced wide discrepancies in the allocations between and within states; Mississippi and New York, for example, received comparable funding. The size and number of programs bore no relation to the number of poor children in a state, a fact to which Congress became more sensitive during the fiscal impoundments and cutbacks of the Nixon administration. A new formula, based on the number of welfare recipients and poor children in each state, was adopted in 1974; a "hold harmless" clause ensured that programs would receive no less than their FY1975 allocations (LaVor and Harvey, 1976).

Illustrating a final issue, the attempt to move Head Start from the Administration for Children, Youth, and Families

(ACYF) of the Department of Health, Education, and Welfare (HEW) into the proposed separate, cabinet-level Department of Education drew intense fire in 1978. The National Head Start Association, with the support of the Children's Defense Fund, lobbied vigorously against the proposed transfer. They insisted that Head Start was not an educational program but a child development program and that the shift would destroy the gains of the last twelve years (Mallory, 1979). Many critics of the proposed move attributed Head Start's success to its diversified delivery system, local control, parent involvement, use of nonprofessional staff, sensitivity to the needs of its minority constituents (65 percent of the enrollment), low overhead costs compared with public schools, and ties to other programs operated by ACYF and HEW. The Carter administration and Senator Abraham Ribicoff, chief sponsor of the Department of Education, quickly removed the Head Start transfer from the bill, fearing the issue would sink the entire department.

In 1982, Head Start continued to be primarily a center-based, comprehensive child development program for low-income children three to five years of age. Its legislative history and the consequences of scores of program evaluations have resulted in a diverse, decentralized, and fairly stable delivery system. Besides the model center-based program, there are several related activities designed to meet the needs of the families of Head Start children and other special populations. The complementary efforts, demonstrating the diversity and creativity of Head Start, include multiple programs. Home Start, a program of home visits by paraprofessionals who teach parents how to teach their own children, reaches about 12,000 children in almost 300 programs (U.S. Congress, Senate Committee on Human Resources, 1978). Parent-Child Centers serve 150 young, pre–Head Start children and their families in about thirty sites, emphasizing early prevention of childhood problems through parent education. Research on their effects is conducted in the experimental outgrowth of the centers, the Parent Child Development Centers (Dokecki, Hargrove, and Sandler, in press). The Child and Family Resource Programs, enrolling 800 families in eleven projects, incorporate the effective aspects of Head Start, Parent-Child Centers, Home Start, and other child development programs (The Comptroller General of the United States, 1979). The Head Start Early and Periodic Screening, Diagnosis and Treatment Collaboration is a pilot program in which 200 Head Start centers are reimbursed for providing specified medical and health services. Project Developmental Continuity links Head Start, preschool, and elementary school to provide continuing educational services to 1,000 children, four to eight years old, in thirteen sites. The Head Start Bilingual-Bicultural Strategy for Spanish-Speaking Children develops curriculum, staff training, and regional resource centers for Head Start programs serving Spanish-speaking children. The Resource Access Projects are regional programs providing consultation and resources for handicapped children in Head Start across the country. The Basic Education Skills Project enables seventeen Head Start programs to give intensive attention to the development of children's language and numerical skills. Follow Through is a demonstration and service program to assist graduates of Head Start or similar early childhood programs to maintain academic gains through early elementary school. Housed now in the Department of Education, Follow Through has maintained a quiet but persistent presence in legislation (Hodges and Sheehan, 1978).

In 1981, Head Start reached over 400,000 children, or about 24 percent of those eligible on the basis of age and family income. About 5,000 children below age three received services through Parent-Child Centers and the Child and Family Resource Programs. In addition, about 80,000 children in kindergarten through grade three participated annually in Follow Through projects in 175 communities.

The federal authorization for Head Start grew from $96 million in 1965 to $700 million in 1981. Funding levels for individual Head Start programs ranged from $966 per child to $2,537 per child in 1977. The funding formulas developed in 1978 were intended to equalize state allocations, but the original competitive grant-funding process created a continuing problem with equalizing per-child allocations. Programs that received higher per-child grant levels in their early years continue to receive higher levels today.

Average costs in the late 1970s of $1,600 per child per

school year (U.S. Congress, Congressional Budget Office, 1978) appear reasonable when compared with group child care ($2,500 to $3,000 for a full year) and private nursery programs ($750 to $1,000 for a half-day program for nine months). Salaries of most Head Start staff, however, are about minimum wage. Utility and transportation costs continue to rise much faster than congressional appropriations, forcing many programs to raise additional money locally or reduce the number of children enrolled. Because of the services mandated by the performance standards, it is usually not possible to reduce services to maintain or increase enrollment.

Although Head Start provides out-of-home care for young children, it is not a child care program in the popular sense. Because it is intended for very low-income families, the guidelines preclude two-parent working families. Even full-day Head Start is defined as a program that operates six or more hours per day, which may not coincide with parents' working hours. The four-day week used by many programs also prevents them from playing a significant child care role. Some centers do provide full-day care, however, using funds from other sources (for example, Title XX); about one third of the total children registered are in full-day Head Start (Kamerman and Kahn, 1976). Head Start's strong emphasis on involving parents in classroom activities and as home teachers also conflicts with the child care function needed by many working families. Although the Congressional Budget Office study of federal child care and preschool policies cited the expansion of Head Start as an option for meeting child care needs (U.S. Congress, Congressional Budget Office, 1978), it referred to expanding coverage to all eligible children, not to lengthening operating hours. The latter form of expansion would be even more expensive than the study's $2 billion estimate.

Parent education, on the other hand, has been an integral component of Head Start almost from its inception. Much of what we now conceive as parent education stems from Head Start's multiple goals of community change, strengthening families, enhancing child development, and developing policy and program models (Mallory, 1979). The four major roles for parents in Head Start are classroom volunteers or paid staff, home teachers of their own children, learners in career-training or child development activities, and participants in policy making. Several studies reported in Chapter Four found that as parents become involved in these activities, their children make cognitive and social gains, both during Head Start and later in elementary school. Because parents are involved in curriculum design and evaluation, the weaknesses of overly pedagogical, professionally defined "parenting" courses are often reduced.

Among early childhood programs, Head Start is unique in the comprehensiveness of its services. It is clearly a developmental program concerned with children's cognitive, social, emotional, and physical growth. Mandated services include education, physical and mental health care, dental care, nutrition education and supplements, transportation, parent involvement, and family support services. Its affiliation with community action agencies and local school systems enables it to provide a broad range of services or to arrange for those services. As a preventive program, it has been a model for other early childhood projects seeking to optimize the preschool period of children's development. Although inflation has caused some Head Start programs to shift away from direct services into information and referral activities, its focus remains comprehensive and preventive.

Does Head Start work? The answer depends on which of Head Start's multiple purposes is under consideration. The numerous evaluations of Head Start over the past fifteen years have addressed the program's four somewhat distinct purposes: cognitive-academic goals, in which the target is the child's developmental status; social service goals, in which the target is the family process and well-being; demonstration goals, in which the target is Head Start policy and programs; and equal opportunity–redistributive goals, in which the target is broad social change in institutions affecting low-income families. We now summarize briefly the findings of Head Start evaluations for over a decade.

Cognitive-Academic Goals. Does Head Start improve children's academic skills? This question has attracted most evaluation attention and has generated the greatest controversy. The history of Head Start evaluations has been similar to that of ESEA Title I, in which early negative findings have been reversed or modified by later studies. The Westinghouse Report (Westinghouse Learning Corporation, 1969) found that Head Start had little effect on academic ability and that such small gains as occurred "faded out" after a few years in elementary school. Controversy immediately swirled around the report; Zigler (1978), for example, criticized it as measuring the wrong thing, stating that improved social competence, not academic performance, was the goal of Head Start. A subsequent synthesis of Head Start research between 1966 and 1969 (Datta, McHale, and Mitchell, no date) was more equivocal, finding that the great diversity among Head Start centers produced understandably different results. Some centers promoted cognitive skills, others were strong on parent training and career development. Datta, McHale, and Mitchell concluded that no single evaluation can ever capture *all* that is Head Start. The subsequent Head Start Longitudinal Study of the effects of Head Start on family processes (such as mothers' participation in and expectations about their children's learning) revealed no significant cognitive gains from Head Start (Shipman, McKee, and Bridgeman, 1977).

The comprehensive reassessment of Head Start by the Social Science Research Group of George Washington University, however, contradicted many of these negative findings (Mann, Harrell, and Hurt, 1977). The group's analysis of sixty Head Start evaluations (related to cognitive gains, social development, child health, family impact, and community change) found improved academic performance for children in full-year Head Start programs, as measured on standardized tests; the children performed as well as or better than their peers at school entry on tests of intelligence or ability. Head Start children also had fewer grade retentions and placements in special education classes than their peers who had not been in the program.

Social Service Goals. Most Head Start evaluations have concentrated on the child's gains, rather than the family's. The Parent-Child Centers and Child and Family Resource Programs—

Head Start projects that focused services on families—have been evaluated mainly in terms of their effects on children's cognitive skills (Sherman, Payne, and Carriker, 1971; U.S. Department of Health, Education, and Welfare, Office of Human Development, 1976). There has been considerable evaluation of Head Start's effects on children's health and nutritional status, however, an important element of the social service goals. The findings have been highly positive. Head Start children have gained greatly in immunizations (90 percent of Head Start children are immunized, versus 50 percent in the general population), dental care (90 percent), and medical care (30 percent receive care beyond routine checkups) (U.S. Congress, Senate Committee on Human Resources, 1978). Head Start children have lower school absenteeism, fewer cases of anemia, better nutritional practices, and better general health (Mann, Harrell, and Hurt, 1977). Furthermore, parents expressed increased satisfaction with the educational progress of their children and participated more often in school programs as their children grew older.

Expression of support for Head Start from parents, which has been overwhelming at times, has carried tremendous weight in Congress. It is clear that policy makers have been moved as much, if not more, by parent testimonials than by evaluations of cognitive gain. Parents' obvious satisfaction with Head Start over the years has given the program its political strength. Thus, one aspect of social service goals, that of supporting parents and increasing their own level of satisfaction, seems clearly to have been met.

Demonstration Goals. Head Start demonstration programs have generally had little effect in providing information that has changed widespread program models or terminated poor programs. However, the demonstrations have provided information about evaluation methodology and implementation problems.

While Head Start as a whole might be considered a demonstration program, two components, the Head Start Planned Variations (HSPV) and the Handicapped Mandate, were designed specifically for experimental purposes. Begun in 1969, HSPV gave grants to eleven sponsors to combine Head Start and Follow Through to experiment with the effects of more sustained intervention. The results were fairly unimpressive, with little difference between the gains for HSPV and regular Head Start children. One evaluation concluded, "On balance, political necessity more than the state of the art has determined HSPV's characteristics" (Datta, 1975, p. 80). The Handicapped Mandate, implemented in 1972, provided a model of services to preschool children at a time of increased pressure on public schools to serve handicapped children. The mandate that Head Start programs serve 10 percent handicapped children, however, seemed to have the effect of encouraging staff to label children as handicapped, rather than serving a new population (Bogdan, 1976). While Head Start served children with mild handicaps (40 to 50 percent of the handicapped total) and health impairments (14 to 25 percent), fewer than 7 percent of the handicapped children served were severely or multiply handicapped. Head Start thus sustained considerable criticism for not serving a sufficiently large number of handicapped children. Lack of resources were cited as an impediment, and in 1976, the Resource Access Projects were established to enhance this endeavor.

On balance, HSPV, the Handicapped Mandate, and other demonstration efforts have had relatively little direct effect on most Head Start programs. However, the demonstrations have broadened the range of delivery models from which local programs may choose, thereby promoting the great diversity that characterizes Head Start. Further, the coexistence of research and service goals has acted as a pressure valve for policy makers, giving them a variety of rationales for continuing public expenditures. If negative evaluations have emerged from research and demonstration activities, pressures to halt public support have been relieved by shifting to service goals, and vice versa.

Equal Opportunity–Redistributive Goals. Head Start was conceived within the community action philosophy and policies of the 1960s. Parental control over programs, training for new careers, and creating change in community institutions have been central to Head Start's mission, but its effectiveness in reaching these goals has been difficult to assess.

Closely related to the antipoverty goals of Head Start is its sponsorship by community action agencies. Even the pro-

grams based in public schools (about one third of the total) reflect a community action orientation rather than a schoollike
format. The proposal to transfer Head Start into the federal Department of Education met stiff opposition from Head Start
primarily on the grounds that most schools are not interested in
community action and change.

The most visible symbol of community action, and therefore the most threatening to entrenched interests, is the role of
parents as volunteers, paid staff, or policy council members
with majority representation and policy-making powers. A 1972
Senate report concluded, "One of the most encouraging aspects
of the successful Head Start program has been its ability to recruit and train nonprofessionals, especially mothers and other
family members, for important staff responsibilities in these
programs" (U.S. Congress, Senate Committee on Labor and
Public Welfare, 1972, p. 11). Whether those powers have been
realized is debatable, but the symbolic use of parents (Farber
and Lewis, 1975) as staff and board members at least creates an
image of redistribution of knowledge, power, and resources.

Conclusions: Head Start. Head Start's multiple goals, constituencies, and evaluation criteria have led to sometimes inconsistent and ambiguous conclusions about its effectiveness. However, the contradictions are not necessarily counterproductive;
in many ways, they have helped to clarify the influence of the
characteristics of specific communities on early intervention
programs. We are beginning to perceive Head Start as an "insti-
tutionalized" program, to use Suchman's (1972) phrase; the
need to justify it as an experimental demonstration program is
declining, both because the means to accomplish empirical justi-
fication are so problematic and because the service delivery
goals of Head Start have gained legitimacy. Since the end of the
planned variation experiments in the early 1970s, Head Start
has been refunded primarily on the basis of intrinsic merit and
political support, rather than empirical grounds.

It is impossible to declare with certainty that Head Start
"works." The local variability in resources, community contexts, and program designs precludes a national assessment of
the effectiveness of the policy and its resultant programs. The

continuation of funding since 1965 is perhaps the clearest indication that Head Start is meeting the needs of both participants and policy makers. The multiple objectives and multiple constituencies of Head Start have been its primary sources of innovation.

The two major weaknesses of Head Start are that it meets only minimally the child care needs of families and that it is means-tested. The second point is very significant, since it limits the number of families and children served and can be demeaning to participants and divisive among societal groups. Therefore, although much good has come from Head Start and many programmatic lessons can be learned from understanding how it has worked, the general situation of American families addressed in this project suggests the need for policies and programs that go well beyond the Head Start approach.

Head Start's strengths have been its local control, its ability to stimulate change in other social systems, and its broad-based constituency, which has included both low-income families and child development professionals. The federal-local administrative structure has bypassed the traditional state role in program administration, delivery, and evaluation and appears to have contributed thus far to Head Start's longevity. In implementing Head Start, sponsoring agencies have been free to develop their own early childhood services without having to conform to a specific model. The result is a plurality of approaches at the state and local levels. Nonetheless, if federal support for Head Start were to end, states would be unlikely to maintain the program as such, in part because state agencies have been bypassed, by and large, in implementation of the program over the years.

There remains a need for a strong federal role in demonstrating new service delivery approaches and creative administrative arrangements. While such model programs may not provide services to all children and their families, they do have the capacity to stimulate multiple approaches that state and local agencies can adapt to their particular social and economic circumstances. Limited fiscal resources in the 1980s may well prevent Head Start from expanding its scope and coverage beyond present levels; the program appears to be as secure for the near future, however, as it has been over its sometimes tumultuous history.

Title XX of the Social Security Act

Title XX of the Social Security Act established a consolidated program of federal financial assistance to the states to encourage the provision of social services. It grew out of a history that saw social services evolving largely in the backwater of public policy; by and large, these social services constituted a highly fragmented approach to meeting the needs of various discrete groups (for example, the poor, the aged, children, the disabled, and Native Americans) through a miscellany of programs (for example, child care, protective services, counseling, and mental health). Passed in 1974, after two years of negotiation between Congress, HEW staff, governors, state welfare officials, and a powerful coalition of twenty or so national organizations, it was seen as landmark legislation for the social services.

Title XX was thus a major attempt at federal funding for comprehensive social services and provided the opportunity, not fully realized, for unified planning and provision of a wide range of services to a diverse population. Rather than requiring that specific services be provided to certain categories of eligible people, Title XX permitted the states a great deal of latitude in choosing the services they wished to offer and in determining where, how, and to whom services would be provided. The services chosen, however, were required to meet at least one of the following five goals: to achieve or maintain economic self-support to prevent, reduce, or eliminate dependency; to achieve or maintain self-sufficiency, including reduction or prevention of dependency; to prevent or remedy neglect, abuse, or exploitation of children and adults unable to protect their own interests, or to preserve, rehabilitate, and unite families; to provide or reduce inappropriate institutional care by providing for community-based care, home-based care, or other forms of less intensive care; and to secure referral or admission for institutional care when other forms of care are not appropriate, or to provide services to individuals in institutions.

Title XX thus shifted the federal role in social services from a dominant one in the choice and planning of services to the less powerful function of specifying the *goals* of services. It made states, generally through their Departments of Public Welfare (or the equivalent agency), responsible for the specific choice of services. It also made the states accountable to their own citizens, rather than to the federal government only, by mandating a planning and accountability process. Each state was required to prepare an annual plan for social services (the Comprehensive Annual Services Program), submitted to the public for review and comment. While the federal government retained program and fiscal auditing functions, Title XX provided for much greater citizen scrutiny and increased participation in the formulation of the service plan than had been true in prior legislation. One sometimes negative consequence of the states' increased discretion has been the intense competition among special interests and particular groups of service providers for Title XX funds.

Social services under Title XX were permitted to people at a somewhat higher income level than was previously possible. The "working poor" and families or individuals outside of the poverty categories—those with incomes up to 115 percent of the state's median income—were eligible to receive Title XX social services if a state so chose. Another feature of Title XX differentiating it from earlier federal social service programs was its allowance of fees for service. The fees were specified as mandatory for most services provided to people with incomes over 80 percent of each state's median income and could be charged to people with lower incomes at the state's option. The fees were permitted to smooth the transition for families from free services for the poorest to full cost for people with higher incomes.

Child care was one of over forty services that states elected to provide with Title XX funds. It has been provided by all the states and has been one of the largest Title XX services in terms of both expenditures and number of people served. In the mid 1970s, states spent approximately 25 percent of their Title XX allocations for child care, although the actual percentage varied widely among the fifty states. A total of $200 million in federal funds were earmarked for child care, over and above the general $2.5 billion Title XX appropriation. The fact that child care was singled out for a separate appropriation and that, in addition, the federal funds required no state matching was an indication of the emphasis on child care.

Interestingly, Title XX constituted the largest federal support mechanism for providing child care through direct service, accounting in the mid 1970s for approximately one third of all federal expenditures for child care and serving at that time an estimated 888,000 children (U.S. Congress, Congressional Budget Office, 1978). Parent education, unlike child care, was not among the specified Title XX services offered by the states, although it is likely that a fair amount of parent education has taken place in the context of other Title XX programs, such as counseling, homemaker services, and child care.

Most families using Title XX child care were reported in the mid 1970s to be employed, seeking work, or in job training; most were one-parent families. Approximately two thirds of the children in Title XX child care were from families receiving Aid to Families with Dependent Children (AFDC); a much smaller proportion (30 percent) were from other income-eligible families (that is, those with incomes above the poverty level but low enough to qualify for services).

Although Title XX allowed service to families with incomes above the level of public assistance, states generally chose to target services, including child care, to very low-income families. In states electing to charge fees for service, the tendency has been to start the fees at fairly low levels of income; although the states had the option of requiring fee payment at income levels as high as 80 percent of the median income, in practice they tended to institute fees at incomes as low as 35 percent of the median. States also tended to restrict access to child care further by narrowing the criteria to families with special needs—single-parent families, those with handicapped children, or those with children in danger of abuse and neglect. The decision of most states to limit eligibility for services, including child care, has generally worked to limit the population served to the very poorest people. Even with this practice, however, Title XX represented an important advance over previous public welfare–related social service policies, which limited eligibility to present, former, and potential welfare recipients, thereby excluding a much larger proportion of the poor population.

Child care services funded through Title XX were generally required to meet standards of care. State regulations vary greatly, from minimum requirements to meet health and safety standards to stringent rules concerning program content. The Federal Interagency Day Care Requirements (FIDCR), which are developmental rather than custodial in orientation, were not formally adopted and were not legally binding. Nonetheless, the National Day Care Study (1979) found that centers receiving Title XX funds by and large complied with those standards. Title XX and FIDCR also provided for parent participation, and although there was considerable variation, the best of Title XX child care probably emphasized parent involvement and soft-pedaled professional domination. Without question, however, the eligibility determination process, no matter how carefully and sensitively performed, placed the professional in control, with little opportunity for the parent to share responsibility and decision making.

Parents chose whether to participate in Title XX services; in the broadest sense, then, they had freedom of choice. However, a more complex issue was the extent to which parents were able to choose particular care arrangements, an issue in which the factor of government-as-purchaser-of-service is important. Under Title XX, state governments decided what modes of care to purchase. While state agencies varied considerably in the percentage of slots purchased in centers, family day homes, and in-home care arrangements, the dominant mode nationally has been center care. Child care providers and children's advocacy groups have generally influenced the state agencies to choose center-based care; providers of center care are well organized, while family day home providers are in an early stage of organization and there is no organization of in-home care providers. It is also important to note that Title XX payments went directly to providers, rather than to parents; the system tended to leave the parents out of the transaction. Parental choice may have been limited further by the uneven distribution of child care arrangements; there are very few choices in rural areas and small communities, and even in larger cities, neighborhoods may have few centers or homes from which parents can choose. Waiting lists were a further problem in some programs, and information and referral services were not plentiful.

Conclusions: Title XX. Title XX of the Social Security Act marked an important phase in the evolution of social service policy in the United States. Services that had developed as part of the cash public assistance program were accorded separate status in recognition of their gradual evolution into services with intrinsic worth beyond utility as an adjunct to poverty, employment, and welfare policy. Some recognition of the value of social services for the nonpoor and encouragement of voluntary-sector provision of services signaled a move toward making services available more broadly to all who may need them. The open planning process and the balance of federal and state authority were fresh approaches to governance. While implementation was uneven, the years of Title XX gave promise of providing a solid base for the development of social services.

The Social Services Block Grant (SSBG) in 1981 changed Title XX to a revenue-sharing program. It removed most of the federal requirements, including income eligibility standards, targeting part of the funds to services for cash welfare recipients, state matching funds, federal regulation of child care services, the open planning process, uniform state reporting, and single state agency administration. And federal funds were reduced.

It can be argued that SSBG was a positive step toward placing responsibility for policy making for social services closer to the point of service delivery; it can further be argued that services *should* be governed and controlled more fully at the state and local levels. On the other hand, diffusion of authority and relaxed federal controls and standards can also have negative consequences. The importance of services can be downgraded, and funds can be more readily used for unintended purposes. Fiscal pressures may tempt states to shift social service money to expanding entitlement programs—Medicaid, for example. The integrative and coordinative intention of Title XX, incompletely implemented at best, may well be lost as funds are spread among state agencies without comprehensive planning. The pressure from states on the federal government to appropriate the authorized SSBG funds may be weakened as Title XX's already diffused and fragmented constituency is spread thinner.

Child care and parent education may retain their shares of social service allocations, but the cutbacks in funds virtually ensure that support for these services will shrink. Some state regulations are less stringent than the former federal standards; child care programs may therefore cost less to run and child care slots may thus be retained. However, there is a risk that developmental daycare, which grew somewhat improbably within the context of welfare-related social services, may be downgraded.

The expansion of child care and parent education within SSBG appears highly unlikely, not only because of stringent funding but also because of historical failure of welfare-related services to reach the nonpoor population. In the short run, SSBG is likely to be an important source of funds for child care and parent education. However, it seems more likely that in the long run, the diverse child care community—education, social work, health, and child development—will unite more effectively with their natural constituents, working parents with young children, to advocate for expanded child care outside the public assistance-related social service system.

Comprehensive Child Development and Family Service Proposals

An obvious possibility for providing child care and parent education is to create a new and comprehensive program for children and their families, comparable in scope to the programs for older people that have grown since the mid 1930s into a major feature of our national life. There were, in fact, serious efforts in the 1970s to pass such a program of services for children and families. The efforts came as close as a presidential veto; with that veto the efforts failed dramatically and the coalition that came so close to success in gaining passage of the legislation gradually fell apart. We review this proposed legislation here briefly as a means of understanding our own national precedent for considering a more comprehensive approach to the provision of services to children and families than is embodied in any of the three major programs just reviewed (see also McCathren, 1980).

In 1971, the Comprehensive Child Development Act, S. 2007, called for a national child care program based on several congressional findings (*Congressional Record*, 1971, p. 31249):

1. Millions of children in the nation are suffering unnecessary harm from the lack of adequate child development services, particularly during early childhood years;
2. Comprehensive child development programs, including a full range of health, education, and social services, are essential to the achievement of the full potential of the nation's children and should be available as a matter of right to all children whose parents or legal guardians shall request them regardless of economic, social, and family backgrounds;
3. Children with special needs must receive full and special consideration in planning any child development programs and, pending the availability of such programs for all children, priority must be given to preschool children with the greatest economic and social need;
4. While no mother may be forced to work outside the home as a condition for using child development programs, such programs are essential to allow many parents to undertake or continue full- or part-time employment, training, or education;
5. Comprehensive child development programs not only provide a means of delivering a full range of essential services to children, but can also furnish meaningful employment opportu-

> nities for many individuals, including older
> persons, parents, young persons, and volun-
> teers from the community; and
>
> 6. It is essential that the planning and operation
>   of such programs be undertaken as a partner-
>   ship of parents, community, and state and lo-
>   cal government with appropriate assistance
>   from the federal government.

This statement of findings and purposes has unusual importance
for two reasons. First, the lofty goals were actually translated
into specific legislation, a rare occurrence. The bill as drafted, if
fully funded and implemented, would in fact have permitted
the services it called for. Second, the remainder of the decade's
experiences with child care legislation was dominated by the
strong response to the findings and purposes of the proposed bill.

The bill passed the Senate in 1971 with a measure of support uncommon for a large and potentially controversial social
program: the vote was 49 to 12. The vote in the House was
closer: 186 to 183. It appeared that this legislation would become reality; but on December 9, 1971, President Richard
Nixon vetoed it, maintaining that child care as proposed in the
bill would foster communal approaches to child-rearing and diminish parental authority. An effort to override the president's
veto gained sufficient votes in the House, but fell seven short in
the Senate of the required two-thirds majority. The congressional support behind the comprehensive child care legislation was
to continue for several years, although it weakened gradually
and ultimately disappeared almost completely.

This is not the place to describe fully the social and political tensions that were manifest in the struggle over this piece of
legislation (see McCathren, 1980). Suffice it to say that the
Comprehensive Child Care Bill of 1971 was flawed by over-
reaching provisions, an underemphasis on the responsibilities of
parents, and language that could easily be misinterpreted, either
in honest dissent or for political advantage.

The unlikely coalition that effectively lobbied for the
passage of the 1971 bill was splintered after the presidential
veto by the defection of the American Federation of Teachers

(AFT) and the American Federation of Labor–Congress of Industrial Organizations (AFL–CIO), whose leadership saw in the need for child care a possible way to put unemployed teachers to work. Nevertheless, it was possible after the 1971 veto to mobilize other advocacy groups and supporters in Congress to draft new child care legislation that would, it was hoped, avoid previous errors and broaden political support for the program in the nation and in Congress. Senators Gaylord Nelson, Walter Mondale, Jacob Javits, and Robert Taft put together a strong bipartisan bill that they titled the Comprehensive Head Start, Child Development, and Family Services Act of 1972 (S. 3617). The measure passed the Senate in June 1972 by a vote of seventy-three to twelve. The bill was not allowed to come to a vote in the House, however.

In 1974, Senator Mondale and Congressman John Brademas sponsored legislation entitled the Child and Family Services Act of 1975 (S. 626). In opening hearings on the bill in February 1975, Senator Mondale described the provisions of the House and Senate bills as follows (U.S. Congress, Senate Committee on Labor and Public Welfare, House Committee on Education and Labor, 1975, pp. 135-136):

> The bills authorize $1.8 billion over the next three years to fund a wide variety of services, including daycare services for preschool children, medical services for expectant and new mothers to reduce the incidence of preventable birth defects, family counseling, education, health diagnosis and treatment programs, and nutrition programs for children.
>
> The bills contain a unique phase-in year for planning, training, and technical assistance, to assure that program funds which become available in the following years can be used as effectively and efficiently as possible.
>
> I want to emphasize that programs authorized by this legislation are totally voluntary and maximize parent control and decision making. They recognize and specifically provide that child care programs must be voluntary and must build upon and strengthen the role of the family as the

primary and fundamental influence on the development of the child.

They assure that parents will have the opportunity to choose among the greatest possible variety of child and family services, including prenatal
care, nutrition assistance, part-day programs like
Head Start, after-school or full-day developmental
daycare for children of working mothers, in-the-
home tutoring, early medical screening and treatment to detect and remedy handicapping conditions, and classes for parents and prospective
parents.

An unprecedented ground swell of public opposition, informed or misinformed by a widely disseminated anti-child care
pamphlet, resulted in the bill's demise; it never came to a vote.
Congress was flooded with letters, most apparently from ultra-
conservative groups and fundamentalist religious denomina-
tions. Senator Mondale's office received as many as 2,100 letters a day, more than had been received on any day during the
Vietnam War.

A subsequent, limited, and seemingly simple child care
bill, the Child Care Act of 1979 (S. 4), was introduced by Senator Alan Cranston in 1979. Finding little unified support among
advocacy groups and active disinterest on the part of the Carter
administration, Cranston soon withdrew the bill, thus ending a
decade of struggle for and against child care legislation.

New coalitions, however, have been forming, and support
for child care legislation continues to be voiced. For example,
the 1980 White House Conference on Families included government provision of child care and parent education among its
top priority recommendations, thus carrying forward and re-
affirming the priority of the 1970 White House Conference on
Children and Youth, which had called for comprehensive child
development programs, oriented toward family needs, that
would include child care, early childhood education, and health
services.

Conclusions: Comprehensive Child and Family Services.
The enormous opposition to the Mondale-Brademas bill, tem-
porarily at least, made child care a politically dangerous issue;

few politicians wanted to have anything to do with it. The Reagan administration's subsequent focus on reducing the size and scope of the federal government has also worked to preclude new initiatives for direct federal support of child care and parent education services. As a result, federal legislative activity in the early 1980s has been directed toward support of child care through indirect means, such as expanding the income tax credit for child care (see Chapter Five) and giving employers tax incentives to provide services (as in the Omnibus Budget Reconciliation Act of 1981). This does not gainsay the fact that a comprehensive approach to services has strong support from many individuals and organizations, however. It seems likely that concern for integrated child care and family support services may again become a major national issue requiring congressional attention at some point in the future.

Value Analysis

In this section, we apply our values criteria to the services option, exemplified by the federal child care and parent education services programs as a group; in doing so, we highlight the special features of each federal initiative that are particularly relevant to the value specifications. Although reductions have been effected in some of the programs, the analysis emphasizes the programs' values as they functioned during the period of their fullest development. Our analysis of services is somewhat more detailed than the analysis of the four major options discussed in Chapter Five, primarily because the nation's experience in providing services to support parents in their childrearing roles is more extensive, better documented, and more thoroughly researched than are the efforts to achieve these objectives through any other policy option.

Does the Policy Enhance Community? This value element stresses that child care and parent education policy and programs should serve not only the participants but the common good; they should enhance a sense of community and mutual concern. Conversely, we are interested in the community's concern for the development of all children as competent and caring members. We pose several questions about the policies to assess their efficacy in enhancing community. Do policies increase shared heritage, mutual aid, and community building? Are they socially divisive? Do they bestow unwarranted advantage? And are they demeaning to the participants?

The major federal programs, ESEA Title I, Head Start, and Title XX, all increase shared heritage, mutual aid, and community building to the extent that they enhance intellectual development of children. ESEA Title I increases the shared heritage insofar as it enables economically and educationally disadvantaged children to share in the educational experiences enjoyed by more advantaged children. By remedying academic deficiencies, ESEA Title I enables academically disadvantaged children to participate in the educational mainstream. As the largest single federal investment in public elementary and secondary schools, the purpose of ESEA Title I has been to ensure an equitable distribution of opportunity for children to achieve basic competencies essential to the economic and humane development of the total community. The program has been successful in remedying deficits in fundamental academic skills, thus adding to the human capital of the nation and diminishing, in some measure, the gap between the competent and the incompetent in the society.

Similarly, Head Start contributes to community cohesiveness and strength through its attention to building children's basic academic skills before they enter elementary school. Although the Head Start curriculum is often unstructured and open-ended, pressures from Congress, school personnel, and parents have led to the frequent inclusion of readiness activities, particularly in the areas of verbal and arithmetic competencies. Project Follow Through and the Basic Education Skills Project indicate Head Start's attention to the maintenance of cognitive skill development into the early elementary grades.

Title XX child care programs have been oriented generally to children's intellectual, social, and emotional development. While the explicit purposes of Title XX child care and parent education services were traditional welfare goals—the promotion of families' economic independence from public assistance and the reduction of abuse and neglect—in practice, Title XX child care programs have adhered to the developmental and competency-oriented goals expressed in the provisions of FIDCR.

While all three programs have contributed to the enhancement of communities through the development of competent children, Head Start especially has been successful in increasing the common bonds among program participants in the interest of stronger communities. These bonds are created and maintained by Head Start's commitment to significant roles for parents in policy-making, program planning and staffing. In local policy councils (made up of a majority of Head Start parents), in regional associations, and in the National Head Start Association, opportunities for group decision making and discussion of concerns common to Head Start families have led to cohesiveness and a sense of shared purpose.

The Title XX planning process has emphasized citizen participation in decisions about social services at the state and local community levels. The planning process was an important feature of Title XX that attempted to move the program away from narrow, public welfare-oriented services and government-controlled planning and give a sense of ownership of public social services to those who use the services and to citizens at large. As implemented, citizen participation in Title XX planning tended toward heavier involvement by special interest groups and providers and lighter participation by consumers. However, the potential for citizen participation in planning services and allocating funds encouraged a sense of shared purpose and community among a broad base of citizens—lay people, professionals, and consumers of services.

These major federal programs also address some of the social divisions in American society. We have already described the contribution of federal service programs to mitigating some of the social divisions between the competent and incompetent by improving disadvantaged children's intellectual and social skills. Another serious social division—that along racial and ethnic lines—persists in spite of progress in recent decades to remove formal barriers to racial justice and equal opportunity.

The federal child care and parent education programs directly address fissures of race and ethnicity, of handicap and special circumstances. As with all federal financial programs, of course, discrimination on the basis of sex, race, color, or national origin is forbidden. Each of the programs discussed, however, has unique features that go beyond the simple absence of discrimination to address goals of social coherence and common purpose.

In the years following its passage, ESEA Title I was amended to include aid for handicapped, neglected, and delinquent children in institutions, American Indian children, and migrant children. The actual racial and ethnic composition of Title I students includes 54 percent white children, 35 percent black children, 10 percent children of Hispanic origin, 8 percent American Indian, and 8 percent of Asian origin.

Head Start has been particularly effective in including disadvantaged, traditionally disenfranchised minorities in its programs. Sixty-five percent of Head Start enrollments have consisted of minority groups (black and Hispanic families primarily), and Head Start has provided these families, as well as other minority groups, such as rural whites, with a forum for community action. Head Start performance standards require ethnic diversity among enrolled children and require the establishment of multicultural classroom curricula to foster intergroup understanding. Multicultural pluralism is also fostered by the Head Start Bilingual-Bicultural Strategy for Spanish-Speaking Children, begun in the late 1970s to stimulate the development of curriculum research, staff training, and resource centers for Head Start centers in Spanish-speaking communities. Additional evidence of Head Start's attention to ethnic pluralism is the concern that assessments of children's development take into consideration factors of socioeconomic status, cultural background, and home environment to establish an accurate and culture-sensitive picture of individual children's needs and abilities. Head Start has promoted social cohesiveness, too, through the 1972 mandate for integrating handicapped children into the classrooms. Although problematic at times, this effort has been relatively successful and has served as a model to other community-based preschool programs.

Finally, Title XX child care programs are more racially integrated than child care programs that do not receive federal funds. According to the *National Day Care Study* (1979, p. 199), "contrary to the expectation of a higher degree of racial segregation in FFP (Federal Financial Participation) centers, the racial mix in subsidized centers is actually more balanced than in non-FFP centers." Furthermore, states tended to include in Title XX child care programs those children with special needs —children in single-parent families, handicapped children, and children in danger of abuse and neglect.

Whether federal child care and parent education services bestow unwarranted advantage on the people served is another important issue from the value perspective of community. In general, we judge that an advantage derived from child care and parent education is warranted if the test of comparative justice is met, that is, if like cases are treated alike. Applying this test, we conclude that federal child care and parent education services policy fails here, since the services have not been made available to all families and children with the same disadvantages. For reasons of policy, as well as failure to provide sufficient funds, the majority of poor children and families do not receive services under the federal programs.

ESEA Title I comes closest to serving the entire target population, reaching an estimated 60 percent of those eligible for services. Nonetheless, the formulas for distributing ESEA Title I funds penalize children in need of special assistance who happen to attend a school with an insufficient number of economically disadvantaged children to qualify for participation in the program. (However, there may be offsetting advantages here in that schools for middle-class children tend to offer better services overall than schools for poor children.)

Both Head Start and Title XX have been able to serve only a minority of poor families, a result of restrictive eligibility standards and inadequate appropriations. Head Start regulations in fiscal year 1980 stipulated that a family of four could make no more than $7,450 to be eligible for services (up to 10 percent of Head Start enrollments may exceed the income guidelines). Limited appropriations have enabled Head Start to serve no more than 20 to 25 percent of those eligible each year since its inception. Families with two working parents who each earn the minimum wage are ineligible because of their combined income; also, such families would find it difficult to take advantage of the services because most Head Start programs are open for only half a day, often for four days a week. Title XX permitted the states to establish income eligibility, as long as families earned below 115 percent of the median income; in practice, however, the states have tended to set much lower eligibility levels. Unlike Head Start and ESEA Title I, which have national income standards for participating children, Title XX eligibility varies greatly from state to state. Further inequity among similarly situated families occurs in the differences among the states in fees charged for Title XX services. While federal law allows states to provide services without charge to families with incomes as high as 80 percent of the median, in practice states have usually instituted fees at income levels as low as 35 percent of the median income. Title XX also bestowed unwarranted advantage on some poor people to the exclusion of others, because half the funds were designated for welfare recipients. Since welfare eligibility varies greatly among the states, similarly situated poor people across the country do not have similar access to services. Further, states' options as to the portion of the overall Title XX allocation devoted to child care and parent education services produced substantial variation among the states in the availability of services. It is apparent that welfare-based programs, fraught as they are with low eligibility levels and state disparities, are least able among federal programs to meet the standard of comparative justice and warranted advantage.

All the federal programs are means-tested, and this is regarded as demeaning because such tests, in our view, are usually administered in a manner that subjects people to actually or potentially humiliating circumstances and communicates that those who participate have an inferior status. Means tests tend to deter people from seeking services and diminish the willingness of people to participate socially. The means tests for the various federal child care and parent education programs are administered somewhat differently from what is generally the case, however, demonstrating that their stigmatizing character can be diminished to some extent. For example, in ESEA Title I, the demeaning attributes of means tests are considerably attenuated by the provision that funds be made available to school districts and schools on the basis of the number of economically disadvantaged children served. Within a particular school, ESEA Title I assistance (remedial instruction, for example) can be provided on the basis of demonstrated need for assistance, without regard to economic status.

Head Start and Title XX, on the other hand, apply a means test to individual families. The Title XX test carries the connotation of greatest stigma, since it is delivered under the auspices of public welfare agencies. The location of Title XX administration within a single state welfare agency undercuts the intent to universalize social services. The welfare association of Title XX was also a deterrent to public acceptability and to the comfortable participation in the programs by many needy families. In addition, complex state fiscal and administrative policies have constituted strong disincentives for child care programs to serve a mix of Title XX and non–Title XX children. As a result, many child care centers were entirely Title XX funded, serving only poor children. Then, too, many small community-controlled programs, whose mission is to serve a socioeconomic mix of families and children, were unable to participate in Title XX owing to lack of sophisticated grantsmanship skills, inability to meet fiscal and program accounting requirements, and lack of matching funds. Thus, the means test and its attachment to the welfare bureaucracy tended, in many communities, to separate Title XX children and programs from the broader community (Morgan, 1977).

Does the Policy Strengthen Families? Strong families are the context for rearing competent and caring children and are the foundation of meaningful community. We judge policies to be in the interest of the community when they assist and support families, not erode or weaken them. Several questions in our value framework help elucidate these issues. Does the policy improve the capacity of families to master developmental tasks, including childrearing? Does it improve liaison or linkage functions related to social resources and supports needed by families? Does it protect families from unwarranted intrusion, allowing parents choice within the constraints of the other value criteria?

Federal child care and parent education service policies are an important facet in the many efforts over the last century to improve families' capacities to develop as social units and raise their children well. Government's attempt to lend a hand to families through the provision of services seems to us a natural means of enhancing family life and not, as the New Right contends, an intended or unintended means of eroding family rights and responsibilities. It is important, however, that government and other large organizations charged with financing and providing services be ever mindful of the need to strengthen, not usurp, family roles. The three major federal child care and parent education service programs do not show evidence of usurping family responsibilities and, in fact, demonstrate, by intent and performance, the capability of government-supported services to strengthen families.

Of the three programs under consideration, Head Start addresses most directly and most successfully the broad needs of families. Head Start has sought to support, not substitute for, poor families by helping them gain access to an array of services and aid. As a comprehensive support system providing educational, social, health, nutrition, transportation, and parent involvement services, Head Start has a tradition of meeting the needs of young children by attending to the ecological systems in which they and their families live. Early in Head Start's evolution, policy makers and researchers saw the need to broaden services beyond children and to their families in order to ameliorate family problems that lead to negative child outcomes. The development of the Parent-Child Centers in 1969 and the Child and Family Resource Programs in 1973 were attempts to strengthen family functioning as a means of improving child development. In addition, the various demonstration projects (Home Start, the Parent Child Development Centers, the Head Start Early and Periodic Screening, Diagnosis and Treatment

Collaboration) have sought to improve the capacity of families to meet intrafamilial needs. Further, Head Start appears to have influenced community services and institutions, making them more responsive to the poor families who seek their assistance. According to evidence from Kirschner Associates, Inc. (1970), educational and health systems located in communities with Head Start programs were found to be affected by the catalytic, community action spirit of Head Start. Public education efforts, involvement of low-income people in decision making, and increased employment opportunities have appeared in many cases as a result of Head Start's presence.

Title XX child care and parent education services, while mainly focused on the explicit goal of enabling families to become economically self-supporting, in practice have helped families in ways quite beyond traditional public assistance purposes. The social service components of many Title XX child care programs—assisting families to gain access to health care, employment services, and parent education opportunities as well as providing child care so that parents may work and support their families—are the means by which Title XX programs have supported and enhanced families. ESEA Title I does not seem to have contributed directly to the strengthening of families, and this is not surprising because the program has not been especially concerned with families, but rather with the competence of children who are deficient in some basic academic skill. However, ESEA Title I does constitute an additional resource for child care that might not otherwise be available, especially in the preschool years. Each of the federal programs places emphasis on support, not supplantation, of families by providing central roles for parents in planning and implementing the services.

All individually means-tested programs, such as Head Start and Title XX, tend to weaken families in that restrictive eligibility criteria may serve to discourage families from working or using services. Families may be caught in the painful dilemma of either foregoing increased wages or losing the very services that enable them to work. The effects of this bind on family morale and family fabric run counter to the intent of the programs to assist families in becoming stronger, more independent, more competent, and at ease in managing their affairs and raising their children.

Head Start has led the way in improving the liaison or linkage function of families so that they may negotiate successfully for the array of resources and services they need. The complex bureaucracies and professional services that characterize contemporary American life are not easy for many families to penetrate and present particular difficulties for families with limited education, limited self-confidence, and low expectations that their needs will be responded to. Head Start has sought to enable parents to maneuver successfully in this arena by teaching parents to cope and by making resources more accessible. As a result, Head Start children have a significantly better chance of receiving timely and adequate medical and dental care than do other low-income children. Parent education, transportation to services, and direct consultation are also provided to parents to increase their knowledge of—and ability to meet—children's physical and psychological needs.

The liaison and linkage functions of families are enhanced, too, by the information and referral services funded in many communities by Title XX. Especially as families seek child care services, information and referral (or resource and referral) centers can be of invaluable assistance not only by helping parents locate child care but by giving them tools to evaluate and monitor the services their children use (Innes, 1980).

Government programs and professionalized services tend, by nature, to raise the specter of intrusion into the lives of families and individuals. And federal child care and parent education services run the risk, of course, of intruding inappropriately. One protection against intrusion is the fact that participation in all three federal programs is voluntary. Further, ESEA Title I and Head Start are subject to the Buckley Amendment (Family Educational Rights and Privacy Act of 1974), and all three programs are subject to state confidentiality statutes concerning the release of personal information. Nonetheless, the protection of family privacy is especially problematic in social service programs. For example, the comprehensive nature of Head Start and of many Title XX programs results in many people, professionals and paraprofessionals, having access to information about the incomes, housing conditions, and personal lives of participating families. Because many enrolled families have multiple needs, pressure from school systems, welfare agencies, and health care providers to share confidential knowledge can be great. A reluctance to share such information may be viewed as uncooperative by community agencies, while a willingness to do so may be seen as intrusive and unethical by many families. Family privacy is likely to be protected best by programs in which all families, the powerful and the powerless alike, are participants. Services that single out poor families or those with special problems and needs have greater difficulty in protecting families from unwarranted intrusion because the families they serve are often less forceful in insisting on guarantees of privacy.

Child care and parent education services can protect families from intrusion not only by ensuring that participation is voluntary and by maintaining the privacy of information but also by ensuring that families have a variety of program options from which to choose. Various federal programs have sponsored a rich array of program options. However, individual families have usually been limited in the choices that are actually available in a given community. Families have access only to the ESEA Title I programs in their public schools, for example, although there may be a variety of other services offered in a school. And in Head Start, parents have no choice as to the days and hours a child may participate; although local variations such as Home Start are possible, parents who want to participate must accept whatever is available. Head Start's centralized regulations, emphasis on part-day schedules, and relatively low level of coverage render it a "love it or leave it" proposition that is usually unable to respond, for example, to the idiosyncratic or employment-related needs of families.

Like ESEA Title I and Head Start, Title XX subsidizes a fairly extensive array of child care and parent education services. There are several modes of child care (in-home, family day homes, group homes, centers), child and family resource centers, parent education projects, and so on. The sponsoring auspices vary, too, from schools to community centers to church-related organizations to parent cooperatives. While these different options exist, the actual choice given to parents is limited to those services that are available in the local community. There are usually few choices in rural areas and small communities. Even in urban areas, neighborhoods may have few centers or homes from which parents can choose, and waiting lists frequently confront eligible families.

Nonetheless, the federal child care and parent education programs of the last twenty years have demonstrated that there is an array of service modes and sponsors that government can develop and support from which families may choose. Making a wide range of choices available to families through creative organizational arrangements for services is a challenge to government at all levels.

Does the Policy Enable Parents To Do Their Job Well? The enabling of parents is the primary program and policy means to strengthen families. Policies that enable parents to make competent decisions for their families rank high on our value scale. We ask, Does the policy minimize stress by making available to parents essential resources? And does it promote shared responsibility between parents and professional service providers?

The federal child care and parent education programs, especially Head Start and Title XX, are effective in making resources available to parents to assist them in rearing their children. Head Start's role in child development and child care—as well as its provision of or arrangement for health services, parent education, transportation, and linking families with other community agencies—enable parents to accomplish the task of childrearing more easily and more capably. Title XX similarly provides care for young children, usually with emphasis on developmental programs and family services. As discussed earlier, Head Start's part-day program and means test limit its success as a support to employed parents (except when it is combined with other forms of child care to provide coverage during parents' working hours). Title XX services, while directed in part to poor working families, most often used a level of eligibility causing some parents real conflict when their wages rose to a level rendering them ineligible for service. When, as frequently happened, families lost eligibility, children were removed from a program, causing undesirable interruption of the consistent, predictable care that is so important for young children. Overall, these service programs have the potential, and frequently the effect, of enhancing and supporting parents' childrearing efforts; on the other hand, their design and the use of eligibility criteria may seriously impede this purpose.

ESEA Title I provides parents a resource in childrearing insofar as it supports educational services. By inference these services should minimize some stress on parents. For example, academic failure in childhood is clearly associated with emotional disturbance in the child and with family discord as well. The repair of academic deficiencies, however, often leads to the remediation of emotional problems. While all children with academic deficiencies are not emotionally disturbed, the repair of academic deficiencies in large populations of children should lead to some reduction in both emotional disturbance and family discord (Hobbs, 1982).

The promotion of shared responsibility between parents and professionals is a strong thread in the value fabric of this project. Many human service professionals foster families' dependency rather than contriving ways to enhance families' capability to function independently. It is important that both care giver–parent relationships and program structures be designed to enable and empower parents.

The federal service programs reviewed here have a mixed history in their approach to parent-professional relationships. ESEA Title I attempts to promote shared responsibility between parents and service providers, especially professionals, and from the beginning, parental participation has been an important feature of the program. Since 1971, for example, each local education agency receiving ESEA Title I funds has been required to establish a parent advisory council, which is involved in the planning, implementation, and evaluation of the local ESEA Title I program. Parent advisory council activities were not explicitly designated in that requirement, however, and "advisory" has been interpreted broadly. Operational characteristics have involved parents in training, classroom observation, field trips, meetings and seminars, work as volunteers and paid aides, and related duties. In 1974, the law was amended to require the establishment of parent advisory councils not only at the district level but also at the individual school level; parents were to constitute a majority of each council, and local education agencies were instructed to provide the councils with materials such as the annual evaluation report.

The 1978 ESEA Title I amendments strengthened parent involvement further by specifying that parents must participate in setting up programs, establishing objectives, and assisting in program operation. Parents must also be informed of their children's progress, and parent advisory council members must receive free copies of the Title I laws, federal and state guidelines, and auditing and evaluation reports for their area. School officials are required to train council members for effective participation in Title I programs, and the Department of Education must sponsor workshops for local school officials on how to work effectively with parents and parent advisory councils. Prior to 1978, programs that focused on the personal development of parents were usually funded from sources other than ESEA Title I. With the new amendments, training for participation is not only legitimate, but required. Quite apart from educational advantages presumed to flow from parent involvement, parents are encouraged to participate in ESEA Title I programs for children as a means of ensuring accountability for the expenditure of public funds. Although the achievement of parent participation still falls short of the requirements, there is now widespread acceptance of the desirability of parent involvement in school programs, especially in the early years. Parents appear to be effectively involved in many preschool programs and, to some extent, in first- and second-grade programs. The expansion of the community school movement, under another title of ESEA, promises to further enhance the relationship between parents and professionals in education.

In contrast to the history of ESEA Title I's sometimes labored attempts to promote shared responsibility between parents and professionals, Head Start has emphasized parent participation on an equal footing with professionals from its inception. In fact, control of the program by community members, especially parents of participating children, has been intrinsic to the Head Start design. The four designated roles for parents (paid staff or classroom volunteers, home teachers of their own children, participants in vocational training and parent education programs, and members of policy councils and parent groups) have given parents opportunities to develop their knowledge and skills and to affect the political process. Although the full realization of the goals of parent and community empowerment is debatable and the effects difficult to measure, the strongly articulated support for the program from Head Start parents attests to the success of the parent participation efforts. The translation of parent empowerment from rhetoric into reality is a Head Start hallmark and has led the way for child care and parent education programs in the welfare and education bureaucracies.

Nevertheless, Head Start has experienced the tension between providing parents opportunities to be independent, on the one hand, and creating reliance on professionals, on the other. There is some danger in Head Start's role as direct service provider that parents may become dependent on the program as the mediator or interpreter of their needs. When programs assume full responsibility for setting medical appointments, taking children to the appointments, and carrying out doctors' recommendations, the parents' role is diminished. It is often simpler and more effective in the short run to be a provider rather than a facilitator, and Head Start programs have struggled with this problem. Direct service goals concerning child development have sometimes conflicted with indirect service goals related to parent education. It is likely that the long-term goals of parental autonomy and community change will always be more difficult to attain.

Title XX child care and parent education programs were somewhat ambivalent in the area of parent-professional relationships. On the one hand, Title XX tended to reflect social work and public welfare traditions, oriented to treating deficits and pathology rather than supporting family strength through the provision of universal, preventive, and developmental services. Social welfare services and eligibility determination procedures clearly tended to place the professional in control. On the other hand, Title XX child care was delivered primarily through the group care network that evolved from the day nurseries of the late 1800s, and their tradition of supporting working parents—who were not viewed as having individual pathology—persists to some extent. Parent participation, through parent advisory councils and parental access to children's classrooms, is detailed in the provisions of FIDCR and was implemented in many Title XX programs in spite of the fact that the provisions of FIDCR were not mandated. The Title XX planning process, which established citizen participation for the purposes of program planning and fiscal accountability, is a further means through which Title XX has given parents the opportunity to share responsibility with service providers. Thus, even in the public welfare bureaucracy, there has been some effort to empower parents.

Does the Policy Enhance Individual Development and Protect the Rights of Individual Family Members? While strong communities and families have salutary effects on individuals, it is important to ascertain the effects of child care and parent education policies per se on individual family members. Thus, the value analysis asks, Does the policy enhance individual opportunities for development of competence and self-realization? Does it protect individual members of the family from abuse and severe neglect?

Federal child care and parent education policies and programs have emphasized the development of individual competence for a particular segment of the population, those whose economic circumstances make them particularly in need of publicly supported services. Head Start and Title XX provide services to the children of poor families, and ESEA Title I incorporates poverty as a criterion for schools' eligibility for federal funds. The programs deal with children's academic deficiencies in the case of ESEA Title I and with a broad range of social and developmental competencies and needs in the case of Head Start and Title XX. Head Start and Title XX also provide a

range of services and opportunities for the individual development of the parents through participation in planning and developing programs. Head Start programs, in fact, have coordinated
their efforts with legal assistance agencies, parent and child advocacy groups, family planning clinics, Comprehensive Employment and Training Act (CETA) programs, and other agencies
capable of ensuring that individual rights to safety, security, and
equitable access to resources are met. Overall, there would appear to be adequate attention in these programs to the development of individuals and to individuals' rights.

A recurrent theme of this project, however, is the community's interest in the optimal development of *all* children and
adults. Each community member has the right to expect that
other people's children will be schooled, intelligent, and capable. A diversity of academic and vocational competencies for
each individual, regardless of economic circumstances, is socially wise and humane. Thus, the criterion of poverty seems a narrow ground on which to identify those who will receive the
benefits of national programs directed to individual development. The rights of individuals who are financially needy, but
who do not quality for services within the state and federal income criteria, may be particularly abridged by current federal
child care and parent education service policy.

Protection of individual family members from abuse and
severe neglect is a minimum expectation of child care and parent education programs, and both Head Start and Title XX
make provisions for child protection services. Child protection
traditionally is a function of public social service agencies, and
indeed Title XX explicitly included the prevention of abuse and
neglect as one of the five goals to which federally funded services could be directed. Increasingly, child care services have
been targeted to children in danger of abuse and neglect, especially as the total funds available have been reduced. Thus, children in need of public protection are likely to continue to be
served by Title XX, even if retrenchment causes services to be
withdrawn from others. Head Start has also played a role in the
identification of child abuse and neglect through parent educa-

tion programs and in-service staff training. Zigler (1978), in fact, declared that prevention of child abuse should be a major goal of Head Start in the next decade.

Conclusions

A great deal of experience in government support of child care and parent education services has accumulated over the past two decades. Although three major direct service programs have been developed and implemented during that time, we still have neither a national child care and parent education policy nor a coordinated or comprehensive services system. Rather, the federal government has supported a variety of programs, directed primarily to the goals of compensating for poor children's academic deficiencies, providing comprehensive services to poor families and children to enhance children's development and empower their families, and enabling poor families to become financially self-sufficient. The services through which these goals have been expressed are highly diverse and have incorporated some experimentation with various program models and organizational sponsors. Several lessons may be drawn from this national experience that suggest directions for future policy.

While the service modes and sponsors have been diverse, a common element in the programs is that they have been intended to support rather than supplant parents in their childrearing functions. Parent participation in all phases of programming—including broad policy making, program design, and program implementation—is a principle that has become embedded in these child care and parent education services. Although implementation of the principle of shared responsibility between parents and professionals has been imperfect, its importance is widely appreciated by policy makers, parents, and professionals alike. The federal, state, and local bureaucracies—public welfare, education, and Head Start—and the professional disciplines—teachers, social workers, and child development specialists—now share a common interest in parents' participation in child-oriented services. It is especially noteworthy that the programs for children administered through the public schools (ESEA Title I

and one third of the Head Start programs) share this adherence
to principles of parent participation. It is difficult to envision a
return to full professional control of child and family services,
although efforts to protect and enhance the gains of parent-
consumers must continue. The fearful specter of usurpation of
parental responsibility for childrearing raised in the mid 1970s
campaign against the Mondale-Brademas bill is belied by the national experience in developing diverse modes of care that embody deepening respect for parents.

Throughout our review of federal child care and parent
education programs, we have observed that national efforts to
provide services have been deficit-oriented. Poverty and academic deficiency have been the targets of federal intervention.
The result has been a two-tiered system, one tier consisting of
services for the poor funded through the categorical (largely
service) programs and the other tier consisting of benefits for
upper-income families, primarily through the tax system (see
Chapter Five). Families with incomes in the $10,000 to $20,000
range, the "working poor," receive few, if any, benefits. In our
view, considerations of equity, as well as the national interest in
building a sense of community, dictate a focus on *all* children.
Means-tested programs are inherently divisive, denying services
to families and children who can profit from them and inevi-
tably creating harmful incentives for families either to reduce
employment or to forgo child development services. Services
that are restricted to the poor are insufficient in the long run to
fulfill a sense of national and local community and fail to move
the nation toward repairing the fissures that separate families
along lines of income and competence.

Both the strengths and deficiencies of the three federal
service programs are instructive. From Title XX, we have
learned that welfare-based programs can, in spite of their narrowly defined purposes, provide high-quality child development
and family-oriented services. On the other hand, the public assistance identification makes it unlikely that universal child and
family programs can develop in the public welfare context. Professional orientation toward a pathology and deficit outlook, as
well as political realities, militate against the development of a

universally available program of preventive and supportive services for families and children within the welfare purview.

Head Start has demonstrated the effectiveness of comprehensive services for poor families and children and has been the catalyst for developing highly diversified modes of care and services. However, the Head Start pattern of intergovernmental relationships, in which administrative and funding lines run directly from the federal government to local community groups and community action agencies, presents limitations for mounting a national, universally available program for children and families. Bypassing state and local officials has sometimes had the virtue of enabling hitherto unserved and underserved populations, especially minority groups, to gain direct access to federal funds. On the other hand, the growing strength of state and local governments and the changes nationally since the early 1960s in protection of minority rights suggest that the capacity of state and local governments to administer child and family programs with wisdom and fairness may have improved.

ESEA Title I has demonstrated the capability of the public schools to channel federal resources successfully into direct educational services in the interests of raising children's academic achievement. The financial cost has been relatively low, and the public school bureaucracies have demonstrated in ESEA Title I the capability to target services to children who have special needs through means tests that have relatively little stigma for individual children and families. Clearly the federal presence in ESEA Title I has forced public schools to wrestle with establishing ways to include parents in school programs, and the involvement and participation of parents in Title I programs represent a significant achievement for the public schools. Directing programs to children with special needs and opening the planning and implementation of programs to parents have not been simple undertakings for the school bureaucracy. However, the ESEA Title I programs have demonstrated the growing capacity of state and local school agencies to succeed in incorporating these essential features in their programs for young children.

Overall, our national experience with the provision of child care and parent education services convinces us that of the five major policy directions examined in the last two chapters, the service provision option comes closest to meeting the values criteria we adopted as being most significant in the nurturance of communities, families, and individual family members. While three of the other major options—developing a national family policy, providing flexibility for families, and providing resources for families—have varied strengths and merits, none meets as many of the values criteria as fully as does the service option. We certainly do not recommend abandoning the other options (save for the Do-nothing position); we do recommend that they take a secondary or complementary place in relation to the provision of services.

If we focus on a service option as the national policy direction of primary importance, we clearly have several additional issues to consider, most of which relate to the potential implementation of such an option on a more comprehensive and integrated basis. One of the major lessons to be derived from our national experience with service provision in the area of child care and parent education is that the focus of responsibility for the implementation of services is quite important. Some of the significant differences in the accomplishments of the three major service programs (ESEA Title I, Head Start, and Title XX) have emerged from the organizational structure and bureaucracies charged with their implementation. Organizational structure is certainly not the only influence on program content and quality, but it does play a major role in determining what is possible and probable within any service program.

In the next chapter, we turn to a consideration of the organizational structures adopted in the course of developing two major and significant statewide programs of child care and parent education. We delve into these programs not only for the information they provide concerning organizational structures well suited to the provision of these services but also for the information that may be gleaned about the processes and purposes observed when the primary initiator of service provision is not the federal government but the states.

SEVEN

ΟΙΟΙΟΙΟΙΟΙΟΙΟΙΟΙΟΙΟΙΟΙΟΙΟΙΟΙΟΙΟΙΟΙΟΙΟΙΟΙΟΙΟ

Exemplary
State Programs

As many who advocate a less centralized approach to human services would argue, the federal government is certainly not the only potential organizer and supervisor of services that support families and children. Although the federal government's role over the last two decades has been critical in our national response to the needs of families (witness, for example, the extent and impact of services provided by ESEA Title I, Head Start, and Title XX), *state* governments have also been active in providing services that meet the needs of children and families.

To survey all the states for initiation and provision of service would clearly be a massive undertaking, as there are up to fifty distinct "stories" that might emerge (assuming only one significant effort per state, a modest estimate at best). Perhaps even more useful, however, is careful descriptive analysis of selected exemplary state efforts, and this is the course we have chosen. We have been able to do this in no small measure because the programs undertaken by two states, California and Minnesota, emerged as particularly consistent with our interests in the family services of child care and parent education and as remarkably consistent with many of our project's values as explicated throughout this volume.

236

Before turning to detailed examination of the programs, it is important to note that the organizational structure used by both states is the public education system. In combination with our earlier observation that all ESEA Title I early childhood services and some Head Start programs are offered through the schools, this fact gave us cause to examine the broader experience in public school provision of services as a means of understanding more fully California's and Minnesota's rationales for giving the state education system major organizational roles in the programs.

The Public Schools in Child Care and Parent Education

That the public schools have been heavily involved in various programs of child care and parent education for many decades was established in Chapter Four and emphasized again in Chapter Six in light of major federal programs. Although early childhood programs evolved historically from disparate approaches—kindergartens in public schools as a means of social reform, child care as welfare for poor families, and nursery schools as educational programs for healthy families (see, for example, Grubb and Lazerson, 1977)—all now share significant characteristics. Each has been heavily influenced by the early intervention programs implemented and evaluated in the last two decades. Teachers and administrators in all programs now receive similar training in colleges and universities. Many would argue that the old distinctions are historic and artificial, that good contemporary early childhood programs, under whatever name, are more alike than different. Child care programs have educational components; many nursery school programs are full-day and in fact provide child care; and public kindergarten and preschool programs, focusing on academic readiness but also including group interaction and play, provide child care to an extent not frequently acknowledged. Parent education and parent involvement are components of each of these types of programs in varying degrees.

Both the states and the federal government have taken initiative in providing child care and parent education in the schools under diverse arrangements. Education has been the traditional domain of the states and local communities, and some states already have considerable experience in child care, preschool, education for parenthood, and parent education. At the same time, and especially since the 1960s, a broad range of federal initiatives has stimulated school sponsorship of child care and parent education, albeit indirectly or as one of several possible sponsorship arrangements. Federally funded programs—such as Head Start, ESEA, Title XX, and the Education for All Handicapped Children Act—have had multiple purposes, including preparation of young children for school entry, assistance to families in achieving economic self-support, and education of handicapped children. These objectives have been pursued in a variety of settings, of which public education is just one. The extent to which these programs are sponsored by public schools varies by program, and within programs by state. As we have seen, some Head Start programs are sponsored by public schools and almost all ESEA Title I programs are in public schools. Even service provision through Title XX varied considerably; for example, in Atlanta, 64 percent of Title XX children received child care through programs administered by the public schools (Levine, 1978), although in most communities Title XX services were provided under nonschool auspices. Public schools are providing early education opportunities for handicapped children in increasing numbers and are eligible for federal preschool incentive grants. Thus, although there is no explicit federal policy promoting child care through the public schools per se, several federally funded programs do in fact provide care in schools as well as in other places. Each of these programs involves, to a greater or lesser degree, parent education. Although parent education was rarely a primary purpose in these programs, it could and did take place in many.

Public and private nursery schools and kindergartens already provide important amounts of child care for three- to five-year-old children, although statistics on child care frequently do not include these important sources, as we noted in Chapter Four. Preprimary programs, which include nursery schools and kindergartens, enroll more than half of the children eligible by age, and the total substantially exceeds the number of children in all other types of formal, out-of-home child care arrangements. The fact that census data show 25 percent of the three-year-olds, 43 percent of the four-year-olds, and 82 percent of the five-year-olds in school in 1978 bears repeating. Two thirds of these preprimary programs were part-time; one third provided care for a full day (Plisko, 1980).

Further, the trend of enrollments in preprimary school programs is steadily upward, as shown in Table 9. The growth in

Table 9. Preprimary School Enrollment: October 1965–October 1980 (in Thousands).

| | Children Enrolled in Nursery Schools and Kindergarten | | | | | |
| | Children Enrolled in Nursery Schools | | | Children Enrolled in Kindergarten | | |
Year	Total	Public School	Private School	Total	Public School	Private School
1965	520	127	393	3,057	2,439	618
1966	688	215	473	3,115	2,527	588
1967	714	230	484	3,313	2,678	635
1968	816	262	554	3,268	2,709	559
1969	860	245	615	3,276	2,682	594
1970	1,096	333	763	3,183	2,647	536
1971	1,066	317	749	3,263	2,689	574
1972	1,283	402	881	3,135	2,636	499
1973	1,324	400	924	3,075	2,582	493
1974	1,607	423	1,184	3,252	2,726	526
1975	1,748	574	1,174	3,393	2,851	542
1976	1,526	476	1,050	3,490	2,962	528
1977	1,618	562	1,056	3,191	2,665	526
1978	1,824	587	1,237	2,989	2,493	496
1979	1,869	636	1,233	3,025	2,593	432
1980	1,987	633	1,354	3,176	2,690	486

Source: U.S. Department of Commerce, Bureau of the Census, 1975b, Table 1; 1981, Table 1.

nursery school enrollment corresponds with legislative interest in early child development, which began in the 1960s: between 1965 and 1970, nursery school enrollment doubled, and in the next decade it doubled again. This rapid increase in enrollment, which occurred despite a decline in the number of births beginning in the early 1960s, means that the *proportion* of all young children enrolled in nursery schools has increased dramatically, from 11 percent of three- and four-year-old children in 1965 to 37 percent in 1980 according to census data. Although nursery school enrollment is predominantly in the private sector, three out of ten children are enrolled in public nursery schools, and this proportion has remained more or less constant over the last fifteen years. In 1980, there were 1,354,000 young children enrolled in private nursery schools and 633,000 children enrolled in public nursery schools. Kindergarten enrollment, relatively stable over the last fifteen years, is overwhelmingly in public school programs.

Data on three- and four-year-olds, for whom preprimary school programs are not universally available, are especially interesting. Participation rates for this group have increased over the last decade for children of both working and nonworking mothers. Children are more likely to be enrolled if their mothers are working, just as they are more likely to be enrolled in full-day programs if their mothers are working. But the difference in enrollment rates for four-year-old children of working and nonworking mothers is surprisingly little: 45 percent compared with 42 percent in 1978. Enrollment was more strongly related to education of the household head than to employment status of the mother (Plisko, 1980), suggesting that nursery school is simply an experience that families want for their children. In any event, for the 2.2 million three- to five-year-old children whose mothers are employed and who are enrolled in preprimary programs—and to a lesser extent, for the 2.9 million enrolled children whose mothers are not in the labor force (Plisko, 1980)—the programs are providing child care as well as educational enrichment.

It can be argued that expansion of programs in the public schools is a natural extension of the already existing framework of nursery school, public preschool, and kindergarten, including, of course, the present focus in many on parent involvement and participation. There are a number of potential advantages of such an expansion: Programs organized through the schools would reduce the fragmentation and duplication of services by

concentrating them within one organizational entity; they
would build on the strengths of existing organizational arrangements, rather than creating new ones; they would rationalize
the allocation of resources; they could well ensure equity by
distributing services uniformly and providing open access to
services; they could contribute to the continuity of care, parent
education, and related services; they could provide a means for
improving the capabilities of care givers and parent educators;
and they could improve accountability by providing for parent
and community participation. There are potential disadvantages
to providing child care and parent education through the
schools. Implementing programs through the schools, it is sometimes argued, would introduce rigidity into child care and possibly into parent education and would undermine the rich diversity that currently exists; it would overburden the public school
system by grafting onto it a new social program; it would stifle
innovation and overemphasize narrow academic preparation; it
would introduce a system of teacher certification and placement
that is sometimes self-serving and has in the past discriminated
against minorities; it would exclude parent and community involvement; and it would be unlikely to promote community
development goals for poor, disenfranchised, and underserved
populations.

All of these arguments, of course, bear at least some grain
of truth; witness the American Federation of Teachers' (1976)
specification of changes (discussed in Chapter Four) that would
be needed in many schools if child care were to be implemented
through the public school system. Robinson and others' (1979)
discussion certainly suggests that the centralization of sponsorship in early childhood programs in an institution such as the
public schools would be optimal if the centralization—critical in
the encouragement of planning, transmission of information
and resources, and guarantee of a basic level of quality—were
complemented by the qualities of decentralization that focus on
valuing consumer (parent) involvement, encouraging creativity,
and responding to local needs. In keeping with these observations, the National Association of Early Childhood Specialists in
State Departments of Education (1978) suggested that state

education agencies, which already provide certain common services to local school districts, are in a position to extend services
to young children. Noting that the schools can provide access
for all children, can coordinate existing services, and can provide support and referral services to preschool children as they
are now doing for school-age children, the association also
stressed the need for programs that are flexible and responsive
to the developmental levels of young children, so that a "back-
to-the-basics" emphasis on skill development in reading and
mathematics is not thrust downward to preschool programs.

Indeed, the need for flexibility and variety is a theme
that is repeated in all the literature examining the possibility of
public school sponsorship of some family services. The evidence
to date indicates that programs through the public schools do
not all look alike. The local programs reviewed by Levine
(1978) are diverse in their goals, program content, and setting.
Indeed, his study revealed a rich variety of arrangements, including a large program operated by a school district (Oakland
Children's Centers), an after-school program run by parents
(Brookline Extended Day Program), a comprehensive child care
program financed primarily with Title XX funds (Atlanta), an
education-for-parenthood project involving a partnership between the schools and a nonprofit agency (Austin), and family
daycare in two school districts in South Carolina. This diversity
is also found *within* state programs. In Minnesota, for example,
parent education programs sponsored by the schools are diverse
in programmatic approach and institutional base.

This diversity in school-based child care and parent education programs diminishes the possibility of generalizing about
schools. Clearly, we need to know more about such issues as
program objectives, access, personnel practices, costs, and parent involvement. For example, the often expressed concern that
schools will stress cognitive development over other child development goals does not appear as yet to have been borne out.
Levine (1978, p. 64) did find a strong emphasis in Atlanta on
"using daycare as a means of early intervention and on achieving and measuring educational objectives," but there is no com-
compelling evidence that this is always the case. In California's

preschool program (which is different from the child care program described later in this chapter), the objectives are broad,
focused on the provision of part-day educational programs that
include services related to educational development, health,
family social needs, nutrition, parent education, parent participation, and staff development. Directors of the preschool programs, when questioned about goals, gave highest priority to
three: developing a child's sense of self-worth, providing a wide
range of experience that will prepare children for school, and
helping children learn to handle their emotions and consider the
feelings of others (California State Department of Education,
1980). All are broad child development goals, rather than the
more narrowly construed academic achievement goals often presumed and feared to be part and parcel of public school involvement in early childhood programs.

It is unfortunate that much of the sponsorship debate in
child care and parent education has been cast in either-or terms
—whether or not the public schools should be *the* prime providers of service. In practice, however, schools are participants in a
variety of service provision arrangements. Perhaps the debate
should be recast in terms of cooperative arrangements between
public schools and other types of providers. Having systematically examined the provision of child care under public school
sponsorship, Levine (1978, p. 4) concluded that "it would seem
unwise to assume categorically that the schools (or any other
agency) are the best possible sponsor or provider of daycare; it
would seem equally unwise for national policy to exclude the
schools as a potential provider of daycare." Arrangements providing for cooperative activity are perhaps one means of addressing the observation by LaCrosse (1977, p. 48), of the
Education Commission of the States Early Childhood Project,
that "when one looks at the obvious advantages of public
schools, it suddenly becomes a challenge to overcome the barriers."

Taking into account some of this rich background of discussion and experience in public school involvement with educationally oriented services for young children and their families, we look at two states—California and Minnesota—which

have elected to develop and implement comprehensive service programs largely through state public education agencies. We review both of these programs in some detail in the next two sections. We have chosen to do this for several reasons, but primarily because it is becoming clear that the development of new and high-quality human services throughout the country often comes from key states serving as models for other states, a kind of state-to-state spread of effect (Lynn, 1980). This does not, of course, negate a potentially fruitful role for the federal government in child care and parent education. Supporters of a federal role, in fact, might read what follows with an eye toward ascertaining how the federal government can encourage and support efforts like California's and Minnesota's in other states.

California: A State Program in Child Care

California's program in child care and development services, which has evolved over the last forty years, offers an interesting model for other states. We examine this diverse system in some detail because California has grappled with several difficult issues: identification of needed services; diversity in program sponsorship and mode of care; interagency coordination; regulation and licensing; responsiveness to ethnic diversity; socioeconomic integration; and cost containment.

Subsidized child care in California is complex. The child care system, reformulated by legislation enacted in 1980, builds upon the long experience of existing programs, recent experiments, and the recommendations of commissions, citizens' groups, and other evaluation efforts. Perhaps no other state has kept such detailed records of its efforts in child development, and at considerable cost. In general, the child care system includes among its purposes the provision of a coordinated and cost-effective system of child care services that allows parents to choose from among many types of care. Thus, the "system" implies a broad range of services under diverse auspices.

California provides child care resource and referral services to *all* families and providers, but subsidized child care services *only* to working parents with low and moderate incomes or to children in need of protective services. The limitation of subsidized care to working parents reflects the origin of the state's early child care programs, begun during World War II with Lanham Act funds to meet wartime needs for women in the labor force. Having placed its child care centers administratively in the Department of Public Instruction, California was one of the few states to continue the centers after the war. The introduction of a means test and sliding fee scale in 1947, however, substantially changed the composition of families using the centers.

The child care centers continued to operate with year-to-year funding until 1957, when they became a permanent part of the state's educational system. "Their goals were mixed, combining elements of educational development with a welfare ideology arguing that the centers kept families economically viable by allowing parents (especially single mothers) to work" (Grubb and Lazerson, 1977, p. 15). Although the centers were placed in the state educational system, only a few local districts contributed funds to their operation (the basic funding formula was composed of two thirds state payments and one third parent fees), and the centers functioned more or less independently of the local school districts in which they were located. In the 1960s, federal education funds became available to the centers. They were renamed *children's centers,* and the state legislature made more explicit their instructional goals. By 1974, the children's centers served about 30,000 children and represented about 62 percent of the publicly subsidized child care in the state (Grubb and Lazerson, 1977).

Although the children's centers in the public schools were the largest and most important stream of child care, other programs and means of subsidizing child care were developed concurrently. County welfare departments, for example, had begun funding centers with federal funds (Title IV-A of the Social Security Act and later Title XX), but in 1970, authority for the programs was transferred to the Department of Education. This is significant because in most other states, Title XX–funded programs were administered by public welfare departments. In the early 1970s, the Department of Education began to contract with community-based groups for the provision of federally funded child care. In a further development, the Alternative Child Care Program (ACCP) was authorized in 1976 and had as its explicit goal the exploration of alternatives for the provision of child care. After a four-year period of experimentation and evaluation, ACCP recommendations were incorporated into the general child care program.

Thus, by 1981, a diverse array of child care programs was in place throughout the state. They are described here in some detail in part to illustrate our finding that all programs under a state education agency need not look alike.

Child Care and Development Services. Overall, the California State Department of Education supports a wide variety of child care and development services. General child development programs constitute the largest single category and are now operated on a contractual basis at the local level by both public and private agencies, such as school districts, offices of county superintendents of schools, county welfare departments, cities, nonprofit organizations, and private proprietary agencies. In addition, there are targeted programs such as migrant child care, campus child care, school-age parenting and infant development programs for high school students, alternative payment programs that provide payments to providers selected by the family, resource and referral programs, programs for handicapped children, and, most recently, a pilot project for intergenerational child care. Families are eligible for child care services under two conditions. First, they must be low income; for example, they must receive income through Aid to Families with Dependent Children (AFDC), Supplemental Security Income (SSI), or the State Supplemental Program, or they must earn less than 84 percent of median income. Second, the parents must be working, seeking employment, in training, or incapacitated. Top priority is given to children who are at risk of abuse or neglect, and second priority is given to children of families in which the parents are working.

A separate state preschool program provides part-day educational programs for three- and four-year-olds. Eligibility for this program is based on the needs of children in low-income families rather than the needs of parents for support in employment or training.

In addition to child care and education programs subsidized by the Department of Education, the state provides other family subsidies (for example, the AFDC income disregard for child care and funding for protective services), some of which are administered through the State Department of Social Services. State income tax credits not to exceed $120 per family are also available to working families. Finally, there are Head Start and Home Start programs, funded by the U.S. Department of Health and Human Services and operated by local community agencies.

Although state efforts are thus diverse, the focus of our inquiry is on programs administered by the State Office of Child Development, in the State Department of Education. We have looked particularly at efforts in direct child care services, alternative payment programs, and resource and referral services.

Although in the early years the largest portion of direct child care was housed in the public schools, child care in California today is characterized by considerable diversity, both in sponsorship (public and private) and type of care (center, family day home, and in-home). By 1979, programs administered by school districts or county offices of education represented 37 percent of all sponsoring agencies and provided 59 percent of all subsidized child care in the state, while other agencies (private, for-profit; private, nonprofit; colleges; and other public agencies) represented 63 percent of the sponsoring agencies and provided 41 percent of all subsidized care. Although 90 percent of the care was provided in centers, a small but growing portion was provided in family day homes by both public and private agencies (California State Department of Education, 1980).

This diverse pattern emerged as the result of a variety of policy initiatives involving both experimentation and evaluation. One of the most important was the Alternative Child Care Program.

The Alternative Child Care Program (ACCP). Authorized in 1976, ACCP was intended to test the cost-reducing features

248   Strengthening Families

of various child care delivery modes, promote parental choice, address unmet geographical needs, encourage community-level coordination, and develop replicable programs. To serve these purposes, $10 million was appropriated to subsidize four different kinds of programs related to child care: center-based care for innovative programs; family daycare associations and networks (which had previously received very little state funding); a vendor-voucher payment program providing subsidies to parents so that they could choose from an array of child care programs; and resource and referral services for all parents, regardless of income.

The entire program was evaluated to an extent remarkable for a state program. The Governor's Advisory Committee on Child Development Programs (GAC) reported on the program after its first year of operation and again at the conclusion of the four-year experiment (Governor's Advisory Committee on Child Development Programs, 1977, 1981). An outside comparative evaluation was conducted by Abt Associates based on information collected in 1978 (Warner, 1979). Additional data collected in March 1979 and extensive discussions of the program were included in the State Department of Education's annual report for 1978-1979 (California State Department of Education, 1980). There is thus a great deal of data on which to draw in assessing the implementation and effectiveness of the four alternative approaches included in ACCP.

The ACCP center-based programs provided care whose quality was comparable to other subsidized centers in terms of child ratios, educational background of the staff, and other such factors. ACCP programs were able to offer care at somewhat lower costs, however, primarily because of lower care giver salaries and the ability of the programs to draw upon other financial resources within their communities. ACCP centers were more likely than other subsidized centers to be run by private, nonprofit organizations (California State Department of Education, 1980; Warner, 1979); contrary to expectations, the ACCP center-based programs did not attract a significant number of proprietary centers. The latter centers apparently found it easier to seek funding through the vendor-voucher component of the ACCP program (Governor's Advisory Committee on Child Development Programs, 1981).

The ACCP efforts in family daycare resulted in a significant expansion of that form of service, although admittedly from a small base. By 1979, there were approximately 3,800 children in family day homes served through ACCP (including both the family day home program and the vendor-voucher program), as compared with the 2,100 children served in family day homes subsidized by other programs. In all, family daycare homes were found to serve about 10 percent of all children in subsidized care and to provide about 25 percent of the subsidized care for infants and toddlers under the age of two (California State Department of Education, 1980). Family day homes in both ACCP and other subsidized systems served predominantly minority populations. Cost differences between ACCP and other systems were not found to be significant (Warner, 1979). Although ACCP envisioned the use of satellite systems—family daycare linked to children's centers—such systems did not develop as fully as had been anticipated (Governor's Advisory Committee on Child Development Programs, 1981).

The ACCP vendor-voucher payment program distributed public subsidies to vendor agencies, which did not provide services directly, but helped eligible families place their children with providers who met the families' needs and preferences. The program drew upon the experience of the Santa Clara County pilot project for vouchers (described in Chapter Five as part of the resources option). Parent fees were set on a sliding scale according to the same criteria as other subsidized care programs in California. The Governor's Advisory Committee on Child Development Programs (1981, p. 10) found that the vendor-voucher program fulfilled "the hopes for promoting parental choice, for addressing unmet geographic needs, and for including both family daycare homes and proprietary centers." Moreover, because fees were set in the marketplace and were affordable to middle-class parents, the programs "promoted economic integration when they included subsidized children" (p. 10). Some vendor agencies paid the subsidy directly to the families—as in a voucher—while others made direct payments to the pro-

viders selected by parents. The vendor payment programs were
the least costly (per child hour) to provide, but in contrast to
the ACCP center-based programs, they did not result in the
levering of additional community resources for child care (Warner, 1979).

A strength of the vendor-voucher program was that many
of the vendor agencies allowed the subsidy to follow the child,
so that a child could move, for example, from a family daycare
program to a center program as needs changed. There were also
some drawbacks to the program, however. Parents' choice of
child care providers was limited to those willing to accept payment within the vendor rate scale, typically lower than the cost
for private center care, and to programs with which the vendor
agencies had agreements. Some vendor agencies only offered
family day home care, for example, while others offered only
center care. In general, however, the vendor-voucher program,
which served about 5,000 children, allowed an expansion of care
for children, particularly groups previously underserved (for
example, infants and school-age children), and expanded availability of family day home care. The children served by the
vendor-voucher program were similar to children served by other California programs: They were largely from income-eligible
families headed by a single parent. However, ethnic minorities
represented only 27 percent of the children subsidized by the
vendor-voucher program, as compared with 63 percent of children in all subsidized programs (California State Department of
Education, 1980).

In contrast to other ACCP services, the resource and referral program provided services to *all* families, regardless of
income. In a sample month, March 1979, thirty-seven resource
and referral agencies in twenty-four counties provided services
to more than 9,500 families (California State Department of
Education, 1980). Families received an average of 4.2 referrals,
usually within one day of a request for information. In addition
to providing referrals for child care, the agencies provided other
services. For example, in 1978, 75 percent of the agencies reported making referrals to parents for other social services, 85
percent published newsletters for providers, 30 percent distrib-

uted newsletters to parents, and 95 percent provided technical assistance and in-service training to family daycare providers (Warner, 1979). Most of the agencies were operated by private organizations, although some were operated by school districts. The agencies provided referrals to those seeking placement for infants (45 percent), preschoolers (39 percent), and school-age children (16 percent) (California State Department of Education, 1980). Many agencies indicated that they followed up their referrals by contacting parents after a period of time.

Equally important were the services made available by the resource and referral agencies to child care providers, such as workshops (on child abuse, crisis intervention, child nutrition, and so on) and technical assistance in preparing funding applications, meeting licensing requirements, developing accounting and budgeting procedures, and designing evaluation plans (California State Department of Education, 1980). Thus, the Governor's Advisory Committee on Child Development Programs (1981, p. 12) concluded that "an unexpected product of these programs was their ability to promote the growth of care through the assistance they gave to persons who wanted to enter the child care field." Moreover, by keeping records of requests for care and requests by providers for information, the agencies became a source of information on unmet needs in specific communities.

In large measure, California's child care legislation of 1980 incorporated ACCP's innovations. Although the cost-reducing features are debatable, ACCP programs have proved to be viable alternatives for achieving the other ACCP objectives. The center-based and family day home care components of ACCP are now part of the general child development programs, and there is explicit legislative intent to have care available through many kinds of agencies. Under the vendor-voucher payment program, now called the alternative payment program, the State Office of Child Development contracts with agencies to provide subsidies directly to certified providers of the parents' selection; subsidies may follow families from one provider to another. This alternative payment program represents 6.3 percent of the total $205 million state budget for child care and development services (an additional 3 percent of the budget is allocated for vendor-style care administered by county welfare departments). Resource and referral programs are now recognized as a priority for every area of the state and receive $4.6 million annually (funding has increased steadily since the first year of the program). They are a permanent part of the child care system and now serve about 90 percent of the population.

ACCP was not the only impetus behind the 1980 legislation, however. The legislation also reflects the recommendations of the Commission on Child Development appointed by Superintendent Wilson Riles and the recommendations of the Governor's Advisory Committee on Child Development Programs (1978). We turn now to some of the issues addressed in these reports: administration, regulation, and licensing; qualifications and compensation of care givers; needs assessment, funding, and expansion; and the roles of citizens and parents. For the most part, these are the critical issues that any state must address in developing a child care program.

Administration, Licensing, and Regulation. Allocation of responsibility for providing child care and development services in the Department of Education has removed, to some extent, the welfare taint that sometimes plagues programs lodged in public welfare agencies. Of equal importance is the fact that this assignment of administrative responsibility has not resulted in education's "capture" of child care and development programs. In 1974, Superintendent Wilson Riles established an Office of Child Development (OCD) within the Department of Education to administer the programs (they had previously been the responsibility of elementary education). This move emphasized the department's commitment to the program and was seen as facilitating the development of diverse programming. Located within the department's administrative offices, the OCD performs the functions of program development, contracting, field service, licensing, and payment. In practice, however, there is still some overlap between education and welfare: responsibility for licensing is shared by the two agencies, and programs, with the exception of resource and referral, are targeted to low-income families who are the traditional clientele of public welfare departments.

Licensing has been one of the most contentious aspects of child care in California, as it has been in the country at large. At least four licensing issues have been addressed during the last five years: the inadequacy of resources to undertake licensing; the division of responsibility for licensing between the Department of Social Services and the Department of Education; the lack of separation of the functions of licensing and technical assistance in the Department of Education; and the application of different licensing standards to programs operated with different funding sources.

Inadequate resources for licensing family day homes in particular had resulted for some time in shifting responsibilities between county welfare departments and the state counterpart, with resultant long delays for providers seeking licensing. In 1981, when the governor proposed deregulation of family day-care, the Governor's Advisory Committee on Child Development Programs (1981) proposed instead a system of registration, then being tested on a pilot basis in three counties; it also advocated the formulation of less complex and burdensome licensing procedures for family day homes. A compromise agreement called for a new system with a simplified application process for family day homes, initial certification by the state for three years, and renewals granted with visits undertaken on a random basis. A major objective of the program was the encouragement of licensing in family day homes. Contrary to the recommendation of the Governor's Advisory Committee, responsibility for licensing remained divided between the Department of Social Services, which licenses all center and family day home programs not under contract with the State Department of Education, and the State Department of Education, which licenses all care programs that it subsidizes. (The Governor's Advisory Committee had recommended the creation of a single and separate Office of Child Care Facilities Licensing.)

Another matter of concern in this area is separation of licensing from the provision of technical assistance. The Governor's Advisory Committee (1981, p. 7) recommended such a step repeatedly, asserting that licensing by the Department of Education conflicts with its "prime functions . . . the provision of technical assistance, support, advice, and program development to the programs which it funds." Creation of a new licensing and compliance unit within the Office of Child Development, separate from the six regional consultant services offices, partially resolved the dilemma.

Until recently, there were three separate licensing standards in the state. Programs receiving federal funds were governed by federal regulations; programs subsidized by state funds were governed by state regulations (referred to as Title 5); and nonsubsidized child care was regulated by yet a different set of state regulations (referred to as Title 22). The three sets of regulations differed principally in their adult-child ratios (one to five, one to eight, and one to twelve, respectively). The federal regulations no longer apply, since in 1981 California completed a process, begun in the mid 1970s, of replacing (buying out) federal Title XX funds for child care with state funds. California chose to buy out Title XX to achieve more flexibility in staffing ratios and to eliminate the need for a complex interagency agreement between the Department of Education (responsible for the subsidized programs) and the Department of Social Services (the single state agency responsible for Title XX funds). Child care advocates supported the buy-out believing, correctly, that services would fare better under full state funding in view of federal budget cuts.

Presently, thus, there are two set of regulations in the state, one for subsidized programs and one for nonsubsidized programs. However, it is important to note that private centers or daycare homes, governed by the less stringent Title 22 regulations, may accept some subsidized children. The intent of this provision is to facilitate the integration of subsidized and nonsubsidized children.

Care Giver Qualifications and Compensation. The issues of care giver qualifications and compensation are not easily resolved in the context of limited resources. The primary difficulty lies in balancing the need for adequate compensation with the need to keep costs down so that care is affordable. For some time, California has required teachers in child development programs to hold a child development permit or a teaching credential issued by the State Commission for Teacher Preparation and

Licensing. Recently added was a requirement that persons holding a teaching credential have, in addition, either twelve units of specific training in early childhood education or at least two years of experience in child care and development programs. The state does not require postsecondary education for aides or assistant teachers, although teachers and aides alike must have a health examination. The intent is to balance the need for training in child development with the need for care givers who are warm, affectionate, and nurturing and who reflect the multicultural and diverse linguistic backgrounds of the children enrolled. Accordingly, the Commission to Formulate a State Plan for Child Care and Development Services in California (1978) recommended the recruitment of ethnic minorities who would serve as positive role models reflecting the children's language and cultural values.

The cost of child care is largely dependent on personnel costs, since about 80 percent of most budgets is for staff. Agencies receiving public funds must pay at least minimum wage. However, this requirement does not apply to self-employed persons, such as providers of family daycare, many of whom do not earn minimum wage unless they care for three or more children (Commission to Formulate a State Plan for Child Care and Development Services in California, 1978). Beyond the requirements of minimum wage, there are no requirements regarding compensation. Salaries are held down in part by the market and in part by the state-established maximum per-child reimbursement rate. When child care is provided by a school district, typically there is a split salary schedule, with employees of the children's centers having one salary schedule and public school teachers having another. The Commisson to Formulate a State Plan for Child Care and Development Services in California (1978) also recommended that compensation in the private sector be enhanced by allowing child care programs to buy into benefit packages, such as health care and retirement programs, through public agencies such as schools, cities, and counties.

Needs Assessment, Funding, and Expansion. Public funding for child care in California increased between 1978-1979 and 1981-1982 from $148 million to $205 million (California State Department of Education, 1980). These figures do not include the $25 million expended annually for state preschool programs. The state has assumed a larger portion of the funding burden as a result of Proposition 13's elimination of local child development taxes in 1978-1979 and the state buy-out of federal Title XX funding for child care.

Despite the ambitious programs of subsidized care, which in 1981-1982 served an estimated 133,000 children, the Commission to Formulate a State Plan for Child Care and Development Services in California (1978) estimated that there was a substantial unmet need for both subsidized and nonsubsidized child care. In 1978, there were spaces available for only one third of the estimated 366,000 children in California eligible for subsidized care; for the estimated 649,000 children requiring nonsubsidized care, there were licensed spaces available for only one quarter. According to the commission, the unmet need was likely to become even more acute in view of the projected increases by 1984 in children whose mothers work. Moreover, the commission found that there were particular populations who did not have access to care. Thus, the commission set forth priorities for expansion of subsidized care during the first year of a recommended five-year plan. First-year priorities included expansion of resource and referral services; expansion of services to infants and toddlers; expansion of care for school-age children; expansion of direct services to isolated geographical areas; and coordination of funding for handicapped children.

Prior to incorporating these priorities into the 1980 child care legislation, the legislature directed a task force to evaluate and recommend methods of allocating additional child care funds. The task force recommended a "hold harmless" policy for presently funded programs, but recommended that allocation of expansion funds be based on five indicators of need: labor force participation of women; number of children; number of families who are income-eligible for child care; number of poor families; and number of children on AFDC. The latter three factors, which are indicators of poverty, account for 45 percent of the formula. These indicators of need were incorporated into the legislation.

In accordance with the new legislation, funds for expansion are allocated by county (or geographical area, within large counties), based on a comparison of existing funding resources and the five indicators of need. There is open competition in the counties for contracts to provide child care services, and the Office of Child Development encourages private agencies to apply for contracts. Although competition for the contracts is keen, new agencies do apply successfully. In 1980–1981, about 40 percent of the awards went to agencies not previously under contract with the State Department of Education. During the first year, the operating agency is monitored very closely; after the first year, contracts are renewed more or less automatically, although all programs are audited each year by an outside firm.

In addition to providing funds for program expansion, the legislature appropriated $4 million in 1980–1981 for capital outlay: small grants to family day homes and revolving loans with no interest to other child care facilities to assist them in meeting licensing standards. The appropriation was an outgrowth of an experiment attempted on a smaller scale under ACCP.

Providers of child care are reimbursed for actual costs on the basis of average daily enrollment (not to exceed $3,523 per child for 1979–1980, increased by a cost-of-living adjustment granted by the legislature). The maximum reimbursement is multiplied by a factor of 1.3 for infants and a factor of 1.1 for handicapped, non-English-speaking, or abused children. In practice, most providers are reimbursed at the rate of about $3,000 per child for full-time care (6.5 or more hours daily).

Families pay according to a sliding fee scale based on their income. Families whose income is below 54 percent of the state's median income pay no fee; families with incomes below 84 percent of the median are eligible to receive partially subsidized care. Once enrolled, income-eligible families can remain with a program until their incomes reach 115 percent of the state's median. At that point, the family must pay the full cost of care. However, families with incomes between 84 and 115 percent are not eligible to *enter* a program. The fee schedule for 1981–1982 assumed a median income of $25,100 for a family of four in California. Accordingly, the daily fee for a family

rises from $0.50 for families with incomes of 54 percent of the
median, to $4.20 for families with incomes at 84 percent of the
median, to $8.20 for families with incomes at the median level.
For families above the median, the fee rises sharply to $14.80
per day, which, when annualized, approximates the maximum
reimbursement to providers—about $3,500.

In theory, this comparatively generous fee schedule allows families with incomes at the median level to receive a subsidy slightly less than half the maximum reimbursable amount.
In actual practice, however, only a small percentage of children
receiving subsidized care are from families with incomes above
84 percent of the median; 40 percent of the families have incomes below 54 percent of the median and 90 percent have incomes below 84 percent of the median (California State Department of Education, 1980). The families' low incomes account
for the small portion of the child care budget that is raised from
parent fees.

In the foreseeable future, there is little likelihood that the
legislature will appropriate additional money for the five-year
expansion recommended by the Commission to Formulate a
State Plan for Child Care and Development Services in California (1978), despite the existence of long waiting lists for subsidized care. Current concerns of the Department of Education
are in the direction of cost containment.

Some increase in the number of children served is anticipated as the general child care programs move from an adult-
child ratio of one to five or one to seven to the ratio of one to
eight permitted in the 1980 legislation. Moreover, the legislation permits care programs to meet children's needs for health
services and social services through referrals to local agencies instead of direct provision of services; the policy is intended to
utilize Department of Education funds for basic child care
services, with other agencies meeting the additional needs of
children eligible for subsidized health and social services.

Community and Parent Participation. California has long
recognized the importance of family and community involvement in the planning of child care programs and the need to include parent education as a component of child care services.
These two elements are explicitly included as indicators of qual-

ity in the 1980 legislation. Moreover, provision is made for the continuation of the Governor's Advisory Committee for several specific tasks: to assist the Department of Education in developing a state plan for child development, to evaluate the effectiveness of programs, and to report to the legislature annually. The participatory significance of this requirement lies in the fact that the committee is broadly representative and includes among its members persons from state agencies; school, family day home, proprietary, and nonprofit child care providers; and parents of children participating in child care programs. The committee issues reports and recommendations after extensive hearings from persons representing diverse interests. The evidence suggests that the recommendations of the Governor's Advisory Committee with respect to vouchers, alternative programs, resource allocation, licensing and regulation, and other issues, as well as the recommendations of the Commission to Formulate a State Plan for Child Care and Development Services in California, have been taken seriously by the Department of Education and by the state legislature.

While there may be substantial parent and citizen input into the policy process at the state level, achieving parent participation at the program level is an elusive goal. The Commission to Formulate a State Plan for Child Care and Development Services in California (1978) recommended that parents be involved in the decision-making process, that parents have the opportunity for education and involvement in center or day home activities, and that members of the community have the opportunity to serve on boards of child programs. However, the Department of Education's efforts to fulfill the objectives of parent education and parent involvement have met with mixed success. Its 1978–1979 annual report noted that parent involvement in program activities was fairly low, although there were differences among various program types; campus programs reported a high rate of parent involvement, while school-age parenting programs reported the lowest rate. The primary cause of lack of involvement reported by both centers and homes was parents' lack of time, followed by lack of interest, lack of knowledge, insecurity, and lack of fluency in English (California State Department of Education, 1980). With respect to parent education, child care staff members attempted to ascertain the needs and preferences of parents through individual conferences and surveys. In general, the types of information and programs preferred by parents were, in order of preference, individual conferences, meetings to discuss problems specific to the children in the program, meetings to discuss child development in general, and school orientation programs. While parents were interested in individual conferences, most facilities reported fairly low rates of parent participation in more formal education-oriented activities. It appeared that working parents simply lack the time to devote to activities beyond the pressing demands of home and job.

Conclusions. Child care in California is distinctive in that state-supported programs, at first predominantly in the public schools, have become, by trial and error and by deliberate policy initiative, diverse in types of providers and types of care. The experience of the Department of Education in administering the programs suggests that placement of child care programs in the state education agency does not necessarily result in the capture of the program by a single profession, nor does it necessarily result in monopolization of services by the schools. An important factor in this regard lies in California's practice of open competition among public and private agencies for contracts to provide subsidized care. Another critical component of California's experience has been the use of personnel who are knowledgeable about child development in program development, licensing, and assessment.

California's experience is instructive for other states in light of its now well-developed policy process that includes identification of needs, implementation and evaluation of pilot programs, expansion of successful programs, and the modification of programs and administrative procedures where warranted. Child care advocacy groups have been well organized for some time and have played an important role in shaping child care legislation. Resource and referral agencies, organized in urban centers even before state funding was available, were important in identifying needed services and in putting parents, providers, and other advocates in touch with one another. Thus, California's programs have a distinctively grass-roots origin.

Innovations of the 1970s resulted from many sources: the prodding of Governors Reagan and Brown and State Superintendent of Education Riles, effective advocacy by consumer and provider groups, marshaling of evidence by the Commission to Formulate a State Plan for Child Care and Development Services in California and the Governor's Advisory Committee on Child Development, and the willingness of the legislature and the Department of Education to take seriously the recommendations presented. The 1980s are not likely to see the expansion that characterized the previous decade. It is more likely that there will be continued refinement of standards of quality, exploration of new ways to ensure quality that are not unduly burdensome to providers or costly to administer, emphasis on resource and referral services to identify needs and link them with existing resources, and emphasis on consumer education. In addition, attention will probably be directed to populations previously underserved and efforts made to involve employers in providing child care. An awareness of limited resources will clearly set the context for these directions.

California's initiatives in child care are likely to be of use to other states for a number of reasons. First, they have been extraordinarily well documented; an unusual amount of data is available regarding needed services, sponsoring agencies, characteristics of families served, parent preferences, qualifications of care givers, and so on. Both data and analyses are available from the agency responsible for administration (State Department of Education) and the Governor's Advisory Committee on Child Development Programs. Second, in the history of its long involvement in child care, California has grappled with difficult issues and to a remarkable extent exemplifies the use of knowledge in the policy development process. We can learn much from the tremendous accomplishments and from the apparent intractability of certain problems. Finally, California offers a model of a state education agency contracting with public school districts *and* community-based organizations to implement a large and diverse system. It is possible that this feature, and many others, could be replicated by other states.

Minnesota: A State Program in Parent Education

A parent education program that is remarkably consistent with good practice as determined by research and with our project's value position is the state of Minnesota's Early Childhood and Family Education (ECFE) program. Established by the state legislature, it focuses on parents and their young children (birth through kindergarten enrollment). Its primary goal "is to enhance and support the competence of parents in providing the best possible environment for the healthy growth of their children" (Council on Quality Education, 1981, p. 20). Major objectives include: "(1) engaging the interest and talents of parents in recognizing and meeting the emotional, intellectual, and physical needs of children; (2) promoting healthy self-concepts among family members; (3) sharing alternative childrearing approaches with parents and offering them a chance to share skills, techniques, and ideas with each other, and (4) providing creative learning experiences for both parents and children" (p. 20).

The program is designed for *all* parents; anyone with children between birth and kindergarten enrollment age may participate, and there are no income or other eligibility standards. Noting that program participants are from a broad range of income levels and ethnic backgrounds, the Council on Quality Education (1981, p. 25) added that "program staff are urged to obtain an approximately pro rata participation rate of persons from all cultural, ethnic, and income groups represented in the community's eligible population." Indeed, special grants have at times been made available to underwrite outreach efforts to achieve these pro rata participation rates, especially among low-income families.

The policy and administrative process that nurtured and maintained this parent education program, enacted in 1974, is impressive. Fortuitously, the program's sponsor, Senator Jerome Hughes, has a background in education and family studies.

Equally fortuitous was the assignment for administration of the program to the Council on Quality Education, established in 1971 by the legislature to promote high-quality and economical programming in local school districts. The Council on Quality Education has nineteen members, ten appointed by the governor (one from each of the state's eight congressional districts and two at-large) and nine from various educational organizations throughout the state. The Council on Quality Education, in turn, appoints a nine-member State Advisory Task Force on Early Childhood and Family Education, whose membership has a majority of parents with young children, as well as several professionals. A staff located in the Division of Special Services of the State Department of Education serves the council in administering the ECFE program.

The Council on Quality Education has played a crucial role in the success of the ECFE program. Although it seemed almost accidental at the outset that the program was delegated to the Council on Quality Education for implementation, members —many of whom are concerned lay people—seized their charge with vigor and managed both to insist on excellence and to steer a course through the difficult political challenges of state government. The council's effectiveness seems largely due to its position at arm's length from state government and to the members' dedicated, competent service. Any state considering parent education programming should give serious consideration to utilizing a mechanism similar to the Council on Quality Education or developing one if none exists.

The first appropriation for ECFE programs in fiscal year 1975 was $230,000. The Council on Quality Education and its staff nurtured the program year by year through gradual funding increases to $1,767,000 in 1980. Funds are deployed through negotiated grants. All of the state's school districts are eligible to apply by submitting proposals. A technical assistance process starts prior to proposal submission and continues throughout a school district's association with the ECFE program. The technical assistance program has a number of functions: to inform people throughout the state when new funding becomes available; to assist proposal writers; to negotiate budgets to ensure that provisions are made for quality programming; to monitor program operation; to provide in-service training for local staff; and to evaluate programs on an ongoing basis.

Although specific services offered in the thirty-six ECFE sites vary, those most frequently offered include center-based parent and family education; home-based parent and family education; center-based child development activities; early health screening; resource libraries; and preparenthood education for adolescents. The particular blend of services offered by a given ECFE program is determined by assessing community and participants' needs; in general, the programs are not supposed to overlap with services provided for families by other community agencies. The goal is to create and maintain the best match between program resources and local circumstances.

Whatever the specific activities chosen, the ECFE focus is clearly on parents. Child care may be a topic in parent education classes, care services may be provided for parents during program activities, and care programs may be offered as a vehicle for teaching parents more about childrearing and children's development; but more extensive child care services are not offered under ECFE auspices. Cooperative agreements and contracts are permitted and encouraged to enable ECFE programs to help participating families secure necessary services, however, and these certainly may include child care.

The background and experience of staff members are varied, befitting the range of program activities. A Minnesota prekindergarten teaching license or its equivalent is required for lead child development teachers, and parent education leaders are usually licensed by the state's vocational-technical education division. Other disciplines represented are home economics, counseling, nursing, social work, family social science, child development, and early childhood education. Paraprofessionals are required to have demonstrated competencies in their areas of responsibility.

The fiscal agents and typical sponsors for ECFE programs are school districts operating instructional programs for kindergarten through grade twelve. Thus, the ECFE program is primarily a public school effort. However, according to the Council on Quality Education (1981), other agencies may participate as providers of services by contracting with local school districts. Presently, nonschool agencies provide the program at seven sites. This is an important option for local school districts, particularly those that would like to see the services made available but do not want—for one reason or another—to provide the services directly.

The program's emphasis on local involvement does not stop at the school district level; there is also "a strong emphasis on neighborhoods and community building" (Council on Quality Education, 1981, p. 16). This has meant in practice that the attendance area of a single elementary school has defined eligibility. The state is now considering modifying this regulation slightly, but there is a continued insistence that "the area to be served should not be of such a size as to offset the community-based structure of these programs" (p. 15).

The ECFE legislation requires further that the local school board appoint an advisory council, whose members are selected from the school attendance area in which the programs are provided. A majority of the members are parents participating in the local programs. These local councils "are responsible for assisting school boards and program staff in the design, administration, and review" of ECFE services (Council on Quality Education, 1981, p. 25).

In its extensive policy study of the ECFE program, the Council on Quality Education recommended strongly the continued use of negotiated grants and associated technical assistance for program development and operation at local sites. The basic argument suggested that if communities are to operate high-quality programs reflecting the overall ECFE goals and objectives, a centralized function is required, especially in the first several years of local program operation. Factors pointing to the importance of this state-local arrangement were the great variability across local communities in initial costs, needs, and types of families served; the potential for local communities to misinterpret ECFE's emphasis on providing assistance to *all* families in enhancing their children's development; the difficulty of the tasks of outreach and communication; the sensitive and difficult process of matching participant needs and learning styles with professional staff resources and teaching styles; the complex demands made on program adminisrators in the early phases of a program's development; the difficulty of locating and outfitting suitable physical facilities; and the need to develop a competent and committed staff. The Council on Quality Education suggested that local communities—if left to operate without program and budgetary oversight and without benefit of the expertise offered by central office personnel—could too easily drift away from the type of programs the legislature wished to establish.

ECFE programs have spread gradually throughout the state to the present thirty-six sites as appropriations have increased. This distribution of programs is based on urban-rural, regional, and related geopolitical factors. Studies have shown that about 16 percent of eligible families within participating areas have taken part in services (Council on Quality Education, 1981). The typical program offers twenty-eight hours of parent education and twenty-seven hours of child development per week. The typical parent participates for 1.8 hours per week, and the typical child for 2.3 hours per week. Costs per participant have been figured at $168 (participation two or more times) and $304 (participation ten or more times). Average costs for different activities were estimated at $1.96 per participant hour for center-based child development group activities, $2.41 per participant hour for center-based family education, and $8.54 per participant hour for home-based parent and family education (Council on Quality Education, 1981). Expenditures on the program in 1980 totaled $1,767,000. The Council on Quality Education recommended gradual and careful expansion of the program at about the rate of fifteen programs per year.

Evaluation data on ECFE have been regularly generated for use by the Council on Quality Education and the state legislature, largely to keep the program on track during the years of development. The weight of the evidence shows clearly that ECFE programs followed the legislative mandate during their early years. There are also indications that ECFE programs are having their intended effects on communities, families, and children, but there has been a recent call for more systematic evaluation of program outcomes. The call is understandable politically and is being heeded by the council. The challenge will be to show with hard data that ECFE programs work and are cost-effective. Many evaluation experts, however, would argue that the council has already generated the evidence most relevant to policy decisions: The overall program is operating according to budget and specifications, and staff, parents, and relevant community members rate it highly. Measurable behavioral outcomes for parents and children will be difficult to demonstrate in the short run, given the state of the art of measurement and program evaluation. Moreover, ECFE was designed to provide readily accessible resources to all families within a program community; it is not intended to be an intensive, long-term intervention for a few problem families. Even in the latter instance, the demand for measurable effects would push the limits of program evaluation technology. Given the broad goals of the program, evidence of accessibility, use, and parents' satisfaction perhaps is all that is possible and all that should be required. That evidence is available, and it is uniformly positive.

Conclusions

We suggested earlier that much of the development of new and high-quality services in child care and parent education has come from key states serving as models for others; and we have examined in some detail two state programs, one providing child care and the other parent education, that are exemplary in many respects. It seems useful to identify those elements common to both programs—and to identify differences as well—that facilitated or impeded the accomplishment of legislative intent.

Although the focus of the California program is on children and the focus of the Minnesota program is on parents, there are striking similarities. Both programs have explicit human development objectives: the support of physical, cognitive, social, and emotional growth and development of children and the enhancement of parents' competence in providing an environment conducive to such growth. Both programs allow, within certain constraints, sufficient flexibility to facilitate the emergence of grass-roots programs responsive to local needs.

The two programs are financed primarily with state funds and are administered by the state education agency. In California, the State Department of Education contracts directly with local agencies, which may or may not be school districts, while in Minnesota the local school district is the fiscal agent responsible for the programs and may, if it chooses to, contract with other agencies to provide services. In both states there is a statewide advisory council, whose members are broadly representative and function at arm's length from those who actually implement the programs. Minnesota's Council on Quality Educaand California's Governor's Advisory Committee on Child Development Programs have provided stimuli for program innovation, development, and evaluation; they have ensured the representation of diverse interests; and they have served as vigorous and effective advocates for continuation and expansion of the programs.

At the local level, community involvement is an explicit objective in both states. Minnesota requires that school boards in districts providing parent education programs appoint an advisory council to assist in the design, administration, and review of services. A majority of the council must be parents who participate in the local programs. While the California legislation does not provide specific mechanisms for local community input, family and community involvement is included as an indicator of quality, and other features of the child care system contribute to the achievement of the objective. Notable in this regard are at least two elements: the contracting system, which facilitates the entry of new, community-based child care programs, and the resource and referral program, which, by gathering information about existing resources, tabulating requests for service, and identifying unmet needs, has stimulated the growth of child care services.

Minnesota and California have taken different paths regarding eligibility and resource allocation. Minnesota's parent education programs are available to all parents who wish to participate. The program has evolved from a few sites in 1975 to thirty-six sites in 1981; incremental expansion of the program has been carefully guided by the Council on Quality Education and its staff. In general, eligibility is defined by elementary school attendance zones; while this policy reinforces the community-based nature of the program, it excludes families who do not live in an area served by the program.

In contrast, California has opted to limit subsidized child care services to low-income working parents, although resource and referral programs are available to all parents. In recent years, California has attempted to allocate child care resources to groups previously underserved (such as infants, school-age children, and children of migrants) and to allocate resources geographically in accordance with a formula that takes into account a county's existing sources of support and various indicators of need for services. Thus, while Minnesota serves all families in a limited number of geographical areas, California has attempted to serve families with greatest financial need throughout the state.

Beyond this very obvious difference in approach regarding eligibility, the way in which funds are allocated is remarkably similar in the two states. In both, there is vigorous competition whenever funding for program expansion is made available. Minnesota employs a negotiated grant approach, in which all school districts are invited to apply for funding and the Department of Education provides technical assistance to local school districts to help ensure the quality of proposals submitted. In California, when expansion funds are available, school districts, cities, nonprofit organizations, and private proprietary agencies are eligible to apply for contracts to provide child care services.

This method of awarding contracts for services, rather than mandating that services be offered, means that the programs in both states are grass roots in their origins; they are not imposed from the top down. One consequence is the implication for community involvement, to which we have already alluded. Another consequence is diversity, both in sponsorship and mode of delivery. Parent education programs in Minnesota are run primarily by public schools, but in seven of thirty-six sites they are sponsored by organizations other than schools. Sponsorship of child care programs in California encompasses a full range, including school districts, cities, higher education institutions, nonprofit agencies, and proprietary agencies. In Minnesota, programs are primarily in centers, typically in the local school itself, but some services are also delivered in the home. In California, child care services are provided in centers, family day homes, and in the child's home.

In both states the maintenance of socioeconomic diversity in programs is an objective. In Minnesota, this has meant a special effort to ensure that low-income families participate. In California, this has meant that various techniques have been utilized to integrate subsidized and nonsubsidized children—by waiving staffing ratios in private centers who accept some subsidized children, by placing children through the alternative payment program, and by using a sliding fee scale.

The issue of quality assurance is an important one in the delivery of human services. California and Minnesota have both done well on this score because program objectives are clearly spelled out in the legislation and because persons responsible for carrying them out (the administrators) have been involved in goal setting. In both states, the programs have evolved over the years as the result of an interactive process that includes administrators, advisory councils, parents, and legislators. In both states, the issue of quality has been addressed by regulatory activities, such as licensing, specified care giver qualifications, and fiscal monitoring, and by procedures such as systematic innovation through demonstration projects, citizen review, and legislative oversight. Licensing has been a difficult matter in California (in contrast to Minnesota), but gradually a consensus has been emerging around some of the particularly vexing issues, such as staff ratios and allocation of the responsibility for licensing. With regard to care giver qualifications, the requirements in both states take into account the need for personnel experienced in child development (by requiring lead teachers to have specific training in child development) and the need for staff members who represent the socioeconomic and ethnic characteristics of participants in the programs. Both states have demonstrated a willingness—and at times an eagerness—to innovate, to test new concepts on a pilot basis, and to use the results of evaluations to refine existing programs. In both states, periodic reports to the legislature are made by the responsible agency and by advisory groups, so that legislative oversight is based on well-documented evidence. In the final analysis, the programs seem to work well because they have clearly articulated objectives, well-defined mechanisms for carrying them out, and commitment on the part of responsible persons to their successful implementation.

Viewed in broad perspective, these programs are important for many reasons, but perhaps most significantly because they are state-initiated efforts to meet the very diverse needs of families seeking to rear their children well. As was true of three federal efforts—ESEA Title I, Head Start, and Title XX—the programs are dynamic and evolving. Centered around sound objectives, the specific aspects of implementation have varied widely between programs and over time. These state experiences are instructive not so much for the detail of implementation and maintenance (although clearly this information adds depth to our understanding of the efforts) but for the principles that have permeated their origins and development. They are instructive also for their clear illustration of the possibilities inherent in cooperative arrangements between various agencies traditionally interested in different aspects of children's and families' well-being. That these cooperative arrangements have been worked out as the responsibility of state education agencies is particularly important. We turn in the next chapter to a consideration of this organizational structure, which has emerged for us as the most well-suited—from the perspective of the values we hold—for the provision of child care and parent education aimed at strengthening the competence and caring capabilities of our nation's families and children.

EIGHT

CRCRCRCRCRCRCRCRCRCRCRCRCRCRCRCRCRCRCRCRCR

Strengthening Families Through Public Schools

A central thesis of this book is that people in communities working together to strengthen families should have as a major goal the building of a competent and caring society, to which the community planning process itself would contribute. This, among other reasons, suggests to us that child care and parent education should be provided primarily through the educational system of the nation.

We have reached this conclusion after carefully examining various alternatives. We have come to it because, in our judgment, the educational system offers the best potential for making opportunities available to *all* families who need and want them. We have reached this recommendation on the basis of the several analyses presented in this volume; we have been particularly influenced by the state experiences exemplified in California and Minnesota, where policy in child care and parent education has capitalized on the potential for universality without sacrificing the richness of diversity or the affinity for local concerns that are so essential for successful programs.

As we have noted in earlier chapters, there is a common body of knowledge derived from three previously separate early childhood traditions—child care, nursery schools, and kindergarten—regarding what constitutes good education for young children and their families. We know that early educational and developmental experiences can make a difference in the lives of children, especially poor children, and that when parents are involved in these efforts, the positive effects are longer lasting. More and more families of all income levels appear to want early childhood experiences for their children, as evidenced by the continuing expansion of preprimary and nursery school enrollment. And many parents are also interested in parent education, as evidenced by their voluntary involvement in classes, purchase of materials, and so on. In view of these interests and needs, it seems sensible, at the least, to make child care and parent education available to all families and children who want them. Saying that, however, does not necessarily point to the educational system as the most appropriate provider, for the evidence suggests that institutional sponsorship per se is not the primary determinant of good programs. Good child care and parent education programs occur in many places, and quality of programming is apparently more dependent on the quality and commitment of the people running the programs than on formal sponsorship arrangements.

However, we judge it to be extremely important to move child care and parent education out of the public welfare bureaucracy. Child care and parent education, if they are to contribute to the achievement of social goals to the benefit of all, should not be available only to the disadvantaged, nor should they be used only for such limited objectives as relieving the welfare rolls. Although it is not possible to implement programs for all families in the current context of limited resources, it seems to us that the schools offer the most appropriate vehicle for the gradual extension of services to all families who need and want them.

We make this recommendation having considered the alternatives very seriously—the welfare system, a mix of community groups and agencies, a predominantly private system, and so on—in short, the range of currently active sponsors described in Chapter Four. It is a decision we have come to in full awareness of the sometimes limited nature of our evidence and

the difficult realities of bringing about the changes necessary in
many school systems before the implementation of our recommendation is possible or sensible. Nonetheless, we believe that
the steps necessary to the implementation of our recommendation are clearly warranted, for the public education system—
long this country's most "regular" socializing agency, reaching
the largest number of families on tasks of critical importance to
societal and individual well-being—is, by virtue of our project
values and more instrumental considerations, the structure best
suited to take on such a task. We emphasize that this recommendation is *not* a prescription that all child care and parent
education take place in schools per se, but rather a prescription
that state and local educational agencies be charged with primary responsibility for implementing these programs through
the mix of school, community, and private offerings that are
most responsive to the needs of any given community.

It is coincidental that we offer this recommendation at a
time when policy-makers and scholars are reexamining the appropriate roles of the federal, state, and local governments in
education. Federal efforts, to date, have concentrated on special
populations (the focus of many categorical programs) in contrast to regular school programs that affect all children. But
even among the most successful federal programs, there is an
important role for local decision making. Rotberg (1981), for
example, suggested that federal programs that are effective—
such as ESEA Title I, serving low-achieving children in schools
with a large proportion of low-income families—are those with
clear and consistent objectives and well-defined methods for
allocating resources. But she also suggested that "although
federal programs can ensure that the intended beneficiaries receive supplemental educational services, it is not at all clear that
the program should attempt to intervene in local decisions
about instructional techniques or planning methods" (p. 29).

There seems to be an emerging consensus that federal initiatives are helpful in stimulating state and local agencies to address certain needs but that the federal role should focus on the
facilitation of local planning and implementation. It appears
that federal program regulations have limited effects on the

quality of local services; more important are the characteristics of local leadership. Thus, in the larger debate, some have argued that the federal government has exercised policy leadership disproportionate to its financial support in recent decades. The Advisory Commission on Intergovernmental Relations (1980) maintained, for example, that while the federal government has provided only 8 percent of the funds for public education, it has exerted heavy influence over all schools because of the requirements that are attached to most grants.

But recently, the states have begun to exercise more leadership in education. The 1970s saw improved staffing for state legislatures and increased availability of education planners and administrators at the state level (positions, interestingly, that were often funded by federal programs); these trends clearly enhanced states' abilities to plan and implement programs (Andringa, 1981; Rosenthal and Fuhrman, 1981). A few states have had long traditions of executive involvement in education, and, increasingly, governors are taking an active interest in education. With their legislatures, many are undertaking initiatives to raise standards, to extend education to kindergarten and even prekindergarten levels, and to improve the quality of teaching.

A widely held belief is that there are certain national purposes that are appropriately addressed by the federal government. Those particularly affecting children and families would include the provision of equal protection against discrimination when a state demonstrates the inability to do so; support for program innovation and experimentation; support for research in education and child development; dissemination of research findings through systems such as Educational Resources Information Center (ERIC); and technical assistance (for example, support for in-service teacher training). If, as we propose, responsibility for child care and parent education is lodged in the state educational authority with services provided in a highly flexible fashion under a diversity of sponsors and funding arrangements, there would still be a very important, though restricted, role for the federal government to play. A widely dispersed system can work to common purpose only if there is effective communication between its component parts; thus, one important function of the federal government would be to facilitate the exchange of ideas and research findings among the states and among the citizenry at large. Similarly, federal assistance in the form of incentives might be required to encourage development of needed services under local sponsorship.

Whatever the outcome of the debate regarding the appropriate functions of the states and the federal government in the field of education, we believe that the schools are well positioned, because of their proximity to the community, to extend child care and parent education to all families and to maximize cooperation with the diverse community groups that are already significant forces in the field. We have already noted the great variety of existing programs, the emergence of federal and state support for child care and preschool programs, and the increased enrollment of children from all families in preprimary programs of many types. Several observers have called for coordination of currently fragmented patterns of funding and provision of services. We believe that this could be accomplished by state education agencies, which could also support and enhance the community-based nature of the programs.

We turn now to an analysis of this recommendation—service provision implemented by state education agencies—through the lens of our values, explicated in Chapter Three. We follow this analysis by briefly considering several specific issues related to actual implementation of the policy option. Throughout the discussion, our analysis is sprinkled liberally with illustrations and reference to the state experiences in California and Minnesota. Implementation of our recommendations clearly implies that states will play a primary role, and the efforts of California and Minnesota, exemplary in some respects, indicate the outlines of possibilities for implementation in many states.

Does the Policy Enhance Community?

We ask first, Has the public education system contributed to community building and what is its potential for doing so in the future? Our public schools, from their origins in the Colonies and their extension westward across the nation, have been a primary instrument for the development of a shared heritage. In the mid-nineteenth century, the movement to formalize education for children and adolescents gained momentum, partly in response to a strong interest in socializing and "Americanizing" the vast numbers of new immigrants entering the country. To this latter purpose mixed motivations have been attributed, among them an enlightened need to have a free and educated citizenry and a covert need to indoctrinate workers into the ideologies and mores of capitalism. Whatever the motives, the idea of a free and compulsory educational system for all youth was a radical idea at the time, an idea that many other nations subsequently adopted. For all their faults, the public schools of America have been one of our most successful expressions of a commitment to community.

It is paradoxical that our public schools, from their beginnings, have been the arena in which myriad community battles have been fought—and it remains so today. Many suggest that public education is in grave danger today because the consensus on which it was built no longer exists. We would suggest, however, that the schools have been extraordinarily resilient as forums in which conflicts such as separation of church and state, the teaching of Darwinian theory, loyalty oaths for teachers, desegregation, and other major battles have been fought. In fact, there would appear to be no place more appropriate or productive than the public schools for experiencing and debating the means for achieving a competent and caring society.

The public schools are simultaneously universal and rooted in local communities; our shared tradition, in fact, is one of great diversity. A prime motivation for establishing public education in the first place was to promote a shared heritage, and this early purpose has been preserved in spite of the vesting of authority for public education in the states (and by tradition in local communities) and the relative absence of federal control over school curricula, teacher certification, requirements for graduation, and other centralizing influences.

Despite the state and local controls—and the absence of an explicit national education policy—there is evidence of remarkable similarity in the experiences offered through the schools. This shared experience in the context of appreciable diversity is brought about by a number of influences, among them the standards set by accrediting organizations, the admissions requirements of colleges and universities, the influence of professional organizations on the practices of teachers and administrators, and the national marketing of books and other instructional materials. Another strong influence in the service of a shared heritage through the public schools is the mobility of the American population from community to community and from lower to higher economic statuses.

From the standpoint of the community criterion as a whole, our schools are clearly less than perfect. But they have shown that they can be responsive both to local needs and to the greater common good, as evident in many systems, including the California and Minnesota programs. In California, the child care and development program enhances community in a number of specific ways: promoting community coordination of child care and development services; encouraging parents' participation in the program at local and state levels; giving financial support to community-based child care services of diverse sponsorship; and establishing a mechanism for citizen input from the broadly representative Governor's Advisory Committee. In the last decade, the legislature has proved to be responsive to the recommendations of citizens' groups, which were funded to involve parents and providers in the policy-making process. Most important, the program recognizes the larger community's interest in supporting the family by providing programs of high quality.

Likewise in Minnesota, community building is the hallmark of the Early Childhood Family Education (ECFE) program at all levels. For example, consider the representative Council on Quality Education and the ECFE advisory committee; the mandate that grants be given to small, local communities; the use of community-based needs assessments and local community advisory councils; the use of community facilities such as the schools; and finally, the use of community development techniques in shaping local programs.

Although our system of public education has contributed

substantially during its history to the unification of the nation as well as to its general vitality, the schools have also been a primary arena for many of our national ideological struggles. In the past, for example, public education has routinely practiced the divisive policies of separating races and isolating children with handicaps. The country has made great strides to overcome these divisions, but not without considerable conflict over the most appropriate means for accomplishing the goals. In time, many of these struggles will likely lead to the enhancement of community, but—as is true of many honest struggles—they can themselves be highly divisive.

Yet, in our view, the option of child care and parent education through the schools offers far greater potential than do other solutions for minimizing divisive influences. The child care program in California, for example, attempts to minimize the divisiveness inherent in a program providing subsidized care for the poor and no subsidy for middle-income groups by promoting socioeconomic diversity within care facilities through the alternative payment program; attempting to meet the diverse needs of ethnic minorities through staffing patterns; providing service on a sliding fee scale, so that families can remain in the programs as their incomes gradually increase; and waiving certain regulations for private facilities that serve a small portion of nonsubsidized children, thereby facilitating the integration of subsidized and nonsubsidized children. In Minnesota there are also efforts to promote age, sex, racial, ethnic, socioeconomic, and other forms of integration. Children are brought together with adults; both mothers and fathers are involved; and all members of the community participate in integrated facilities and programs. Although fees may be charged, often on a sliding scale, they do not single out individuals for special treatment and can be waived when necessary.

We believe that child care and parent education programs should be offered in such a way as to avoid bestowing unwarranted advantage to anyone. Our long-range goal of universal eligibility for programs through the schools certainly meets this criterion. In the meantime, as our nation copes with resources and priorities allowing for less than universal eligibility, California's program has met the test of *warranted* advantage in its efforts to allocate resources to groups previously underserved and to distribute resources geographically in accordance with a formula that takes into account an area's existing sources of support and various indexes of need for services. Similarly, Minnesota has responded to the observation that families already disadvantaged sometimes have difficulty in availing themselves of new opportunities; when difficulties in recruiting low-income families were discovered, special outreach activities were undertaken to increase diversity of participation, and program activities were modified to better fit varying family circumstances.

A final concern of this project relating to community is that programs not be demeaning to any group. By this we mean that programs should not be means-tested and should not separate out poor children in ways that are stigmatizing. In fact, our strong belief that program participation should not be stigmatizing is one of the very compelling reasons for placing the programs in the domain of education rather than welfare. The ECFE program in Minnesota explicitly recognizes the common need of all parents, and future parents, for some assistance in developing the requisite knowledge and skills to perform the parental role. This issue was fully debated at the time of the program's establishment, and a deliberate decision was made to establish programs for *all* families in a small number of communities rather than to begin by offering the program only to disadvantaged families. All programs make a major effort to recruit participants representative of the local community, with staff sensitivity to individual needs and freedom to shape educational experiences to fit all needs of all participants. A different decision was made in California, where child care services at the present time are primarily for disadvantaged families. The intent of the California legislature is for all families to have access to child care and development services. It has provided for resource and referral services for all families, regardless of income. Although the Commission to Formulate a State Plan for Child Care and Development Services in California has advocated subsidized care for middle-income parents as a long-range goal, this objective has not been met owing to the considerable gap between identified need for services and available resources. In fact, only about one third of the families needing subsidized care receive it, and there is a similar shortage of licensed care for families who do not need subsidization. For the latter group, the policy has been to encourage expansion of nonsubsidized care, primarily through state-funded resource and referral agencies. In the context of limited resources, the policy seems to be a sensible one.

Overall, the implementation of a child care and parent education program through the public schools meets the community enhancement criterion very well. Although the schools, by virtue of history and current circumstances, are certainly not without problems in this area, their strengths outweigh the liabilities, especially in light of the clear demonstrations in California and Minnesota that community-threatening difficulties can be resolved.

Does the Policy Strengthen Families?

We ask in our analysis if policies strengthen families by enhancing their capacity to master developmental tasks; by improving their abilities to obtain social resources and supports when needed (liaison and linkage functions); by protecting families from unwarranted intrusion; and by allowing parents choice within the constraints generated by other criteria.

In our view, providing child care and parent education through the public education system draws on a long tradition of schools helping people master various developmental tasks. We believe that if schools opened themselves to greater participation by all family members, they could contribute significantly to strengthening families. Such openness to family members is one of the important purposes of the community school movement, for example. Although it can be argued that the public schools have traditionally been unconcerned with family functioning in general, a number of federally funded programs (for example, Head Start, ESEA, and the Education for All Handicapped Children Act) have required that schools identify children and families in need of special assistance, engage them in significant ways in planning school activities for the children, and provide them with experiences enhancing to parents' and children's development. In most states, the schools have responded well to this requirement. Further, state programs through the schools have also incorporated such objectives. The goals of the California legislature in establishing the child care program were to help families attain financial stability through employment, maximize growth and development of children, and enhance parenting skills. Threaded through numerous reports on the program is the persistent objective of enhancing family functioning and viability. This criterion is also one of the key orienting principles of Minnesota's ECFE program. Its operational philosophy involves assessing the diverse needs of individual families, recognizing that families face different developmental tasks, and recognizing that the same family has different developmental needs at various times in its life cycle.

Ideally, child care and parent education programs through the schools would empower families by serving a liaison function, introducing parents to the other services already available in the community, and enhancing parents' capacity in their executive function as decision makers for their families. In this vein, one of the objectives of California's resource and referral program is to assist families in utilizing other support services within their communities; the evidence to date suggests that families who initiate inquiries are indeed assisted in this liaison or linkage function. In Minnesota, state-developed program guidelines specifically mandate that ECFE staff learn about and help participants use the many social resources and supports, both formal and informal, available in local communities. If school programs in child care and parent education were to pursue this liaison function actively, much could be accomplished in reducing the fragmentation that currently characterizes the various services upon which families draw.

Clearly, programs in the schools must also protect parents from unwarranted intrusion and allow them choice. Over the years, national and state laws have been enacted that allow the sharing of sensitive information by those who need to know and yet protect such information from disclosure. The protections incorporated in the federal Family Educational Rights and Privacy Act of 1974 could easily be extended to child care and parent education programs in the schools. As to choice, participation would of course be voluntary, and programs could be devised so that families may choose from a wide variety of services. In California, for example, families are given information about many child care options from which they may choose, including different types of care and different providers. Within certain constraints (such as waiting lists for available programs), families clearly have a range of choices. In Minnesota, participation in parent education programs is also strictly voluntary, and the program seems characterized by great sensitivity to families' needs for confidentiality and privacy. Taken together, freedom from intrusion and having choice contribute to parents' effective functioning as family decision makers, thus confirming our conclusion that family strength can be enhanced by child care and parent education programs offered through the public schools.

Does the Policy Enable Parents to Do Their Job Well?

Enabling parents is the primary policy and program means to strengthen families. Thus, a good program should enable parents to do their job well; should minimize stress by making available to parents essential resources such as time, energy, and knowledge; and should promote shared responsibility between parents and professionals.

Through good child care in community locations, the schools could diminish stress on families by providing parents and other family members the time needed for employment and other personal and family purposes. Simultaneously, of course, there is a need for parents to invest time and energy if they are to be involved in programs and maximize the benefits for their children. Therefore, this possibility does not allow for unilateral diminution of time pressures on parents; it could be expected overall, however, to contribute to parents' store of resources for good parenting.

The schools should have a major advantage in enabling parents to do their job well. Schools are teaching places and

should be prepared to provide the kinds of knowledge, understanding, and skills that parents need for rearing children well
until they achieve independence. This may, in fact, constitute a
major advantage of the schools over other kinds of child care
arrangements, which by tradition end at the time of the child's
entry into elementary school.

A recurrent theme in this project is the need for *shared*
responsibility between parents and service providers, including
professionals. Thus, we are speaking here of empowering parents to be capable decision makers rather than having professionals take over childrearing functions. We see it as critically
important that professionals treat parents with full respect and
mutual positive regard. It is on this criterion that the schools do
not fare well in the eyes of many. Schools have a reputation for
indifference to parents (with the possible exceptions of preschool and kindergarten programs). If the public schools are to
be considered seriously as providers or supervisors of child care
and parent education services, many will have to change the
character of their relationships with parents. We would give this
specific criterion high value in determining whether or not child
care and parent education programs should be made the responsibility of the educational system.

Some see contemporary administrators and teachers as
changing their views of parents, as being much more willing
than formerly to invite parent involvement and assume a role
in enabling parents. And indeed we have observed that many
early childhood programs have attempted to involve parents in
meaningful ways. Parent involvement, for example, is an explicit component of quality for California child care programs.
However, the evidence about parents' participation and shared
responsibility is mixed, and many working parents feel that
they do not have the time to be actively involved in the planning of programs. There is, of course, tremendous variability
among California programs on this dimension, given the diversity of programs offered. The Minnesota ECFE programs perform better on this criterion, probably because parents are the
explicit focus of the programs. Parents at all levels of the program, state and local, perform advisory functions for program

operation. Additionally, the programs use an adult pedagogical model wherein parents are active agents in planning, implementing, and evaluating program activities. Program evaluators have noted tendencies for some failure to deliver on this second item, with some scattered concern for parents becoming dependent on programs. But staff members at all levels have taken note of this tendency and have worked to correct it.

In sum, schools clearly appear to have the possibility of enabling parents to do their job well; they are designed as educational institutions, and many seem to be responding to findings over the last decade that families are in fact an important part of children's educational prospects and outcomes. Thus, the possibility of meaningful response on this criterion is clear. Nonetheless, many schools have a long way to go before being able to enter into a pattern of full respect for parents at a minimum, and shared responsibility with parents at a higher level of mutual cooperation. That they *can* do so is illustrated well in the cases of California and Minnesota; the prospects and programs of various states' efforts in this regard will bear scrutiny.

Does the Policy Enhance Individual Development and Protect the Rights of Individual Members of the Family?

Although the emphasis of this project is on families, we are also concerned about the needs of individual family members. Our argument has been that strengthening families and enabling parents will have salutary effects for *all* family members. Still, it is worth repeating the issue here with a focus on individual family members. We thus favor policies that enhance individual opportunities for the development of competence and self-realization and, at the same time, protect the rights of individual family members.

To the extent that individual competencies are strengthened, we believe that the potential for abuse and neglect of family members diminishes. That such goals may be realized through child care and parent education programs delivered through the public schools has been demonstrated in both California and Minnesota. One specific aim of the California program, in fact, is to reduce tension between parent and child in order to prevent abuse and neglect. This objective is accomplished through child development programs for children and the enhancement of parents' skills, which together are seen as facilitating the family's achievement of economic and emotional stability. Indeed, children who are at risk of abuse or neglect are given priority for child care services. In the same light, the Minnesota ECFE program is also seen as a preventive education program that focuses on helping parents and parents-to-be understand the duties and privileges of parenthood so that their parental behavior will be effective and responsible.

Many families, of course, are able to provide their children—from their own resources, both personal and economic—with rich opportunities to grow strong and healthy, agile in thought, and humane in motivations by providing and purchasing special opportunities for their children from birth through graduate or professional school. Our national experience indicates that children who are less fortunate, both economically and educationally, need a supplement of public resources to realize their full potential. Additional expenditures are often required to repair the disadvantages the nation allowed to develop in earlier generations. The California program offers opportunities for the support of physical, cognitive, social, and emotional development in children, opportunities that would not otherwise be available. The State Department of Education provides technical assistance to care providers and monitors compliance with standards of quality to ensure that these objectives are met. The focus of the ECFE program in Minnesota is on parents, but young children and adolescents are also involved. The ECFE legislation originally was offered as a form of preventive education, its goal being to help all participants to master family and individual developmental tasks and avoid problems in development.

One of the very purposes of education, of course, is the enhancement of individual development and competence. While schools have been faulted for their performance at times, there can be little doubt that the weight of school resources and educational planning has been oriented toward the improvement of individual competence. Thus, schools seem by their very nature appropriate to the meeting of this criterion. Here, too, however, they are not without faults, and the adequacy of their performance—on which full implementation of our recommendations hinges—clearly bears monitoring, with reference, perhaps, to the success of the child care and parent education programs in California and Minnesota in meeting these challenges.

Instrumental Considerations

We turn now from our values analysis—indicating the appropriateness of a leading role for public education in child care and parent education services—to considering several instrumental issues of importance to implementing such a policy.

The State Education Agency and Pluralism. In our view, the most effective way to accomplish the objective of expanding family-strengthening services of high quality to all who need or desire them is to organize child care and parent education programs at the state level in the education agency. Responsibility for administering the program could be entrusted to the division responsible for elementary and secondary education or, alternatively, to a separate office of child development within the education department, as has been done in California. Primary responsibility for implementation could be retained by the state education agency or delegated to the local school district. Whether the program is run by the state or by the local school district, there are numerous possibilities for service delivery: Local schools could provide all services, or the responsible agency could contract with other groups—public or private—to provide some or all services. Some local school districts may not wish to take on these functions, in which case the state agency or the local districts could contract for services. One state might adopt one strategy, and another state might adopt a different approach, depending on local interest and capability.

Both California and Minnesota have demonstrated that child care and parent education programs organized by the state education agency need not result in programming cut from a single mold. California, especially, has demonstrated that it is possible to implement programs responsive to diversity of geography and ethnicity. Openness and flexibility are necessary for any plan to find a congenial setting in the many cultural niches of our nation, to encourage invention of new patterns of service in response to local needs, opportunities, and constraints, and to ensure that the development of child care and parent education is not inhibited by orthodoxy.

Our arguments for pluralism should not be misconstrued, however, as condoning abdication of social responsibility on the convenient assumption that the problem will be cared for locally without the need for guidance or support from the state capitol or Washington. Our analyses suggest that child care and parent education are too important for the common good to ignore either the development of broad principles to guide program development or a broad concern for the adequacy of local solutions to the problem. Nor does our emphasis on local initiative blunt our insistence that minority groups are not to be denied the opportunities that are available to more privileged groups. Assurance that this does not happen is, as we have already noted, an appropriate federal function.

Child care and parent education should be provided in a variety of settings. Group care in centers is the predominant mode presently in school-sponsored child care and in nursery schools. However, several school systems—in states as diverse as California and South Carolina—have successfully implemented care through networks of family day homes, an alternative that is especially attractive for very young children. A school district, in addition to offering center care, could if it chose to do so, establish a system of sponsored family day home care, building on the strong, viable, and highly decentralized family day home structure that presently exists. A small but important portion of family daycare homes (estimated to be 30,000) are already affiliated with family daycare systems, which are generally related to larger social service agencies both public and private (*National Day Care Home Study Final Report,* 1981).

Public and Private Participation. Although we have developed the argument that public support for child care and parent education programs should be regarded as an essential component of our national commitment to the building of community

and our common societal good (and we have noted the complementary rationale focused on improving the quality of children
and thus of future workers and parents), we do not assume that
these arguments necessarily create a presumption for public programs. In fact, the literature reviewed and the analysis developed in earlier chapters suggest that the type of sponsorship—
whether public, private nonprofit, or private for-profit—is not a
reliable predictor of quality with regard to child care and parent
education. Other variables, such as staff training, are more closely related to high quality than is sponsorship per se. Programs,
wherever they are located, are frequently as good or as limited
as the individuals who carry them out.

Many have argued that public and private provision of human services should not be viewed as a dichotomy, however,
and that programs can be implemented by the private sector in
ways that serve the public interest (Schultz, 1977). There are
several advantages to using the private sector. Such use taps expertise developed by the private sector, fosters diversity in service delivery, and permits the rapid expansion or contraction of
services without incurring governmental obligations to employees. With respect to child care and parent education, some
very good programs have developed under private auspices, both
with and without the infusion of public funds. Public support of
nonprofit agencies has the additional advantage of levering additional community resources in support of programs that serve
the common good. Some would approve the involvement of
nonprofit organizations but would exclude the for-profit sector
because of alleged deficiencies, such as marginally trained staff,
low wages, and low parental participation. Yet the evidence
does not suggest that this is always or even frequently the case.
Moreover, historically an important portion of child care (both
in centers and family day homes) and parent education has been
provided by this sector.

Rather than excluding any particular set of providers
from participation, our preferred course of action would be to
build in various requirements for quality and participation and
then provide technical assistance to achieve these goals. (We do
regard it as essential, however, that child care and parent educa-

tion programs of all types be required, at the very least, to conform to state and local law.) Thus, we believe that one of the strengths of our recommendation lies in the designation of the state education agency as the implementer of policy but not the sole provider of service. It seems to us, in fact, that one of the primary strengths of the California and Minnesota programs lies in the encouragement of local school districts to contract with whatever community or private agencies are most able to meet identified community needs. Our recommendation of a primary role for the public sector through the state's educational system in no way creates the presumption of excluding private and other community groups; in fact, we would recommend that they be encouraged as complements to the educational agency, providing services that the public sector is unable or unwilling to provide.

   Parent Participation and Information and Referral. Parent education should be built into all types of child care services, both family day home and center care; in addition, an independent program of parent education should be made available on a voluntary basis to families who desire it. We see the community school movement, given federal encouragement by the 1978 extension of ESEA, as a particularly felicitous concept for integrating child care and parent education as a natural part of a number of other services that have been associated with community schools. The integration of child care and parent education is consonant with the community education philosophy, which, according to Cottom (cited in Hobbs, 1978, p. 762), "seeks to relate the school to the community by opening up the schools, using the schools as the catalysts for bringing community resources to bear on community problems."

   As we envision child care and parent education programs, parents would be active participants in ongoing activities. Although some federal mandates for parent participation in policy making have been dropped and there is disagreement among researchers as to whether parents wish to be involved in actual decision making, most early childhood specialists agree that parent involvement is important. While the schools have not always viewed parents as equal partners, there is evidence that some are making the effort. Parent involvement and parent education are two of the criteria by which California evaluates its programs, for example; there, the conclusions are that teachers and care givers try to promote parent involvement and that it is difficult to achieve. Many have emphasized the necessity for parent participation to ensure that local values and objectives are pursued and that individual needs of children are met. These objectives should not be abandoned, even if they are difficult to attain.

We would consider information and referral services to be a high priority for funding and implementation because of the vital role that they can play in assisting parents to make informed choices about supplemental care for their children. Some states have developed information and referral programs that compile data indicating need for services; distribute consumer's guides to child care; compile child care directories, including information about style and content of programs; place counselors in communities to receive inquiries from parents and give them information about alternatives; and offer technical assistance to care providers. In some communities, the effect of these activities has been to encourage new providers to enter the child care field and "old" providers to upgrade the quality of services. Information and referral services would seem quite important in the early stages of developing a program of child care and parent education through state education agencies.

Quality Assurance. In addition to parent participation and dissemination of information, there are other issues related to assurance of quality that a program of child care and parent education through the schools must address. Few would disagree that regulations are required to ensure that children are cared for in safe places and that minorities do not receive discriminatory treatment. We now know, however, that while it is possible to achieve compliance with regulations, it is much more difficult to ensure quality of service. Assurance of quality involves a balance between monitoring compliance with regulations (a sort of minimum guarantee) and nurturing capacities for local leadership that can engender the delivery of services of truly high quality.

Compliance with regulations is a function of the clarity

of objectives as embodied in legislation or charter and the regulations themselves; the level, range, and dependability of public and professional support of the program; the extent of agreement on technical procedures for carrying out the regulations; and the organizational and managerial capability of the unit from which compliance is expected. But as Hargrove (1983) noted, it is often necessary to supplement formal requirements with a number of informal arrangements, sensitively attuned to local circumstances, to make the system work. Compliance with regulations does not necessarily mean that the quality of services will be improved; meeting observable and countable standards may have little relationship to the quality of work being done. A statewide program is likely to benefit from regulations that encourage local experimentation and the evolution of new organizational forms, especially when actual service providers are highly competent.

There are probably few areas as contentious as licensing and regulation of human service facilities. Licensing of care providers is essential, however, to ensure protection of the children and to assure parents that at least minimum standards are being met. But licensing and regulation are expensive activities and licensing requirements may reduce the supply of services by increasing costs. Time lags between application for licenses and inspection and approval may be considerable. Some states have experimented with registration of family day homes and periodic, rather than annual, review of facilities. Regulations to ensure safety and fiscal accountability are essential, but beyond that, it may be preferable to obtain agreement on broad principles and goals for programs as a whole, leaving the design of methods to achieve those goals to local units and individual providers well supported by technical assistance programs. In the design of human development programs, a flat organizational arrangement that gives substantial authority and autonomy to small teams or individual workers and that provides technical backup when needed is generally preferred over an organization where control is exercised hierarchically from the top down. However, organizations within which authority and responsibility are widely shared require an imaginative and sustained investment in communication. Teams and local units must be informed of what other groups are doing, and they need an opportunity both to share their own experiences and to discover operational discrepancies where improvements in programming might be made. Thus, it has frequently been observed that some state and national human development programs have worked well not so much because of the formal administrative structure or the technical adequacy of the regulations but because there was an informal communications network of professionals who worked closely with other providers in seeing that the objectives of the programs were achieved.

Regulations can have a salutary effect on factors such as group size or child-staff ratios, provided that the requirements are reasonable. A dramatic example of this is the adoption by many federally funded child care centers of staffing ratios in *anticipation* of the adoption of the Federal Interagency Day Care Requirements. The proposed staffing ratios may have contributed to the now common belief that certain ratios should be maintained for children of a certain age.

Clearly, we do not disagree with the assertion that regulations are needed to ensure that children are cared for in a safe environment by caring providers using developmentally appropriate activities. But additionally, and perhaps even more importantly, we suggest that there is a need for supportive measures—such as technical assistance, training, and adequate salaries—to help care givers do their jobs well.

Technical assistance should be offered by the state education agency or local school district, both of which are well positioned to build on existing information networks and both of which have considerable experience in providing technical assistance to schools. Presently, technical assistance in child care is provided by a variety of formal and informal mechanisms: child care advocacy groups, information clearinghouses, and so on. But additional assistance is clearly needed—for example, in coordinating the development of sponsored family daycare, a task that might involve any of the following: assessing the supply and need for day home services; encouraging providers to join a support network of care givers; screening providers for health, experience, and suitability of the home; providing in-service training for care givers in nutrition and child development; providing technical assistance regarding record keeping, insurance, and taxes; administering USDA Child Care Food Program funds; and providing other supports, such as the distribution or loan of supplies, toys, and equipment. A sponsored family day care system could also assist parents by providing information about child care options, serving as a liaison with health and other social services, and assisting in the placement of children in homes. Similar assistance should be given to center care providers, whether they are under direct school sponsorship or are private providers under contract.

Training and Salaries. The *National Day Care Study* (1979) suggested that of the many items considered in relation to quality of care, specialized training appropriate to young children is usually more important than care givers' years of formal education. For providers who are not already well trained in child development, there are two useful approaches to training that could be used. The first emphasizes making opportunities available to them, including in-service training, on-site supervision, and financial support for released time to attend continuing education programs. The second approach involves the accreditation of care givers, using, for example, the Child Development Associate (CDA) credential, which measures specific competencies. Whichever approach is adopted, in-service training involving work with young children should be emphasized.

The issue of "who shall train" needs more careful consideration than we give it in this section, since it goes to the heart of the issue of professional control of child care. Training and technical assistance for child care providers have been funded by Title XX and Head Start, as well as other federal and state programs. Institutions as diverse as state agencies (welfare and education) and postsecondary educational institutions (schools of social work and education, community colleges, and so on) and independently operated private, nonprofit training organizations have offered programs for child care providers. In addition, there is a technical assistance component focused on training in the licensing activities of many state agencies. The training and technical assistance offered by these diverse organizations within the social work, child development, and early childhood education traditions now share a common pedagogy for the most part. The common body of child and family development knowledge, expanded and enriched so greatly during the past twenty years, should serve as the basis of training and technical assistance programs provided by the education agency.

The question of training is closely related to that of salaries. Salaries of child care workers are extremely low. In 1977, for example, the median full-time annualized salaries in child care centers were $6,136 for teachers and $5,138 for aides. While most earned more than the federal minimum wage, according to the *National Day Care Study* (1979), they were paid far less than public school teachers, whose average salary in 1977 was $13,400. Their counterparts working in family daycare homes fared even worse; the average hourly wage in 1977 was $1.25, a figure well below the minimum wage of $2.30. Measured against the Bureau of Labor Statistics' low-income budget for an urban family of four—$10,000—child care workers did quite poorly.

Child care is labor-intensive in centers and homes, whatever the sponsorship arrangements. Salaries are the major part of costs, and raising wages to a more livable level would raise the cost of care substantially. Despite low salaries, center care staff tend to be well educated and experienced when compared with the total female labor force. According to the *National Day Care Study* (1979), neither education nor experience, however, seems to affect wage rates for center care givers. Family day home providers tend to have somewhat less formal education than care givers and only limited training opportunities; neither years of experience nor education affect family day home wage rates (*National Day Care Home Study Final Report,* 1980).

The policy option of providing child care through the schools raises the question of whether staff should be paid on the same scale as public school teachers. Strict economic considerations alone do not justify increasing salaries greatly; there appears to be a pool of eager young people who are trained and willing to work in child care for low salaries. However, the low salaries for child care workers are indicative of the low value society places on caring for children. Policy considerations such as the continued assurance of a corps of highly able and qualified child care providers suggest that society must demonstrate its commitment to the task by paying child care staff adequately. While it is unlikely that child care workers will soon be paid at the level of public school teachers, at some point society must face the issue of whether child care staff should be subsidizing this important public service through the very low wages they receive.

Financing. In a few states, child care and parent education are part of the regular education budget, and providers are thus assured of a stable, ongoing source of support. However, in most cases of school sponsorship, funding has come through a variety of sources—federal, state, local, and private—and financing has been problematic. Levine (1978, p. 119) argued that child care "affiliated with the schools or *any other organizations* will not achieve more financial stability unless significant actions are taken at both the federal and state levels. An infusion of federal funds is needed along with aggressive state implementing of Title XX sliding fee scales, the only existing means of broadening both eligibility and parent payments for daycare."

Ultimately, in our judgment, child care and parent education should be available at no cost and on a universal basis, that is, with no means test. Currently, kindergarten is almost universally available to all families who choose to have their five-year-old children attend. However, most prekindergarten child care programs in public schools are specified for low-income families, partly because of the requirements of federal funding sources on which many programs depend. Low-income children were targeted for school-sponsored services in four of the five programs reviewed by Levine; this is also the case in California's child care program but not in Minnesota's parent education efforts. Aggregate census data on enrollment in nursery school programs indicate that children in families with incomes below

$10,000 are more likely to be in public prekindergarten programs, whereas children in families with incomes above $10,000 are primarily in private nursery schools.

The argument as it has developed thus far, which emphasizes the contribution of child care and parent education to the common good, implies clearly that the costs of child care and parent education services should be shared widely among the citizenry as a community responsibility and not paid for solely by families with children. The human capital rationale would add that families who rear children well make a substantial contribution to the economic strength of the nation, to the security of our aging population, and so on. It is arguably equitable on both grounds, then, for the cost of child care and parent education to be paid for out of general tax revenues, much as the public schools are supported.

The pattern of funding that would appear to give greatest assurance of adequate programming without loss of local control would derive revenue from state taxes supplemented by local and federal funds, the federal investment being required by the interest of the larger society in the adequacy of child care and parent education. In fact, our analysis of the problem leads inexorably to a requirement for a substantial federal investment in child care and parent education, perhaps up to 15 percent of the total cost. The unequal distribution of resources among states, as well as within states and across population groups, requires, in our judgment, substantial national investment in child care and parent education for the good of the country. Given current economic and political constraints, we do not expect an eager response to this recommendation, but we do expect, in time, a revival of concern for equity and community in our national life and, with that, a renewed interest in the federal government's role in strengthening families, in sharing the burden of caring well for new generations. In the meantime, and at some point concurrently, the challenge must be picked up by the states if progress toward those goals is to be made.

We assume in the recommended system of child care and parent education that participation will be completely voluntary and that parents who wish to purchase services from private providers will be completely free to do so. With regard to services either provided by or under contract with public agencies, it might be desirable to establish, as an interim measure, some kind of sliding scale of fees to ease the immediate burden of the total cost of providing services, to speed the development of services, to facilitate socioeconomic integration, and to provide continuity for the child as family income changes.

Very little information is available about the implementation of sliding scale fees in programs serving nonpoor children. In child care centers that receive subsidies from outside sources and serve low-income children predominantly, a very small portion of the typical budget is raised from parent fees; the difficulties associated with ascertaining and collecting fees seem to outweigh any monetary gain. Yet there is some evidence to suggest that child care centers serving diverse populations have developed workable fee schedules that have several features in common. For example, no family pays more than the actual cost for its own child, and fees are set at a relatively constant percentage of family income, typically between 9 and 12 percent (Child Care Information Exchange, 1979). The *National Day Care Study* reported that centers charge different rates, based on factors such as source of payment, hours of care per week, family income, family size, age of child, and number of children in care (*National Day Care Study*, 1978). Despite the difficulties inherent in administration, a sliding scale fee schedule may make possible the expansion of coverage to a greater number of beneficiaries and the integration of poor and nonpoor children at the same site. The long-term objective, of course, is the development of non-means-tested programs, programs open to all children.

Political Feasibility. We must now ask the question, Is it realistic to assume that the states would be willing to commit the resources required to provide programs of child care and parent education through the schools, even if they begin on a modest scale, with gradual expansion throughout the state and to all children? Rosenthal and Fuhrman (1981) provided an incisive look at education policy making in state legislatures. They noted that during the 1970s, state legislatures became increasingly important in policy making for at least two reasons. The first was the expansion of the state's role in education, especially in matters relating to financing. This occurred in part because of pressures to relieve the burden of local property taxes and in part because of court decisions on school financing. The second reason was the improved capacity of the legislatures, enhanced by better staffing, improved committee structures, and the specialization and expertise of the legislators themselves. As we have seen, the 1970s were also a period that saw the expansion of state and local government spending in education and human services, spurred on partly by federal matching grant incentives. The California and Minnesota programs developed during this period, and legislators took an active role in shaping these policies. State education agencies expanded, in part because the federal government provided some funding for new positions; some have suggested that the state education agencies also improved their capability to administer programs. The Education Commission for the States recently documented a diverse array of school improvement initiatives undertaken by the states during the last five years (Odden and Dougherty, 1982).

A critically important issue in feasibility is whether the states are currently in a position to replicate programs of broad scope, like those in California and Minnesota. In general, states undertaking innovative programs are likely to have healthy economic and tax bases, which provide adequate resources to fund programs, and well-organized interest groups capable of coalescing for the enactment of programs. Such was the case in California, where interest groups came together at various strategic points in time to push for change, expansion, and experimentation in state-supported child care. The role of interest groups was actually formalized by their inclusion on the Governor's Advisory Committee on Child Development.

In California, the legislature is only one of several influential actors in education policy (Kirst, 1981). The elected state superintendent of schools has considerable power and visibility; the governor is important in the process because of extensive appointment authority; there are well-staffed interest groups in

Sacramento; and the State Department of Education has a sophisticated planning and evaluation staff (the latter, for example, were quite evident throughout the planning and experimental phases of child care program development). Noted Kirst, "California is a high state-control state; each year legislated programs and regulations become more specific. In elementary and secondary education the legislature examines any idea that circulates in the national marketplace and often mandates it" (p. 42).

Minnesota is a state long known for its progressive policies and generous funding of human services and education at the elementary, secondary, and higher education levels. The political climate is somewhat different from California's, however, especially in that the population is more homogeneous, and policy makers need not be as explicitly attentive to ethnic diversity as in California. Nonetheless, there were some important debates in Minnesota, about whether the Early Childhood and Family Education program should be universal or aimed only at disadvantaged groups and whether the schools should be given responsibility for programming.

Interestingly, in both states innovations have occurred under the general rubric of promoting cost-effectiveness. The Council on Quality Education was established by the Minnesota legislature in 1971 to promote cost-effective innovations in local school districts. Similarly, the innovations in California under the Alternative Child Care Program (1976) included cost-effectiveness as one of several objectives.

It seems quite likely that in the future education will continue to compete with other interests for its share of scarce resources. This may be a particularly difficult time to propose adding yet another new function for education, especially when current policy interest centers on improving educational qualities of existing offerings at the elementary and secondary levels. One line of analysis suggests that when faced with fiscal constraints, any agency will tend to preserve what are regarded as core functions, because the agency will be judged according to how well it carries out those particular functions; it will resist adding new tasks regarded as peripheral.

If the function of child care and parent education is to receive adequate attention in this context, enabling legislation should establish a clear legal framework, assigning responsibility to the state's department of education and board of education. This is necessary if the new programs are to receive adequate oversight and leadership in early formative stages. Particular attention must be paid to the involvement of the private sector. In some states, departments of education have strong biases against the private sector; and indeed, the private sector may be apprehensive about oversight from the state departments. Yet clearly, the two have a common interest, especially in receiving ongoing support from the legislature in appropriations for child care and parent education. The cooperative relationships forged in California and Minnesota are instructive and indeed would serve as a model for contracting, oversight, placement, technical assistance, and a myriad of other concerns. There is also a very real question as to whether there will be a well-organized coalition of interested parties to advocate for the allocation of resources to child care and parent education. It is not at all clear that the traditional education lobby (colleges and universities, school board associations, teachers associations, and so on) will welcome a newcomer to the group, for they will likely have strong interest in allocating resources to and improving existing programs. They may well be wary of new mandates, especially when funding for existing programs sometimes meets only a small portion of the actual costs. All of these considerations point to the fact that programs for child care and parent education are most likely to materialize in states and communities where there is effective grass-roots advocacy.

If the programs are to be allocated the priority that we believe they should have, it is important to be aware of the nation's long-run stake in the outcome. A federal role may be essential to support states' movement in these areas, for many factors militate against adding new programming, especially in human services. Nonetheless, we believe that in the long run the challenge of strengthening families will be placed again on national and state agendas, for the interests of all levels of community in this society require it.

Conclusions

We recommend that child care and parent education services be made available through the public education system of the nation to all families who need and want them. We have reached this recommendation after serious consideration of many alternatives, most of which are represented in current service provision; further, we have come to this recommendation with full awareness of the limitations of the public education system that must be addressed if our recommendation is to be successful. These limitations—primarily in the ability of the schools to share responsibility with parents and serve as the administrative locus of public and private offerings—must be addressed successfully if developmentally sound, community-based child care and parent education services are to strengthen and complement family functions. We are persuaded by the successful experiences of many communities, particularly in California and Minnesota, that such a resolution is both possible and promising.

The schools thus emerge as the most appropriate of the many "regular" socializing agencies to take on the developmental and educational functions central to well-designed and family-strengthening programs of child care and parent education. Our values in particular argue strongly for the community-enhancing functions of services offered by the public education system and the potential of such programs, if well supported and responsive to parent needs, to enhance parent abilities and the development of all family members.

NINE

CRICRICRICRICRICRICRICRICRICRICRICRICRICRICRICRIC

Conclusion: Enhancing the Well-Being of Children, Families, and Communities

Our goal is the development of strong families in caring communities, families rich in the qualities needed to nurture healthy and competent people. Central to this task is the creation of environments that promote competence and caring—caring manifest in commitment to family, friends, the immediate community, and the broader "community of strangers" that constitutes society.

We have discussed two major rationales for national attention to families, one focused on human capital and the other on human development. The former is based on the solid ground of concern for the quality of the work force in the new generation. Clearly, as families have become smaller and the proportion of older, dependent people in the population has grown, the nation has developed a strong economic interest in ensuring competence in the new generation. The simple demographic fact is that smaller numbers of people will be responsi-

303

ble for the productivity needed to sustain growing numbers of
older and economically dependent people. Concurrently, as increasing numbers of women enter the work force, by choice
and necessity, it has become clear that continued attempts to
rely on traditional means of caring for children will meet, at
best, with limited success. It is no longer reasonable to assume
that most families will have a mother at home to care for the
children and a father in the work force to support the family.
It is also clear that as the number of children who spend some
time in single-parent homes increases, both they and their families will need new forms of community support to complement
traditional family resources.

These demographic realities do not negate traditional emphases on strong, able parents caring well for their children. Indeed, they emphasize the centrality of these concerns. The
conditions of life that they create, however, necessitate alternative and supplementary means of helping parents with these socially critical functions. Previous forms and possibilities are
changing and are no longer available to many families, who
nonetheless remain deeply concerned with the quality of life
they give to their children. The human capital rationale supports this position, insofar as good child care and education are
important to developing individual competence and productivity. The rationale does not go beyond the nation's economic
well-being, however, in justifying attention to individuals' lives.

The human development rationale asserts that national
concern with human life should encompass much more than the
transmission of marketable skills to children, much more than
functional competence for productivity. The rationale focuses
on the creation of environments rich in the qualities needed for
optimal human development. It calls forth fundamental social
responsibility for the development of competent and caring
citizens, people who are skilled and productive, to be sure, but
who are equally well developed in the qualities of caring and
commitment necessary to the well-being of fellow citizens,
friends, and strangers alike.

The patterns of competence and caring implied in the human development rationale emerge early in life; for most peo-

ple they begin in the family. Because families are fundamental
to the healthy development of children and the well-being of
all members, we have sought ways of supporting families in raising their children with satisfaction to themselves and responsiveness to the needs of both their children and their communities.

We emphasize the capacity of child care and parent education services to contribute to the development of competent
and caring individuals and propose these services as ways of
meeting families' needs for community support in gaining the
time, energy, resources, and knowledge critical to successful
childrearing. We choose them not because we believe them to be
the only ways of achieving individual, family, and community
well-being, but rather because they are the means most directly
responsive to pressing family needs and because the nation has
accumulated varied and successful experience in their provision.
We propose them not as means of curing social pathology or
bandaging social wounds, but as a way of enabling families to
rear their children well and participate simultaneously in the life
of the workplace and community. We propose them as means of
meeting children's needs for sound and healthy environments as
they grow into patterns of competence and caring.

The child care services we envision are designed to support family abilities to rear children effectively with the skills
and energy requisite to the task. We speak of supplements and
complements to family functions, services provided to enhance
parents' abilities, not replace them; we speak of child care as a
variety of familylike alternatives from which parents may
choose to augment their own caring capacities. In parent education, we speak of services designed to complement parents'
responsibilities and knowledge, focused on increased understanding of children, heightened competence in caring for
them, and increased abilities to protect the rights and well-being
of all family members. These services involve shared responsibilities and reciprocal relationships between parents and professionals, with both groups of participants bringing knowledge
and expertise to the solution of problems and the development
of increased competence in childrearing and family functioning.

We have proposed several criteria related to individual,

family, and community well-being by which to evaluate the adequacy of family policy alternatives. The commitments inherent in these values are neither new nor radical; indeed, they represent long-standing concerns in our society, manifest throughout our history. But they are qualitatively different from the commitments of a human capital rationale. We stress this point not to assert error in concern for the economic vitality of the nation but to underscore the insufficiency of such concerns. Taken alone, human capital concerns are inadequate to realizing the full promise of life to individuals who are citizens in a democracy. The sometimes conflicting purposes of a democracy, we suggest, are best served not by the singular pursuit of liberty, equality, or community but rather by a careful balancing of all three in the interests of strengthened individuals, families, and communities.

Thus, we speak of our historically rooted commitment to the value of strong and capable *individuals,* both children and adults. Valuing children as individuals leads logically to committing resources to those institutions in which children live, play, study, and grow to adulthood—their families and the many supportive community services selected by parents to complement family functions. Those services have long included schools, recreation programs, parks, and health programs, to name but a few. We suggest that to those traditional family supplements the nation now explicitly add child care and parent education.

A belief in the value of adults as individuals leads to similar conclusions. Parents need support if they are to do their job well—raising children and nurturing their own adult talents, skills, and abilities. Adults who bear no direct responsibility for children also need these supports, albeit indirectly. At a minimum, their own well-being, particularly as they retire, depends on the success of their peers who have raised children. Beyond this minimum, the well-being of all adults may be seen as dependent, at least in part, on participating in the maintenance of a society that is a healthy and generative place for the development of new members.

We speak also to the value we have placed historically on strong *families.* We suggest that allocating the resources families need to do their tasks well will enable individual members to develop fully and will offer, simultaneously, the best opportunity for healthy development of society as a whole. There is a considerable body of evidence and experience indicating that healthy families are the most important environment for the nurturance of competent individuals; they are, at the same time, the first and most significant context from which children learn the ways of reciprocity, the patterns of giving and receiving that bespeak shared commitments. We value healthy families and familylike environments in promoting the continuous development of all individuals, adults and children alike. We assert further that families should not be viewed only as means to ends, but should be valued as ends in their own right.

We suggest finally the clarification and implementation of a national commitment to the development of *community*. We speak of community as manifest in thousands of diverse localities, responsive to the needs of members, sustained by their work and contributions. We speak also of community as our pluralistic society knit together with the common threads of shared heritage and purpose. The nation needs strong communities to enhance the life chances and opportunities of individuals and their families. And the nation needs the full participation of those individual and family constituents so necessary to sustain the community. We believe that the quality of human community plays a major role in determining the strength of families and their abilities to raise their children well; the adequacy of community support for families is especially fundamental to childrearing functions.

After serious consideration of several alternative plans for implementing child care and parent education services, we have recommended their implementation through the public education system. We have chosen this direction with clear awareness that this system is far from perfect. We are also well aware that significant challenges must be met before our recommendation can be undertaken successfully; these challenges lie particularly in combining public and private provision of service under school auspices and sharing program responsibilities between parents and professionals. Nonetheless, we believe public education to be the most appropriate and well-suited means of ensuring services to *all* families who need and want them, without the divisiveness and harmful stigma of eligibility requirements, means-testing, and the emphasis on pathology that has historically characterized most services for families.

We have concluded, in short, that the public schools are the best situated of all "regular" socializing agencies to take on the tasks of child care and parent education. Further, we believe that public education, which has been remarkably successful over the broad sweep of its history in accomplishing tasks of large proportion and broad mandate, has the capacity and the will—expressed through professional and consumer members—to make changes necessary to the full realization of developmental services for all families. The Minnesota and California experiences, and countless other small and large experiments, indicate that this is possible. With technical assistance and shared leadership from various levels of government, it is not only possible, but normal in the course of community life.

We have emerged as advocates of a strong position in the final stages of this project. We have done so with full awareness that such a course is perhaps startling in a volume devoted to the usually dispassionate work of policy analysis, startling perhaps even in a volume explicitly committed to value-conscious policy analysis. We have come to this position through value-based analyses of the national experience in the design and implementation of thousands of efforts, locally based as well as federally sponsored, that constitute a rich national background in child care and parent education. Our position is consonant with many social purposes prominent in the national heritage. It may be seen as a contemporary call to the vision of an earlier generation, decades ago, when the nation decided to ensure children's learning through the provision of free and universal public education. We suggest nothing more than a similar commitment to the provision of supplementary child care and parent education services to families who need and choose them; we recommend nothing less.

Ours is an age marked by awareness of the need to allocate limited resources wisely and carefully among competing interests. We do not suggest that the commitments we recommend be undertaken recklessly, nor do we suggest that they can be accomplished without expense. We do assert that this commitment of resources is essential to the well-being of our nation —its health, its security, its vitality, its culture—and warrants reallocations necessary for its accomplishment.

The choices will be hard, given patterns of existing commitment and a theme of lingering nostalgia for the return to a time when strong independent families took care of their own and raised children to socially responsible adulthood. We suggest that this historical memory bears truth, but only limited truth; more importantly, we live today in a world that has changed and will continue to see profound change. A fundamental contribution to this changing world—and to the creative continuation of our own society—lies in the empowerment of parents and families, for they are our best means to the nurturance of competent and caring individuals, strong in abilities and strong in commitments to the community in which we all live.

References

○I○I○I○I○I○I○I○I○I○I○I○I○I○I○I○I○I○I○I○I○I○I○I○

Aaronson, M. *Directory of Child Rearing Programs Suitable for School-Age Parents.* (Prepublication copy, unedited.) Washington, D.C.: National Institute of Mental Health, 1978.

Adams, D., and Macht, M. "Rural Family Day Care." *Child Care Quarterly,* 1976, *5,* 292-306.

Advisory Commission on Intergovernmental Relations. *The Federal Role in the Federal System: The Dynamics of Growth.* Washington, D.C.: Advisory Commission on Intergovernmental Relations, 1980.

Ainsworth, M. D. "The Effects of Maternal Deprivation: A Review of Findings and Controversy in the Context of Research Strategy." In *Deprivations of Maternal Care: A Reassessment of Its Effects.* Public Health Papers, No. 14. Geneva: World Health Organization, 1962.

Ainsworth, M. D. "Discussion of Three Models for Parent Education." Paper presented at the biennial meeting of the Society for Research in Child Development, Denver, April 1975.

Allen, G. B., and Masling, J. M. "An Evaluation of the Effects of Nursery School Training on Children in the Kindergarten, First and Second Grades." *Journal of Educational Research,* 1957, *51,* 285-296.

American Federation of Teachers. *Putting Early Childhood and Day Care Services into the Public Schools: The Position of the American Federation of Teachers and an Action Plan for*

311

Promoting It. New York: American Federation of Teachers, 1976.

Amidon, A., and Brim, O. G., Jr. "What Do Children Have to Gain from Parent Education?" Paper prepared for the Advisory Committee on Child Development, National Research Council, National Academy of Sciences, 1972.

Andringa, R. C. "A Statehouse View on the Federal Role in Education." In R. A. Miller (Ed.), *The Federal Role in Education: New Directions for the Eighties*. Washington, D.C.: Institute for Educational Leadership, 1981.

Bane, M. J. *Here to Stay: American Families in the Twentieth Century*. New York: Basic Books, 1976.

Bane, M. J., and others. "Child Care Settings in the United States." In B. Berger and S. Callahan (Eds.), *Child Care and Mediating Structures*. Washington, D.C.: American Enterprise Institute for Public Policy Research, 1979.

Barnes, M. L., and Dunlop, K. H. "The Effects of Day Care on Children, Parents and Families." Working paper, Institute for Public Policy Studies, Vanderbilt University, 1978.

Beck, D., Tileston, C., and Kesten, S. *Educational Programs of Family Agencies: Who Is Reached?* New York: Family Service Association of America, 1977.

Beilin, H. "The Status and Future of Preschool Compensatory Education." In J. C. Stanley (Ed.), *Preschool Programs for the Disadvantaged: Five Experimental Approaches to Early Childhood Education*. Baltimore: Johns Hopkins University Press, 1972.

Belsky, J., and Steinberg, L. D. "The Effects of Day Care: A Critical Review." *Child Development*, 1978, *49*, 929-949.

Berger, B. "The Family and Mediating Structures as Agents for Child Care." In B. Berger and S. Callahan (Eds.), *Child Care and Mediating Structures*. Washington, D.C.: American Enterprise Institute for Public Policy Research, 1979.

Berger, P. L., and Neuhaus, R. J. *To Empower People: The Role of Mediating Structures in Public Policy*. Washington, D.C.: American Enterprise Institute for Public Policy Research, 1977.

Biber, B. *Goals and Methods in a Preschool Program for Disad-*

vantaged Children. New York: Bank Street College of Education, 1970.

Bledstein, B. J. *The Culture of Professionalism: The Middle Class and the Development of Higher Education in America.* New York: Norton, 1978.

Blehar, M. "Anxious Attachment and Defensive Reactions Associated with Day Care." *Child Development,* 1974, *45,* 683–692.

Bloom, B. S. *Stability and Change in Human Characteristics.* New York: Wiley, 1964.

Bogdan, R. "National Policy and Situated Meaning: The Case of Head Start and the Handicapped." *American Journal of Orthopsychiatry,* 1976, *46,* 229–235.

Bohen, H. H., and Viveros-Long, A. *Balancing Jobs and Family Life.* Philadelphia: Temple University Press, 1981.

Bonney, M. E., and Nicholson, E. L. "Comparative Social Adjustments of Elementary School Pupils with and Without Preschool Training." *Child Development,* 1958, *29,* 125–133.

Boocock, S. S. "A Crosscultural Analysis of the Child Care System." In L. G. Katz (Ed.), *Current Topics in Early Childhood Education.* Vol. 2. Norwood, N.J.: Ablex, 1979.

Bowlby, J. "The Nature of the Child's Tie to His Mother." *International Journal of Psychoanalysis,* 1958, *39,* 1–34.

Bowlby, J. *Child Care and the Growth of Love.* (2nd ed.) London: Penguin, 1964.

Braun, S. J., and Caldwell, B. M. "Emotional Adjustment of Children in Day Care Who Enrolled Prior to or After the Age of Three." *Early Child Development and Care,* 1973, *2,* 13–21.

Brim, O., Jr. *Education for Child Rearing.* New York: Russell Sage Foundation, 1959.

Bronfenbrenner, U. *Is Early Intervention Effective? A Report on Longitudinal Evaluations of Preschool Programs.* Vol. 2. Washington, D.C.: Office of Child Development, Department of Health, Education, and Welfare, 1974.

Bronfenbrenner, U. "Toward an Experimental Ecology of Human Development." *American Psychologist,* 1977, *32,* 513–531.

Bronfenbrenner, U. "Who Needs Parent Education?" *Teachers College Record*, 1978, *79*, 767-787.

Brookhart, J., and Hoch, E. "The Effects of Experimental Context and Experiential Background on Infants' Behavior Toward Their Mothers and a Stranger." *Child Development*, 1976, *47*, 333-340.

Bruner, J. S. "Poverty and Childhood." In R. K. Parker (Ed.), *The Preschool in Action: Exploring Early Childhood Programs*. Boston: Allyn & Bacon, 1972.

Caldwell, B. M., and Smith, L. E. "Day Care for the Very Young—Prime Opportunity for Primary Prevention." *American Journal of Public Health*, 1970, *60*, 690-697.

Caldwell, B. M., and others. "Infant Day Care and Attachment." *American Journal of Orthopsychiatry*, 1970, *40*, 397-412.

California State Department of Education. *Summary of the Final Child Care Pilot Study Report*. Sacramento: California State Department of Education, 1978.

California State Department of Education. *Child Development Guidelines*. Sacramento: California State Department of Education, 1979.

California State Department of Education. *Annual Report on Publicly Subsidized Child Care Services, 1978-79*. Sacramento: California State Department of Education, 1980.

Caplan, G. *Support Systems and Community Mental Health*. New York: Behavioral Publications, 1974.

Child Care Information Exchange. "Sliding Fee Scales." *Child Care Information Exchange*, June 1979.

Clarke, A. M., and Clarke, A. D. B. *Early Experience: Myth and Evidence*. New York: Free Press, 1976.

Cochran, M. M. "A Comparison of Group Day and Family Child-Rearing Patterns in Sweden." *Child Development*, 1977, *48*, 702-707.

Cohen, D. K. "Loss as a Theme in Social Policy." *Harvard Educational Review*, 1976, *46* (4), 553-571.

Cohen, D. K., and Farrar, E. "Power to the Parents? The Story of Education Vouchers." *The Public Interest*, 1977, *48*, 72-97.

Commission to Formulate a State Plan for Child Care and Development Services in California. *Child Care and Development Services, 1978.* Sacramento: California State Department of Education, 1978.

The Comptroller General of the United States. *Early Childhood and Family Development Programs Improve the Quality of Life for Low-Income Families.* Report to the Congress of the United States. U.S. General Accounting Office Publication No. HRD-79-40. Washington, D.C.: U.S. General Accounting Office, Feb. 1979.

Congressional Record, Sept. 9, 1971. Washington, D.C.: U.S. Government Printing Office, 1971.

Cooke, R. *Recommendations for a Head Start Program by a Panel of Experts.* Washington, D.C.: Office of Economic Opportunity, 1965.

Coons, J. E., and Sugarman, S. D. *Education by Choice: The Case for Family Control.* Berkeley, Calif.: University of California Press, 1978.

Cornelius, S. W., and Denney, N. W. "Dependency in Day Care and Home Care Children." *Developmental Psychology,* 1975, *11,* 575-582.

Council on Quality Education, State of Minnesota, Department of Education. *A Study of Policy Issues Related to Early Childhood and Family Education in Minnesota.* St. Paul: Minnesota Council on Quality Education, 1981.

Craig, J. H., and Craig, J. *Synergic Power: Beyond Domination and Permissiveness.* Berkeley: Proactive Press, 1973.

Datta, L. E. "Design of the Head Start Planned Variation Experiment." In A. M. Rivlin and M. P. Timpane (Eds.), *Planned Variation in Education: Should We Give Up or Try Harder?* Washington, D.C.: Brookings Institution, 1975.

Datta, L. E., McHale, C., and Mitchell, S. *The Effects of the Head Start Classroom Experience on Some Aspects of Child Development: A Summary Report of National Evaluations, 1966-1969.* Washington, D.C.: Office of Child Development, Department of Health, Education, and Welfare, n.d.

Davis, D. C. *Patterns of Primary Education.* New York: Harper & Row, 1963.

Dennis, W., and Najarian, P. "Infant Development Under Environmental Handicap." *Psychological Monographs,* 1957, *71,* 1-13.

Dewey, J. *Theory of Valuation.* Chicago: University of Chicago Press, 1939.

Dokecki, P. R. "Bureaucratic Schools and Families: Toward a Renegotiation with Policy Implications." *Peabody Journal of Education,* 1977, *55,* 56-62.

Dokecki, P. R. "Inventing, Explaining, and Conserving America: Garry Wills's Relevance to Community Psychology." *Journal of Community Psychology,* 1981, *9,* 371-378.

Dokecki, P. R., Hargrove, E. C., and Sandler, H. M. "An Overview of the Parent Child Development Center Social Experiment." In R. Haskins (Ed.), *Parent Education and Public Policy.* Norwood, N.J.: Ablex, in press.

Dokecki, P. R., Roberts, F. B., and Moroney, R. M. "Families and Professional Psychology: Policy Implications for Training and Service." Paper presented at the annual meeting of the American Psychological Association, New York, Sept. 1979.

Dolbeare, K. M., Dolbeare, P., and Hadley, J. A. *American Ideologies: The Competing Political Beliefs of the 1970s.* (2nd ed.) Chicago: Markham, 1973.

Donzelot, J. *The Policing of Families.* (R. Hurley, Trans.) New York: Pantheon Books, 1979.

Doyle, A. B. "Infant Development in Day Care." *Developmental Psychology,* 1975, *11,* 655-656.

Doyle, D. P. "The Politics of Choice: A View from the Bridge." In *Parents, Teachers, and Children.* San Francisco: Institute for Contemporary Studies, 1977.

Dunlop, K. H. "Rationales for Governmental Intervention into Child Care and Parent Education." Working paper, Institute for Public Policy Studies, Vanderbilt University, 1978.

Dunlop, K. H. "Child Care and Parent Education: Reformist Rationales for Governmental Intervention." *Education and Urban Society,* 1980, *12,* 175-191.

Dunlop, K. H. "Maternal Employment and Child Care." *Professional Psychology,* 1981, *12,* 67-75.

Edelman, M. W. "An Interview with Marian Wright Edelman." *Harvard Educational Review,* 1974, *44* (1), 53-73.

Edmonds, R. R. "Making Public Schools Effective." *Social Policy,* 1981, *12,* 56-60.

Education Commission of the States. *Early Child Development: Alternatives for Program Implementation in the States.* Denver: Education Commission of the States, 1971.

Education Commission of the States. *The Role of the Family in Child Development: Implications for State Policies and Programs.* Denver: Education Commission of the States, 1975.

Emery, F. E., and Trist, E. L. *Towards a Social Ecology: Contextual Appreciation of the Future in the Present.* London: Plenum, 1972.

Evans, E. D. *Contemporary Influences in Early Childhood Education.* New York: Holt, Rinehart and Winston, 1978.

Farber, B., and Lewis, M. "The Symbolic Use of Parents: A Sociological Critique of Educational Practice." *Journal of Research and Development in Education,* 1975, *8* (2), 34-43.

Farran, D. C., and Ramey, C. T. "Infant Day Care and Attachment Behavior Toward Mothers and Teachers." *Child Development,* 1977, *48,* 1112-1116.

Fein, G. G. "Infant Day Care and the Family: Regulatory Strategies to Ensure Parent Participation." Report prepared for the Office of the Assistant Secretary for Planning and Evaluation, Department of Health, Education, and Welfare, 1976.

Fein, G. G. "The Informed Parent." In S. Kilmer (Ed.), *Advances in Early Education and Day Care.* Vol. 1. Greenwich, Conn.: JAI Press, 1980.

Fein, G. G., and Clarke-Stewart, A. *Day Care in Context.* New York: Wiley, 1973.

Finkelstein, N. W., and Wilson, K. "The Influence of Daycare on Social Behaviors Toward Peers and Adults." Paper presented at the biennial meeting of the Society for Research on Child Development, New Orleans, March 1977.

Finkelstein, N. W., and others. "Social Behavior of Infants and Toddlers in a Day Care Environment." *Developmental Psychology,* 1978, *14,* 257-262.

Florin, P. R., and Dokecki, P. R. "Changing Families Through Parent and Family Education: Review and Analysis." In I. Sigel and L. Laosa (Eds.), *Changing Families.* London: Plenum, 1983.

Fowler, W., and Kahn, N. "The Development of a Prototype Infant and Child Care Center in Metropolitan Toronto: Year 4 Progress Report." Unpublished manuscript, Ontario Institute for Studies in Education, 1975.

Freud, A., and Dann, S. "An Experiment in Group Upbringing." *The Psychoanalytic Study of the Child*, 1951, *6*, 127–168.

Frost, J. L., and Kissinger, J. B. *The Young Child and the Educative Process*. New York: Holt, Rinehart and Winston, 1976.

Galinsky, E., and Hooks, W. H. *The New Extended Family: Day Care Programs That Work*. Boston: Houghton Mifflin, 1977.

The Gallup Organization, Inc. *American Families—1980: An Indepth Survey and Analysis*. Newport Beach, Calif.: American Research Corporation, 1980.

General Accounting Office. *Project Head Start: Achievements and Problems*. Washington, D.C.: Office of Child Development, Department of Health, Education, and Welfare, May 1975.

Ginsberg, S. "The Child Care Center Chronicle." In J. L. Hymes, Jr. (Ed.), *Early Childhood Education: Living History Interviews*. Book 2: *Care of the Children of Working Mothers*. Carmel, Calif.: Hacienda Press, 1978.

Glaser, E. M. "Knowledge Transfer and Institutional Change." *Professional Psychology*, 1973, *4*, 434–444.

Glass, N. "Eating, Sleeping and Elimination Habits in Children Attending Day Nurseries and Children Cared for at Home by Mothers." *American Journal of Orthopsychiatry*, 1949, *19*, 697–711.

Glick, P. C. "Children of Divorced Parents in Demographic Perspective." *Journal of Social Issues*, 1979, *35* (4), 170–182.

Goldsmith, C. "The New York City Day Care Unit." In J. L. Hymes, Jr. (Ed.), *Early Childhood Education: Living History Interviews*. Book 2: *Care of the Children of Working Mothers*. Carmel, Calif.: Hacienda Press, 1978.

Goldstein, J., Freud, A., and Solnit, A. J. *Beyond the Best Interests of the Child*. New York: Free Press, 1973.

Golembiewski, R. T., and Hiles, R. J. "Drug Company Workers

Like New Schedules." *Monthly Labor Review*, 1977, *100*, 65-69.

Gordon, I. J. "Parent Education and Parent Involvement: Retrospect and Prospect." *Childhood Education*, 1977, *54*, 71-79.

Gordon, I. J. "Parent Education: A Position Paper." In Education Commission of the States, *Families and Schools: Implementing Parent Education*. Denver: Education Commission of the States, 1979.

Governor's Advisory Committee on Child Development Programs. *The Alternative Child Care Program (AB 3059) 1976-77*. Sacramento: Governor's Advisory Committee on Child Development Programs, 1977.

Governor's Advisory Committee on Child Development Programs. *Child Care Licensing and Regulation*. Sacramento: Governor's Advisory Committee on Child Development Programs, 1978. (Reissued 1981.)

Governor's Advisory Committee on Child Development Programs. *AB 3059: A Report to the Governor on the Alternative Child Care Programs, 1976-80*. Sacramento: Governor's Advisory Committee on Child Development Programs, 1981.

Gray, S. W., and Klaus, R. A. "The Early Training Project: A Seventh Year Report." *Child Development*, 1970, *41*, 909-924.

Greenblatt, B. *Responsibility for Child Care: The Changing Role of Family and State in Child Development*. San Francisco: Jossey-Bass, 1977.

Grubb, W. N., and Lazerson, M. "Child Care, Government Financing, and the Public Schools: Lessons from the California Children's Centers." *School Review*, 1977, *86* (1), 5-37.

Hargrove, E. C. "The Search for Implementation Theory." In R. J. Zeckhauser and D. Leebaert (Eds.), *What Role for Government? Lessons from Policy Research*. Durham, N.C.: Duke University Press, 1983.

Harman, D., and Brim, O. G., Jr. *Learning to be Parents: Principles, Programs, and Methods*. Beverly Hills, Calif.: Sage, 1980.

Havelock, R. G., and Lingwood, D. A. *R & D Utilization Strategies and Functions: An Analytical Comparison of Four Sys-*

tems. Ann Arbor, Mich.: Institute for Social Research, University of Michigan, 1973.

Heinicke, C. M. "Some Effects of Separating Two-Year-Old Children from Their Parents: A Comparative Study." *Human Relations,* 1956, *9,* 105–176.

Hendrix, N. L. "Demographic Parameters of the Need for Child Care." *New Human Services Review,* 1979, *5,* 5–6.

Hendrix, N. L. "Childcare Usage Patterns as Estimates of Childcare Need." *Journal of Sociology and Social Welfare,* 1981, *8,* 665–673.

Hightower, H. H. "Perceptions of Ideal and Actual Parent Involvement in Educational Decision-Making." Unpublished doctoral dissertation, Arizona State University, 1977.

Hill-Scott, K. "Citizen and Parent Participation in Policy Making and Program Implementation." Paper presented at the annual meeting of the American Psychological Association, San Francisco, August 1977.

Hirschowitz, R. G. "Groups to Help People Cope with the Tasks of Transition." In R. G. Hirschowitz and B. Levy (Eds.), *The Changing Mental Health Scene.* New York: Spectrum, 1976.

Hobbs, N. *The Futures of Children: Recommendations of the Project on Classification of Exceptional Children.* San Francisco: Jossey-Bass, 1975a.

Hobbs, N. (Ed.) *Issues in the Classification of Children: A Sourcebook on Categories, Labels, and Their Consequences.* San Francisco: Jossey-Bass, 1975b.

Hobbs, N. "Families, Schools, and Communities: An Ecosystem for Children." *Teachers College Record,* 1978, *79,* 756–766.

Hobbs, N. *The Troubled and Troubling Child: Reeducation in Mental Health, Education, and Human Services Programs for Children and Youth.* San Francisco: Jossey-Bass, 1982.

Hodges, W. L., and Sheehan, R. "Follow Through as Ten Years of Experimentation: What Have We Learned?" *Young Children,* 1978, *34* (1), 4–14.

Hoffman, L. W. "Effects of Maternal Employment on the Child: A Review of the Research." *Developmental Psychology,* 1974, *10,* 204–228.

Hunt, J. M. V. *Intelligence and Experience.* New York: Ronald Press, 1961.

Innes, S. M. "Information and Referral Services: One Aspect of the Child Care Service Delivery System." Working paper, Institute for Public Policy Studies, Vanderbilt University, 1980.

Innes, S. M., and Dunlop, K. H. "A Descriptive Analysis of Child Care Programs in the United States." Working paper, Institute for Public Policy Studies, Vanderbilt University, 1979.

Innes, S. M., and Dunlop, K. H. "Descriptive Observations About Day Care Programs." Working paper, Institute for Public Policy Studies, Vanderbilt University, 1980.

Internal Revenue Service. *Statistics of Income—1972: Individual Income Tax Returns.* Washington, D.C.: U.S. Government Printing Office, 1974.

Internal Revenue Service. *Statistics of Income—1975: Individual Income Tax Returns.* Washington, D.C.: U.S. Government Printing Office, 1978.

Internal Revenue Service. *Statistics of Income—1976: Individual Income Tax Returns.* Washington, D.C.: U.S. Government Printing Office, 1979.

Internal Revenue Service. *Statistics of Income—1977: Individual Income Tax Returns.* Washington, D.C.: U.S. Government Printing Office, 1980.

Internal Revenue Service. *Statistics of Income—1978: Individual Income Tax Returns.* Washington, D.C.: U.S. Government Printing Office, 1981.

Internal Revenue Service. *Statistics of Income—1979: Individual Income Tax Returns.* Washington, D.C.: U.S. Government Printing Office, 1982.

Internal Revenue Service. *Statistics of Income—1980: Individual Income Tax Returns.* Washington, D.C.: U.S. Government Printing Office, 1983.

Joffe, C. E. *Friendly Intruders: Childcare Professionals and Family Life.* Berkeley, Calif.: University of California Press, 1977.

Johnson, A. S. *Recommendations to the White House Conference on Families.* Pamphlet from Family Impact Seminar, Institute for Educational Leadership, George Washington University, May 1980.

Kagan, J., Kearsley, R. B., and Zelazo, P. R. "The Effects of Infant Day Care on Psychological Development." *Evaluation Quarterly,* 1977, *1* (1), 109-142.

Kahn, A. J. "The Inevitability and the Hazards of Family Policy." Paper presented at a conference sponsored by the Australian Council of Social Welfare Ministers, Sidney, Australia, May 1980.

Kamerman, S. B. "Family Policy: A Comparative Review." Paper presented at a conference sponsored by the Australian Council of Social Welfare Ministers, Sidney, Australia, May 1980.

Kamerman, S. B., and Kahn, A. J. *Child Care, Family Benefits, and Working Parents.* Philadelphia: Temple University Press, 1976.

Kamerman, S. B., and Kahn, A. J. "The Day-Care Debate: A Wider View." *The Public Interest,* 1979, Winter (54), 76–93.

Kanter, R. M. *Work and Family in the United States: A Critical Review and Agenda for Research and Policy.* New York: Russell Sage Foundation, 1977.

Kaplan, B. A., and Forgione, P. D. "Parent Involvement in Compensatory Education Programs: Problems and Potential Strategies Across 32 School Districts." Paper presented at the annual meeting of the American Educational Research Association, Toronto, Canada, March 1978.

Kearsley, R. B., and others. "Separation Protest in Day-Care and Home-Reared Infants." *Pediatrics,* 1975, *52,* 171–175.

Keesling, J. W., and Melaragno, R. J. "Parents and Federal Education Programs: Some Preliminary Findings from the Study of Parental Involvement." In R. Haskins (Ed.), *Parent Education and Public Policy.* Norwood, N.J.: Ablex, in press.

Keniston, K., and the Carnegie Council on Children. *All Our Children: The American Family Under Pressure.* New York: Harcourt Brace Jovanovich, 1977.

Keyserling, M. D. *Windows on Day Care.* New York: National Council of Jewish Women, 1972.

Kilmer, S. "Infant-Toddler Group Day Care: A Review of Research." In L. G. Katz, M. X. Glockner, C. Watkins, and M. J. Spencer (Eds.), *Current Topics in Early Childhood Education.* Vol. 2. Norwood, N.J.: Ablex, 1979.

Kirschner Associates, Inc. *A National Survey of the Impacts of Head Start Centers on Community Institutions.* Washington, D.C.: Office of Child Development, Department of Health, Education, and Welfare, May 1970.

Kirst, M. "California." In S. Fuhrman and A. Rosenthal (Eds.), *Shaping Education Policy in the States*. Washington, D.C.: Institute for Educational Leadership, 1981.

Knox, A. B. *Adult Development and Learning*. San Francisco: Jossey-Bass, 1977.

LaCrosse, E. R. "The Early Childhood Project of the Education Commission of the States." *Theory into Practice*, 1977, *16*, 47-48.

Ladd, E. C. "Traditional Values Regnant." *Public Opinion*, 1978, *1*, 45-49.

Lambie, D. Z., Bond, J. T., and Weikart, D. P. "Framework for Infant Education." In B. Z. Friedlander, G. M. Sterritt, and G. E. Kirk (Eds.), *Exceptional Infant*. Vol. 3: *Assessment and Intervention*. New York: Brunner/Mazel, 1975.

Largman, R. "The Social-Emotional Effects of Age of Entry into Full-Time Group Care." Unpublished doctoral dissertation, University of California, Berkeley, 1975.

Lasch, C. *Haven in a Heartless World: The Family Besieged*. New York: Basic Books, 1977.

Lasch, C. "Life in the Therapeutic State." *New York Review of Books*, 1980.

Laslett, P. "Characteristics of the Western Family Considered over Time." *Journal of Family History*, 1977, *2* (2), 89-115.

LaVor, M., and Harvey, J. "Headstart, Economic Opportunity, Community Partnership Act of 1974." *Exceptional Children*, 1976, *42*, 227-230.

Lazar, I. "Social Research and Social Policy—Reflections on Relationships." In R. Haskins and J. J. Gallagher (Eds.), *Care and Education of Young Children in America: Policy, Politics, and Social Science*. Norwood, N.J.: Ablex, 1980.

Lazar, I., and others. *Summary: The Persistence of Preschool Effects*. Department of Health, Education, and Welfare Publication No. OHDS 78-30129. Washington, D.C.: U.S. Government Printing Office, 1977.

Lazar, J. B., and Chapman, J. E. "A Review of the Present Status and Future Research Needs of Programs to Develop Parenting Skills." Paper prepared for the Interagency Panel on Early Childhood Research and Development, 1972.

Lazerson, M. "The Historical Antecedents of Early Childhood

Education." In I. J. Gordon (Ed.), *Early Childhood Education: The Seventy-First Yearbook of the National Society for the Study of Education.* Chicago: University of Chicago Press, 1972.

Leeper, S. H., and others. *Good Schools for Young Children.* (3rd ed.) New York: Macmillan, 1974.

Leler, H. "Parent Education and Involvement in Relation to the Schools and to Parents of School-Aged Children." In R. Haskins (Ed.), *Parent Education and Public Policy.* Norwood, N.J.: Ablex, in press.

Levine, J. A. *Day Care and the Public Schools: Profiles of Five Communities.* Newton, Mass.: Education Development Center, 1978.

Lieberman, A. F. "The Social Competence of Preschool Children: Its Relations to Quality of Attachment and to Amount of Exposure to Peers in Different Preschool Settings." Unpublished doctoral dissertation, Johns Hopkins University, 1976.

Lortie, D. C. *Schoolteacher.* Chicago: University of Chicago Press, 1975.

Lynn, L. E. *The State and Human Services: Organizational Change in a Political Context.* Cambridge, Mass.: M.I.T. Press, 1980.

McCathren, R. R. "The Demise of Federal Categorical Child Care Legislation: Lessons for the '80s from the Failures of the '70s." In H. C. Wallach (Ed.), *Approaches to Child and Family Policy.* Boulder, Colo.: Westview Press, 1980.

McCutcheon, B., and Calhoun, R. S. "Social and Emotional Adjustment of Infants and Toddlers to a Day Care Setting." *American Journal of Orthopsychiatry,* 1976, *46,* 104–108.

McInerny, T. K., Roghmann, K. J., and Sutherland, S. A. "Primary Pediatric Care in One Community." *Pediatrics,* 1978, *61,* 389–397.

McLaughlin, M. W. *Evaluation and Reform: The Elementary and Secondary Education Act of 1965, Title I.* Cambridge, Mass.: Ballinger, 1975.

McMillan, D. "Sense of Community: An Attempt at Definition." Unpublished manuscript, George Peabody College for Teachers, 1976.

Macrae, J. W., and Herbert-Jackson, E. "Are Behavioral Effects of Infant Day Care Programs Specific?" *Developmental Psychology*, 1975, *12,* 269–270.

McWilliams, W. C. *The Idea of Fraternity in America.* Berkeley, Calif.: University of California Press, 1974.

Majteles, D. H. "V is for Voucher, Valuable, Viable." *Day Care and Early Education*, 1979, *6* (4), 18–21.

Mallory, B. L. "Project Head Start: The Interaction of Policy Making and Program Evaluation." Working paper, Institute for Public Policy Studies, Vanderbilt University, 1979.

Mann, A. J., Harrell, A., and Hurt, M. *A Review of Head Start Research Since 1969 and an Annotated Bibliography.* Washington, D.C.: Social Research Group, George Washington University, May 1977.

Marmor, T. "On Comparing Income Maintenance Alternatives." *American Political Science Review*, 1971, *65,* 83–96.

Masnick, G., and Bane, M. J. *The Nation's Families: 1960–1990.* Cambridge, Mass.: Joint Center for Urban Studies of M.I.T. and Harvard University, 1980.

MIDCO Educational Associates. *Perspectives on Parent Participation in Head Start: An Analysis and Critique.* Department of Health, Education, and Welfare Publication No. 05-72-45. Washington, D.C.: Project Head Start, Office of Child Development, Department of Health, Education, and Welfare, Nov. 1972.

Moore, K. A., and Hofferth, S. L. "Women and Their Children." In R. E. Smith (Ed.), *The Subtle Revolution: Women at Work.* Washington, D.C.: Urban Institute, 1979.

Morgan, G. G. *The Trouble with Title XX: A Review of Child Daycare Policy.* Washington, D.C.: Day Care and Child Development Council of America, 1977. (Available through ERIC Document Reproduction Service, ED-143-443.)

Moroney, R. M. *Families, Social Services, and Social Policy: The Issue of Shared Responsibility.* Department of Health and Human Services Publication No. ADM 80-846. Washington, D.C.: U.S. Government Printing Office, 1980.

Moskowitz, D. S., Schwarz, J. C., and Corsini, D. A. "Initiating Day Care at Three Years of Age: Effects on Attachment." *Child Development*, 1977, *48,* 1271–1276.

Mueller, O., and Cole, M. "Concept Wins Converts and Federal Agency." *Monthly Labor Review,* 1977, *100,* 71-74.

Naparstek, A., and others. *Neighborhood and Family Services Project.* Los Angeles: University of Southern California, Washington Public Affairs Center, 1978.

National Academy of Sciences. *Toward a National Policy for Children and Families.* Washington, D.C.: National Academy of Sciences, 1976.

National Association of Early Childhood Specialists in State Departments of Education. "Contributions of State Departments of Education in Early Childhood Program/Services Coordination: A Position Paper." Unpublished paper, August 1978.

National Childcare Consumer Study: 1975. Vol. 1: *Basic Tabulations.* Washington, D.C.: Office of Child Development, Department of Health, Education, and Welfare.

National Childcare Consumer Study: 1975. Vol. 2: *Current Patterns of Childcare Use in the United States.* Washington, D.C.: Office of Child Development, Department of Health, Education, and Welfare.

National Childcare Consumer Study: 1975. Vol. 3: *American Consumer Attitudes and Preferences on Child Care.* Washington, D.C.: Office of Child Development, Department of Health, Education, and Welfare.

National Day Care Home Study Final Report. Vol. 2: *Family Day Care in the United States: Research Report.* Department of Health and Human Services Publication No. OHDS 80-30283. Washington, D.C.: Department of Health and Human Services, 1980.

National Day Care Home Study Final Report. Executive Summary: *Family Day Care in the United States.* Department of Health and Human Services Publication No. OHDS 80-30287. Washington, D.C.: Department of Health and Human Services, 1981.

National Day Care Study. Vol. 3: *Day Care Centers in the U.S.: A National Profile 1976-1977.* Final Report of the National Day Care Supply Study. Cambridge, Mass.: Abt Associates, 1978.

National Day Care Study. Vol. 1: *Children at the Center: Summary Findings and Policy Implications of the National Day Care Study.* Cambridge, Mass.: Abt Associates, 1979.

National Institute of Education. *Compensatory Education Study: Final Report.* Washington, D.C.: Department of Health, Education, and Welfare, 1978.

Nelson, R. R. *The Moon and the Ghetto.* New York: Norton, 1977.

Nisbet, R. A. *The Quest for Community.* New York: Oxford University Press, 1969.

Odden, A., and Dougherty, V. *State Programs of School Improvement: A 50-State Survey.* Denver: Education Commission of the States, 1982.

Palmer, F. H. "The Effects of Early Childhood Intervention." Paper presented at the annual meeting of the American Association for the Advancement of Science, Denver, December 1977.

Parker, R. K., and Day, M. C. "Comparisons of Preschool Curricula." In R. K. Parker (Ed.), *The Preschool in Action: Exploring Early Childhood Programs.* Boston: Allyn & Bacon, 1972.

Pifer, A. *Perceptions of Childhood and Youth.* Annual Report for the Fiscal Year Ended September 30, 1978. New York: Carnegie Corporation of New York, 1978.

Plisko, V. H. "Preprimary Education." In National Center for Education Statistics, *The Condition of Education: 1980 Edition.* Washington, D.C.: U.S. Government Printing Office, 1980.

Portnoy, F. C., and Simmons, C. H. "Day Care and Attachment." *Child Development,* 1978, *49,* 239-242.

Powell, D. R. *The Interface Between Families and Child Care Programs: A Study of Parent-Caregiver Relationships.* Detroit, Mich.: Merrill-Palmer Institute, 1977.

Powell, D. R. "Organizational Problems in Institutionalizing Parent Education in the Public Schools." In Education Commission of the States, *Families and Schools: Implementing Parent Education.* Denver: Education Commission of the States, 1979.

Project Head Start, 1969-1970: A Descriptive Report of Programs and Participants. Washington, D.C.: Research and Evaluation Division, Office of Child Development, Department of Health, Education, and Welfare, July 1972.

Racki, G. H. E. M. "The Effects of Flexible Working Hours." Unpublished doctoral dissertation, University of Lausanne, 1975.

Ragozin, A. S. "Attachment Behavior of Young Children in Day Care." Unpublished doctoral dissertation, Harvard University, 1976.

Ramey, C., and Smith, B. "Learning and Intelligence in Disadvantaged Infants: Effects of Early Intervention." *American Journal of Mental Deficiency,* 1977, *81,* 318-324.

Raph, J. B., and others. "The Influence of Nursery School on Social Interaction." *American Journal of Orthopsychiatry,* 1968, *39,* 144-152.

Ravenscraft, P. "Day Care on Campus." *Day Care and Early Education,* 1973, *1,* 22-25.

Ravitch, D. "In the Family's Way." *The New Republic,* 1980, *182,* 18-21.

Rawls, J. *A Theory of Justice.* Cambridge, Mass.: Belknap Press, Harvard University Press, 1971.

Resch, R. C., and others. "Infant Day Care as a Treatment Intervention: A Follow-Up Comparison Study." *Child Psychiatry and Human Development,* 1977, 7 (3), 147-155.

Rice, R. M. *American Family Policy: Content and Context.* New York: Family Service Association of America, 1977.

Rivlin, A. *Systematic Thinking for Social Action.* Washington, D.C.: The Brookings Institution, 1971.

Roberts, F. B., and Dokecki, P. R. "A Summary of Findings and Policy Issues Related to Parent Education Within the Health Care Delivery System." Working paper, Institute for Public Policy Studies, Vanderbilt University, 1980.

Robinson, H. B., and Robinson, N. M. "Longitudinal Development of Very Young Children in a Comprehensive Day Care Program: The First Two Years." *Child Development,* 1971, *42,* 1673-1683.

Robinson, N. M., and others. *A World of Children: Daycare and Preschool Institutions.* Monterey, Calif.: Brooks/Cole, 1979.

Rosenthal, A., and Fuhrman, S. *Legislative Education Leadership in the States.* Washington, D.C.: Institute for Educational Leadership, 1981.

Ross, H., and Sawhill, I. *Time of Transition: The Growth of Families Headed by Women.* Washington, D.C.: Urban Institute, 1975.

Rotberg, I. C. "Federal Policy Issues in Elementary and Secondary Education." In R. A. Miller (Ed.), *The Federal Role in Education: New Directions for the Eighties.* Washington, D.C.: Institute for Educational Leadership, 1981.

Rubenstein, J. L., Howes, C., and Boyle, P. "A Two-Year Follow-Up of Infants in Community Based Infant Day Care." Paper presented at the biennial meeting of the Society for Research in Child Development, San Francisco, March 1979.

Rubenstein, J. L., Pedersen, F. A., and Yarrow, L. J. "What Happens When Mother Is Away: A Comparison of Mothers and Substitute Caregivers." *Developmental Psychology,* 1977, *13,* 529-530.

Rubin, L. *Worlds of Pain: Life in the Working Class Family.* New York: Basic Books, 1976.

Sassen, G., and Avrin, C. *Corporations and Child Care: Profit-Making Day Care, Workplace Day Care and a Look at the Alternatives.* Roslindale, Mass.: Women's Research Action Project, 1974.

Schaefer, E. S. *Parent-Professional-Child Interaction and Involvement.* Three Year Continuation Report. Chapel Hill, N.C.: School of Public Health, Frank Porter Graham Child Development Center, University of North Carolina, 1977.

Schickendanz, J. A. "Parents, Teachers, and Early Education." In B. Perksy and L. Colubchich (Eds.), *Early Childhood.* Wayne, N.J.: Avery Publishing Group, 1977.

Schlossman, S. L. "Before Home Start: Notes Toward a History of Parent Education in America, 1897-1929." *Harvard Educational Review,* 1976, *46,* 436-467.

Schlossman, S. L. "The Parent Education Game: The Politics of Child Psychology in the 1970's." *Teachers College Record,* 1978, *79,* 788-808.

Schultz, C. L. *The Public Use of Private Interest.* Washington, D.C.: Brookings Institution, 1977.

Schwarz, J. C., Krolick, G., and Strickland, B. S. "Effects of Early Day Care Experience on Adjustment to a New Environment." *American Journal of Orthopsychiatry,* 1973, *43,* 340-346.

Schwarz, J. C., Strickland, R. G., and Krolick, G. "Infant Day Care: Behavioral Effects at Preschool Age." *Developmental Psychology,* 1974, *10,* 502-507.

Sherman, A., Payne, J. S., and Carriker, W. S. "Is Head Start Dying?" *Training School Bulletin,* 1971, *68,* 113-130.

Shipman, V. C., McKee, D., and Bridgeman, B. *Stability and Change in Family Status, Situational and Process Variables, and Their Relationship to Children.* Princeton, N.J.: Educational Testing Service, 1977.

Short, E. C. "Knowledge Production and Utilization in Curriculum: A Special Case of the General Phenomenon." *Review of Educational Research,* 1973, *43,* 237-301.

Shortlidge, R. L., Jr., and Brito, P. *How Women Arrange for the Care of Their Children While They Work: A Study of Child Care Arrangements, Costs and Preferences in 1971.* Columbus: Center for Human Resource Research, Ohio State University, 1977.

Silverman, P. R. "Mutual Help." In R. G. Hirschowitz and B. Levy (Eds.), *The Changing Mental Health Scene.* New York: Spectrum, 1976.

Smith, M. S., and Bissell, J. S. "Report Analysis: The Impact of Head Start." *Harvard Educational Review,* 1970, *40,* 51-104.

Spitz, R. A. "Hospitalism: An Inquiry into the Genesis of Psychiatric Conditions in Early Childhood." In A. Freud and others (Eds.), *The Psychoanalytic Study of the Child.* Vol. 1. New York: International Universities Press, 1945.

Steiner, G. Y. *The Children's Cause.* Washington, D.C.: Brookings Institution, 1976.

Steiner, G. Y. *The Futility of Family Policy.* Washington, D.C.: Brookings Institution, 1981.

Steinfels, M. O. *Who's Minding the Children?* New York: Simon & Schuster, 1973.

Stoddard, S. "Vouchers for Child Care: The Santa Clara Child Care Pilot Study." In P. K. Robins and S. Weiner (Eds.), *Child*

Care and Public Policy. Lexington, Mass.: Lexington Books, 1978.

Stolz, L. M. "The Kaiser Child Service Centers." In J. L. Hymes, Jr. (Ed.), *Early Childhood Education: Living History Interviews. Book 2: Care of the Children of Working Mothers.* Carmel, Calif.: Hacienda Press, 1978.

Suchman, E. A. "Action for What? A Critique of Evaluation Research." In C. N. Weiss (Ed.), *Evaluating Action Programs: Readings in Social Action and Education.* Boston: Allyn & Bacon, 1972.

Surrey, S. S. *Pathways to Tax Reform: The Concept of Tax Expenditures.* Cambridge, Mass.: Harvard University Press, 1973.

Swift, J. W. "Effects of Early Group Experience: The Nursery School and Day Nursery." In M. C. Hoffman and L. W. Hoffman (Eds.), *Review of Child Development Research.* Vol. 1. New York: Russell Sage Foundation, 1964.

U.S. Congress. *Economic Opportunity Act of 1964,* Sec. 2 of P.L. 88-452; 78 Stat. 508, 1964. Washington, D.C.: U.S. Government Printing Office, 1964.

U.S. Congress. *Elementary and Secondary Education Act,* Sec. 101 of P.L. 95-561; 92 Stat. 2143, 1978. Washington, D.C.: U.S. Government Printing Office, 1978.

U.S. Congress, Congressional Budget Office. *Child Care and Preschool: Options for Federal Support.* Washington, D.C.: U.S. Government Printing Office, 1978.

U.S. Congress, House Committee on Education and Labor. *House Report No. 92-1367: Economic Opportunity Amendments of 1972,* 92nd Congress, 2nd session. Washington, D.C.: U.S. Government Printing Office, 1972.

U.S. Congress, House Committee on Science and Technology. *Statement by Kenneth Prewitt in Hearings Before the Subcommittee on Science and Technology.* February 20, 1980. Washington, D.C.: U.S. Government Printing Office, 1980.

U.S. Congress, Joint Committee on Internal Revenue Taxation. Unpublished data, September 23, 1974.

U.S. Congress, Joint Committee on Internal Revenue Taxation. *General Explanation of the Tax Reform Act of 1976,* H.R.

94-10612. Washington, D.C.: U.S. Government Printing Office, 1976.

U.S. Congress, Senate Committee on Human Resources. *Senate Report No. 95-892: Economic Opportunity Act Amendments of 1978,* 95th Congress, 2nd session. Washington, D.C.: U.S. Government Printing Office, 1978.

U.S. Congress, Senate Committee on Human Resources, Subcommittee on Employment, Poverty, and Migratory Labor. *Economic Opportunity Amendments of 1977-1978,* 95th Congress, 1st session, 2nd session, S. 2090. Washington, D.C.: U.S. Government Printing Office, 1978.

U.S. Congress, Senate Committee on Labor and Public Welfare. *Senate Report No. 92-793: Comprehensive Headstart, Child Development, and Family Services Act of 1972,* 92nd Congress, 2nd session. Washington, D.C.: U.S. Government Printing Office, 1972.

U.S. Congress, Senate Committee on Labor and Public Welfare, Subcommittee on Children and Youth and Subcommittee on Employment, Poverty, and Migratory Labor; House Committee on Education and Labor, Subcommittee on Select Education. *Child and Family Services Act of 1975,* 94th Congress, 1st session, S. 626 and H.R. 2966. Washington, D.C.: U.S. Government Printing Office, 1975.

U.S. Department of Commerce, Bureau of the Census. "General Characteristics of Families." *Subject Reports,* Series P-ENO. 2A. Washington, D.C.: U.S. Government Printing Office, 1950.

U.S. Department of Commerce, Bureau of the Census. "Household and Family Characteristics: March 1975." *Current Population Reports,* Series P-20, No. 291. Washington, D.C.: U.S. Government Printing Office, 1975a.

U.S. Department of Commerce, Bureau of the Census. "School Enrollment—Social and Economic Characteristics of Students: October 1974 (Advance Report)." *Current Population Reports,* Series P-20, No. 278. Washington, D.C.: U.S. Government Printing Office, 1975b.

U.S. Department of Commerce, Bureau of the Census. "Projections of the Population of the United States: 1977 to 2050."

Current Population Reports, Series P-25, No. 704. Washington, D.C.: U.S. Government Printing Office, 1977.

U.S. Department of Commerce, Bureau of the Census. Unpublished tabulations, 1980.

U.S. Department of Commerce, Bureau of the Census. "School Enrollment—Social and Economic Characteristics of Students: October 1980 (Advance Report)." *Current Population Reports,* Series P-20, No. 362. Washington, D.C.: U.S. Government Printing Office, 1981.

U.S. Department of Commerce, Bureau of the Census. "Projections of the Population of the United States, 1982–2050 (Advance Report)." *Current Population Reports,* Series P-25, No. 922. Washington, D.C.: U.S. Government Printing Office, 1982.

U.S. Department of Health, Education, and Welfare, National Center for Education Statistics. *Projections of Education Statistics to 1988–89.* Washington, D.C.: U.S. Government Printing Office, 1980.

U.S. Department of Health, Education, and Welfare, Office of the Assistant Secretary for Planning and Evaluation. *The Appropriateness of the Federal Interagency Day Care Requirements (FIDCR): Report of Findings and Recommendations.* Washington, D.C.: U.S. Government Printing Office, 1978.

U.S. Department of Health, Education, and Welfare, Office of Child Development, Federal Panel on Early Childhood. *Federal Interagency Day Care Requirements.* Pursuant to Sec. 522(d) of the Economic Opportunity Act. Washington, D.C.: U.S. Government Printing Office, 1968.

U.S. Department of Health, Education, and Welfare, Office of Human Development, Office of Child Development. *The Child and Family Resource Program: An Overview.* Department of Health, Education, and Welfare Publication No. OHD 76-31087. Washington, D.C.: U.S. Government Printing Office, 1976.

U.S. Department of Health, Education, and Welfare, Office of the Secretary. 45 CFR Part 71, HEW Day Care Regulations. *Federal Register,* 1980, *45* (55), 17870–17885.

U.S. Department of Labor, Bureau of Labor Statistics. *U.S.*

Working Women: A Data Book. Washington, D.C.: U.S. Government Printing Office, 1977.

U.S. Department of Labor, Bureau of Labor Statistics. *Employment in Perspective: Working Women.* Report 631, Fourth Quarter. Washington, D.C.: Department of Labor, 1980.

Valentine, J., and Stark, E. "The Social Context of Parent Involvement in Head Start." In E. Zigler and J. Valentine (Eds.), *Project Head Start: A Legacy of the War on Poverty.* New York: Free Press, 1979.

Vickers, G. *Value Systems and Social Process.* New York: Basic Books, 1968.

Wade, M. *Flexible Working Hours in Practice.* New York: Halsted Press, 1973.

Waite, L. J. "U.S. Women at Work." *Population Bulletin,* 1981, *36* (2), 1-44.

Waldman, E., and others. "Working Mothers in the 1970's: A Look at the Statistics." *Monthly Labor Review,* 1979, *102* (10), 39-49.

Wandersman, L. P. "Parenting Groups to Support the Adjustment to Parenthood." *Family Perspectives,* 1978, *12,* 117-128.

Warner, D. D. *Comparative Evaluation of AB 3059 Alternative Child Care Programs: Summary Report.* Cambridge, Mass.: Abt Associates, 1979.

Watson, D. *Caring for Strangers: An Introduction to Practical Philosophy for Students of Social Administration.* London: Routledge & Kegan Paul, 1980.

Weeks, K. "Tax Credits and Child Care Expenses: Implementation and Implications for Policy." Working paper, Institute for Public Policy Studies, Vanderbilt University, 1980.

Weikart, D. P. "Longitudinal Studies in Early Childhood Education." In R. Haskins (Ed.), *Parent Education and Public Policy.* Norwood, N.J.: Ablex, in press.

Weikart, D. P., Deloria, D. J., and Lawson, S. "Results of a Preschool Intervention Project." In S. Ryan (Ed.), *A Report on Longitudinal Evaluations of Preschool Programs.* Vol. 1. Department of Health, Education, and Welfare Publication No. OHD 74-24. Washington, D.C.: Department of Health, Education, and Welfare, 1974.

Westinghouse Learning Corporation. *The Impact of Headstart: An Evaluation of the Headstart Experience on Children's Cognitive and Affective Development.* Athens: Ohio University Press, 1969.

White, S. H. *Federal Programs for Young Children.* (4 vols.) Cambridge, Mass.: Huron Institute, 1973.

Whitfield, R. C. *Education for Family Life: Some New Policies for Child Care.* London: Hodder & Stoughton, 1980.

Wills, G. *Inventing America: Jefferson's Declaration of Independence.* New York: Doubleday, 1978.

Winett, R. A., and others. "A Cross-Sectional Study of Children and Their Families in Different Child Care Environments: Some Data and Conclusions." *Journal of Community Psychology,* 1977, *5* (2), 149-159.

Woolsey, S. H. "Pied Piper Politics and the Child-Care Debate." *Daedalus,* 1977, *106* (2), 127-145.

Wright, L. "Parent Consultation and Other Methods of Indirect Treatment." In L. Wright and A. B. Schaefer (Eds.), *Encyclopedia of Pediatric Psychology.* Baltimore: University Park Press, 1979.

Yankelovich, Skelly, and White, Inc. *Raising Children in a Changing Society.* Minneapolis: General Mills, Inc., 1977.

Yurchak, M. J., and Bryk, A. S. *ESEA Title I Early Childhood Education: A Descriptive Report.* Cambridge, Mass.: Huron Institute, January 1979.

Zigler, E. "America's Head Start Program: An Agenda for Its Second Decade." *Young Children,* 1978, *33* (5), 4-11.

Zigler, E., and Anderson, K. "An Idea Whose Time Had Come: The Intellectual and Political Climate for Head Start." In E. Zigler and J. Valentine (Eds.), *Project Head Start: A Legacy of the War on Poverty.* New York: Free Press, 1979.

Index

338   Index

ents' attitudes toward, 85, 88; preprimary school enrollment in, 83-84, 86-87, 88, 89, 239-240; provider relations with children in, 124-126, 138-140; and social development, 96-101; types of, 81-83. *See also* Child care and parent education

Child Care Act of 1979 (S. 4), 214

Child care and parent education: analysis of national experience with, 54-126; by colleges and universities, 70-72; conclusions on, 303-309; cooperative and self-help groups for, 58-61; financing, 296-298; guidelines for program development in, 108-126; individual, private provision of, 56-58; institutional arrangements for, 109-114; and instrumental considerations, 287-302; leadership for, 113-114; needs for, 4-5, 131; and parental role, 114-124; participation effects of, 91-108; and privacy, 224-225, 282-283; private, for-profit sponsorship of, 74-76; from private, nonprofit organizations, 61-64; programs of, 54-79; by public schools, 64-70, 237-244; shared responsibility in, 122-124; summary on, 78-79, 90-91, 107-108, 126; utilization of, 79-91; workplace-sponsored, 72-74. *See also* Child care; Parent education

Child Care Information Exchange, 298, 314

Child Development Associate (CDA) credential, 294

Childrearing: leaves for, 143-145; as public trust, 1-6

Children: allowances for, 154-157; care givers in relationships with, 124-126, 138-140; as economic assets, 21, 34; as individuals, 306. *See also* Handicapped children

Children's Defense Fund, 196

Clarke, A. D. B., 45, 314

Clarke, A. M., 45, 314

Clarke-Stewart, A., 123, 139, 317

Cobb, S., xi

Cochran, M. M., 98, 105, 314

Cognitive development: and child care, 101-107; and Head Start, 199-200

Cohen, D. K., 28, 159, 314

Cohen, W., x

Cole, M., 143, 326

Colleges, child care and parent education by, 70-72

Commission on Child Development (California), 252, 258, 259, 261, 280

Commission to Formulate a State Plan for Child Care and Development Services in California, 255, 256, 314-315

Community: analysis of support in, 30-53; aspirations for, 39; concept of, 41-42; families and human development related to, 43-45; value of, 35-37, 40-43

Community enhancement: criteria for policies for, 46-49; and flexibility option, 146-147; and public schools, 276-281; and resources option, 171-173; and services option, 215-221

Comprehensive Annual Services Program, 206

Comprehensive Child Development Act of 1971 (S. 10007), 131, 211-213

Comprehensive Employment and Training Act (CETA), 231

Comprehensive Head Start, Child Development, and Family Services Act of 1972 (S. 3617), 213

Comptroller General of the United States, 197, 315

Congressional Budget Act of 1974, 167

Consortium for Longitudinal Studies, 104, 106

Cooke, R., 193, 315

Coons, J. E., 158, 159, 315

Cooperative groups, for child care and parent education, 58-61

Core, M., xi

344   Index

Title I in, 185-193; exemplary state programs in, 236-271; and family strengthening, 221-226; goals of, 183; Head Start in, 193-205; and individual rights, 230-232; and intergovernmental relationships, 183-184; and parent enabling, 226-230; parent participation in, 232-233; program elements in, 184; Title XX in, 205-210; value analysis of, 215-232, 235
Sesame Street, 62
Sheehan, R., 197, 320
Sherman, A., 201, 330
Shipman, V. C., 200, 330
Short, E. C., 8, 330
Shortlidge, R. L., Jr., 80, 330
Silverman, P. R., 59, 330
Simmons, C. H., 94, 327
Sloan, F., xi
Smith, B., 103, 328
Smith, L. E., 96, 102, 314
Smith, M. S., xi, 194, 330
Smith, S., xi
Social development, and child care, 96-101
Social policy, economic policy related to, 33-34
Social Security Act, 33; Title IV of, 61, 117n, 245. See also Title XX
Social Security system, 18, 20, 48, 154
Social Services Block Grant (SSBG), 182, 209-210
Society, competent and caring, 4, 35, 40, 43, 131, 133, 304-305
Solnit, A. J., x, 45n, 318
South Carolina, school programs in, 242
Southwest Educational Development Laboratory, 77
Spitz, R. A., 93, 330
Spock, B., 77
Stark, E., 116-117, 334
State Advisory Task Force on Early Childhood and Family Education (Minnesota), 263
State Commission for Teacher Preparation and Licensing (California), 254-255

State Department of Education (Hawaii), 78
State Department of Education (Minnesota), 269; Division of Special Services of, 263
State Department of Social Services (California), 247, 253, 254
State programs: for child care, 244-262; conclusions on, 267-271; exemplary, 236-271; for parent education, 262-267; in public schools, 237-244; quality assurance in, 270-271; role of, 275
State Supplemental Program (California), 246
Steinberg, L. D., 124, 312
Steiner, G. Y., x, 3, 45n, 130, 131, 134-135, 330
Steinfels, M. O., 66, 72, 74, 75, 330
Stetten, N., x
Stoddard, S., 161, 330-331
Stolz, L. M., 72, 331
Strickland, B. S., 97, 98, 99-100, 330
Strupp, L., xi
Suchman, E. A., 203, 331
Sugarman, S. D., 158, 159, 315
Supplemental Security Income (SSI), 246
Surrey, S. S., 167, 331
Sutherland, S. A., 76, 324
Sweden: childrearing leave in, 144, 148; national family policy in, 133, 148
Swift, J. W., 94, 96, 97, 101, 331
Switzerland, flexible working hours in, 142-143

T

Taft, R., 213
Tax credits: assessment of, 163-171; conclusions on, 170-171
Texas, schools program in, 69, 242
Texas Institute for Families, 73
Thoreau, H. D., 40
Tileston, C., 63, 312
Title XX of Social Security Act: assessment of, 205-210; background on, 61, 74, 181-185, 198; buy out of, 254, 256; and commu-